museum of the Bible

Volume 2
Samuel through the Prophets

Museum of the Bible
Volume 2 – Samuel through the Prophets

Editor-in-Chief:	Jerry A. Pattengale, Ph.D., Indiana Wesleyan University
Senior Editor:	Gil Ilutowich, Compedia
Senior Review Editor:	Timothy Dalrymple, Ph.D., Polymath Innovations
Research:	Tzvi Shimon, Ph.D., Bar Ilan University
Convergent Media Producers:	Jeffrey Schneider, Museum of the Bible; Elad Brandes, Compedia
Project Manager:	Tal Yanai, Compedia
Art Director:	Gennady Arkulis, Compedia
Graphic Production and Design:	Merrav Babad, Sigalit Svetlit, Compedia
Editing:	David Dekker, Lesley Richardson, David Simmer, Compedia; Stan Guthrie, Stacey L. Douglas, Nick DeNeff, Jared N. Wolfe, Ph.D., Allison Brown, Museum of the Bible
Instructional designer:	Mati Schwarcz, Ph.D., Matthew Lipman, Hagit Shabtai, Sharon Duek, Devorah Katz, Adam Drucker, Chaya Golan, Compedia
Augmented Reality development and implementation:	Elad Brandes, Tal Einat, Noam Geva, Roman Pselk, Hana Polk, Anna Elfassy, Hadas Rutenberg, Hadas Gur-Zeev, Irene Shteinberg, Maya Belkovskiy, Zohar Schoenmann, Sivan Mendel, Oded Ben Hefer, Compedia
Animation and 3-D design:	Eli Botzimbski, Compedia
Maps:	Eli Itzak, Ph.D., Bar Ilan University
Bible Translations:	Bible translations are used by permission and owned by their respected copyright holders as follows:

Scripture quotations marked (ESV) are taken from the *ESV® Bible (The Holy Bible, English Standard Version®)*. Copyright © 2001 by Crossway, a publishing ministry of Good News Publishers. Used by permission. All rights reserved.

Scripture quotations marked (KJV) are taken from the King James Version.

Scripture texts marked (NABRE) in this work are taken from the New American Bible, revised edition © 2010, 1991, 1986, 1970 Confraternity of Christian Doctrine, Washington, D.C. and are used by permission of the copyright owner. All Rights Reserved. No part of the New American Bible may be reproduced in any form without permission in writing from the copyright owner. "This curriculum was not reviewed or approved by the United States Conference of Catholic Bishops."

Scripture quoted by permission. Quotations designated (NET) are from the NET Bible® copyright ©1996-2006 by Biblical Studies Press, L.L.C. http://netbible.com All rights reserved.

Scripture quotations marked (NIV) are taken from the Holy Bible, New International Version®, NIV®. Copyright © 1973, 1978, 1984, 2011 by Biblica, Inc.™ Used by permission of Zondervan. All rights reserved worldwide. http://www.zondervan.com The "NIV" and "New International Version" are trademarks registered in the United States Patent and Trademark Office by Biblica, Inc.™

Scripture quotations marked (NJPS) are taken from the Tanakh: The Holy Scriptures: The New JPS Translation According to the Traditional Hebrew Text (NJPS). Copyright © 1985 by the Jewish Publication Society. Used by permission.

Scripture quotations marked (NKJV) taken from the New King James Version®. Copyright © 1982 by Thomas Nelson. Used by permission. All rights reserved.

Scripture quotations marked (NLT) are taken from the Holy Bible, New Living Translation, copyright ©1996, 2004, 2007, 2015 by Tyndale House Foundation. Used by permission of Tyndale House Publishers, Inc., Carol Stream, Illinois 60188. All rights reserved.

Scripture quotations marked (NRSV) are from New Revised Standard Version Bible: Catholic Edition, copyright © 1989, 1993 National Council of the Churches of Christ in the United States of America. Used by permission. All rights reserved.

© 2016–2017 Museum of the Bible and Compedia Software & Hardware Ltd. All rights reserved.

No part of this work may be reproduced or transmitted in any form or by any means, electronic or mechanical, without written permission from the copyright holder.

PRINTED IN THE UNITED STATES

This product has been developed for private school, home school, and independent study settings.

© All rights reserved

Table of Contents

1	King David	1-10
2	"House of David"	11-16
3	Psalms	17-22
4	Music	23-30
5	King Solomon	31-40
6	Hazor, Megiddo, and Gezer	41-46
7	Proverbs	47-52
8	The Song of Songs	53-58
9	Ecclesiastes	59-64
10	Elijah	65-72
11	Sennacherib's Assault	73-78
12	King Josiah's Reform	79-84
13	Prophets of a Future Hope	85-92
14	Job	93-98
15	Esther	99-104
16	Daniel	105-110
17	Coming Home from Babylon	111-118
18	Rediscovered People	119-126
19	The Septuagint	127-132
20	The Hebrew Bible	133-138
21	The "Obscure" Books of the Bible	139-144
22	Daily Life in Bible Times	145-152
23	The Dead Sea Scrolls	153-160
24	Digging Up Jerusalem	161-170
25	Education	171-176
26	Early America's Charters and Laws	177-184
27	Early State Constitutions	185-192
28	Early American Culture	193-198

King David
Seduction, Violence, and Betrayal
From Shepherd Boy to King of Israel?

"Then Samuel said to Jesse, 'Are all your sons here?' And he said, 'There remains yet the youngest, but behold, he is keeping the sheep.'"

1 Samuel 16:11 (ESV)

Phase 1

Read the Story:
1 Samuel 7; 8; 12
2 Samuel 5:1-12; 7:1-17; 11; 12:1-14

The Story in a Nutshell

The story of David is one of the most dramatic sections of the entire Old Testament. It contains a wide range of actions and emotions. We encounter murder, adultery, betrayal, revenge, rebellion, jealousy, and seduction. But we also read about friendship, loyalty, sacrifice, justice, and redemption. The chapters about David contain some of the key turning points in the long narrative about the people of Israel. With its tense drama, memorable characters, and moral lessons, the story feels surprisingly contemporary.

The story begins, however, on a peaceful, innocent note. David is a teenager herding sheep, strumming his lyre, and slaying the occasional lion or bear that threatens his flock.

Vocabulary

> **Contemporary** [adjective]
belonging to or occurring in the present; or occurring at the same time

King David 1

Archaeological site of the ancient city of Socoh in the Elah Valley of Israel. Here David the shepherd boy and the giant Goliath are said to have fought each other.

After David's victory over Goliath in battle, he holds up the giant's head. ***David with Goliath's Head,*** Caravaggio, 1606–1607. Kunsthistorisches Museum, Vienna.

But Israel faces a larger, more serious threat: the dreaded Philistines. On the battlefield, the Philistine champion, Goliath, challenges the Israelite army to send a soldier to fight him. (Said to be more than nine feet tall, Goliath is no ordinary warrior!) The outcome will decide the war between the two armies.

Neither King Saul nor any of his soldiers has the courage to accept Goliath's challenge. David shows up with lunch one day for his older brothers and hears Goliath's mocking challenge. When no one else will step forward, David accepts the challenge. David rushes toward the giant, slings one of his stones, and hits Goliath squarely in the forehead. The giant falls to the ground, dead. With Goliath's own sword, David cuts off the giant's head!

As David grows into manhood, additional military victories follow. David's rise to glory reaches its peak when he is crowned king. He unites all the tribes into a single kingdom, leaving a lasting imprint on Israelite history and the arc of the Old Testament narrative. He conquers Jerusalem, makes it his royal capital, and brings the Ark of the Covenant, containing the Ten Commandments, to Jerusalem.

If the story ended there, David would simply have become known as a great military leader. Instead, the story takes a series of tragic turns. David gives in to temptation, which sets off a chain of events that shapes the lives of many.

One afternoon, David is looking over the city. He notices a beautiful woman taking a bath. He finds out who she is and summons her to the palace, where he sleeps with her. The woman, Bathsheba, becomes pregnant. The king tries to cover up his action. When that attempt fails, he has Bathsheba's husband, Uriah killed in battle. Soon thereafter, Bathsheba becomes one of David's wives. (Like many kings in ancient times, David was said to have multiple wives and concubines; the latter had a lower status than a wife.)

2   King David

"You Are the Man!"

None of us likes to be criticized. That is true of king and commoner alike. The Bible depicts some kings as though they consider themselves above criticism and above the laws they apply to their subjects. As portrayed in the Bible, the law of the time does not allow this luxury for David or any of the kings of Israel.

Record-Breaking Fame
The name *David* is mentioned more often in the Hebrew Bible (about 1,000 times) than any other name.

In 2 Samuel 12, the prophet Nathan comes to the palace not long after David's affair with Bathsheba. Nathan tells the king a parable about a very rich man who, although he has many sheep, takes the only and beloved lamb from a poor man. Offended by the injustice presented in this parable, David interrupts Nathan to declare, "As the LORD lives, the man who has done this deserves to die" 2 Samuel 12:5 (ESV). Nathan responds with a phrase that has entered our vocabulary: "You are the man!" David realizes the story is about him. He, who has so much, has stolen Bathsheba from Uriah. Nathan warns the king of God's coming punishments. In bitter sorrow, David admits his sin. Psalm 51, which expresses remorse for sin, is traditionally understood to have been written by David.

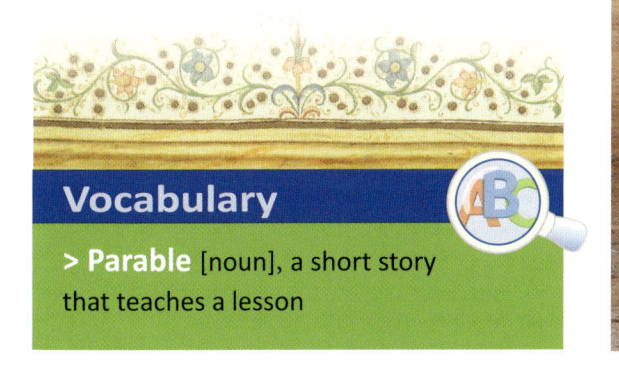

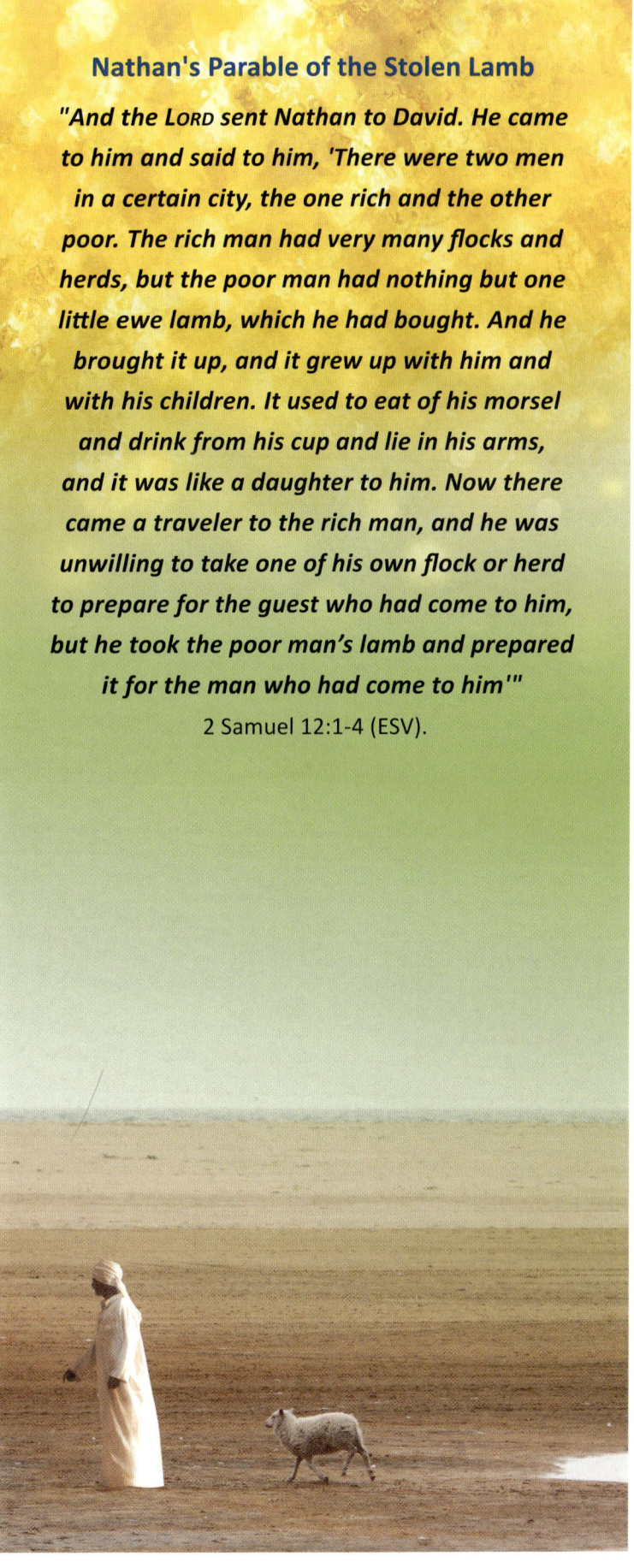

Vocabulary
> **Parable** [noun], a short story that teaches a lesson

Nathan's Parable of the Stolen Lamb

"And the LORD sent Nathan to David. He came to him and said to him, 'There were two men in a certain city, the one rich and the other poor. The rich man had very many flocks and herds, but the poor man had nothing but one little ewe lamb, which he had bought. And he brought it up, and it grew up with him and with his children. It used to eat of his morsel and drink from his cup and lie in his arms, and it was like a daughter to him. Now there came a traveler to the rich man, and he was unwilling to take one of his own flock or herd to prepare for the guest who had come to him, but he took the poor man's lamb and prepared it for the man who had come to him'"
2 Samuel 12:1-4 (ESV).

King David 3

The prophet Nathan pointing to King David and declaring "you are the man" after exposing his adultery with Bathsheba. Detail from a relief on the gate of La Madeleine Church, Paris, ca. 1840.

Replica of Michelangelo's famous *David*, in front of the Palazzo della Signoria, Florence, Italy.

Vocabulary

> **Reprimand** [verb], to rebuke severely

The Messenger's Message

The Bible tells of many kings and many prophets. Often the prophet's role is to remind the king what God would have him do. At this point in the story of David, the prophet is named Nathan. Nathan reprimands the king, who acknowledges his mistakes. Yet he still has to face the consequences of his actions:

- The early death of the first child he has with Bathsheba
- Public humiliation
- A household in chaos, with some of his children violently turning against each other, and against him

Although his reputation is marred by his mistakes and their serious consequences, the Bible portrays David as a great leader who also has many strengths and positive characteristics.

On the Criticism of Kings

The Bible often exposes the wrongdoings of even its greatest hero figures. No one, not even the most renowned of the kings, is exempt from prophetic criticism and judgment. This stands in contrast with many other annals and chronicles from the Ancient Near East, many of which were court histories commissioned by the rulers themselves to boast of their virtues and victories. The criticism in the Bible suggests that biblical writers considered even the highest leaders accountable; they thought leaders' lives provide moral lessons from which all people can learn.

Artwork from the 16th century on the floor of the Cathedral in Siena, Italy, depicting David's son Absalom hanging by his hair from a tree.

Absalom's Death

The death of David's rebellious son, Absalom, counts as one of the Bible's stranger stories for modern readers. In the account in 2 Samuel, Absalom is known for his head of long, thick hair. One day, as he flees his father's forces, the son's prized locks become entangled in the branches of a tree. Absalom hangs there in midair, helplessly, until the military commander Joab kills him with three spears (2 Samuel 18:9-15).

Tomb of King David's Son Absalom

Absalom, King David's beloved son, rebels against him in an attempt to become the next king of Israel.

This ancient tomb is located in the Kidron Valley in Jerusalem and is traditionally considered to be Absalom's burial site. Scholars believe the existing monument was built in the first century AD.

The traditional site of the ancient tomb of Absalom in Jerusalem, Israel.

King David

David's Harp, a Modern Symbol

Images of King David and his lyre are often seen today in art, stamps, coins, and even festivals across Israel.

Mount Gilboa, in northern Israel, where King Saul and his son Jonathan are, according to the biblical account, slain in battle. David and Jonathan are described as close friends. David laments their death by writing a poem that is still celebrated today.

Vocabulary

> **Lament** [noun or verb], an expression of grief or sorrow

David's Many Talents

David is a rare figure in the Bible: a great military leader who is also well versed in the fine arts. He is called "the sweet psalmist of Israel" (1 Samuel 23:1, ESV) and for good reason. In the biblical account, he composes, sings, plays the lyre, and dances. Many of the songs and poetry in the Book of Psalms are attributed to David. The stories suggest that he could act, too: once David escaped death by pretending to be insane (see 1 Samuel 21).

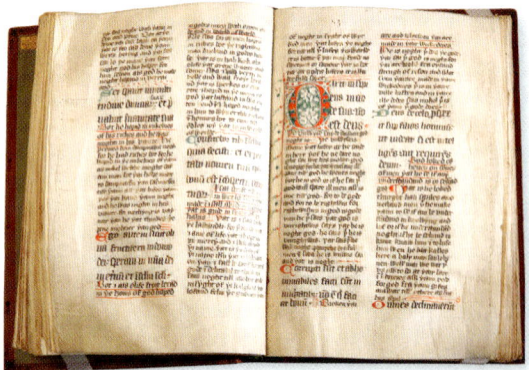

A page from Psalms, The Rosebery Rolle. This vellum text includes one of the earliest English translations of the Bible. Richard Rolle (a brilliant but eccentric hermit, who died in 1349) created it at the request of an anchoress, Margaret Kirkby. This designation of "anchoress" was given to a woman who voluntarily lived an ascetic life. Kirkby isolated herself in a walled-in space for much of her life.

True Friendship

David is still a young man when Saul becomes the first king of a united Israel. As David's popularity grows, Saul becomes envious of David and repeatedly tries to kill him. David never retaliates, even though he has many opportunities to do so. Why not?

Aside from the fact that David and Saul's son Jonathan are close friends, David considers Saul to be the legitimate king of Israel, chosen not just by the people, but by God. When news reaches David that both his friend Jonathan and his enemy Saul have been killed in a battle on Mount Gilboa, he writes a touching lament. Even today, this lament (found in 2 Samuel 1:17-27) is considered one of the most beautiful Hebrew poems ever written.

Phase 2
Travel through Time

When we survey the story of Israel covered so far in the Bible, we learn that David is only the second king in Israel's history. After a disappointing first king (Saul), David too makes serious mistakes. Prior to Saul, the story suggests that there were no kings over the people of Israel. In fact, the Bible says, the prophets told them that God alone is their king, and that he has led them well. For example, according to the biblical story:

- God leads Abraham and Sarah safely to the Promised Land.
- The Israelites are welcomed to Egypt when famine strikes Canaan.
- God rescues the Jews from Egypt, even parting the Red Sea for them.
- God provides the Law to Moses and his people, including the Ten Commandments.
- Every morning, for 40 years in the desert, they awake to find food called manna.
- God provides a pillar of fire by night and a pillar of cloud by day to guide them through the wilderness.
- God leads them to conquer the city of Jericho and then gradually most of Canaan.
- God provides judges to guide them as they became a more populous nation.

Wanting to Be Like Everybody Else

Despite the prophet's reminders of God's blessings, the people see the other nations' kings of flesh and blood and want the same for themselves. Although God warns that they will be sorry, they insist. So he lets them have their way. The prophet Samuel helps them choose Saul as their first king. Saul is described as tall and handsome. At times, he is an able leader and warrior, but often, we read, he is consumed by jealousy and rage. God eventually rejects Saul and sends Samuel to find another king. Samuel finds David, at the time still a young shepherd.

Vocabulary

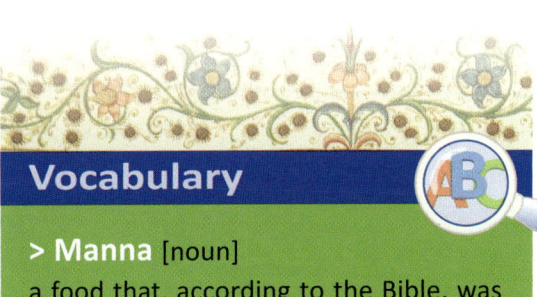

> **Manna** [noun]
a food that, according to the Bible, was miraculously supplied to the Israelites on a regular basis for 40 years in the wilderness

King David 7

Time Travel

The Battle Location
Valley of Elah, ca. 1010 BC

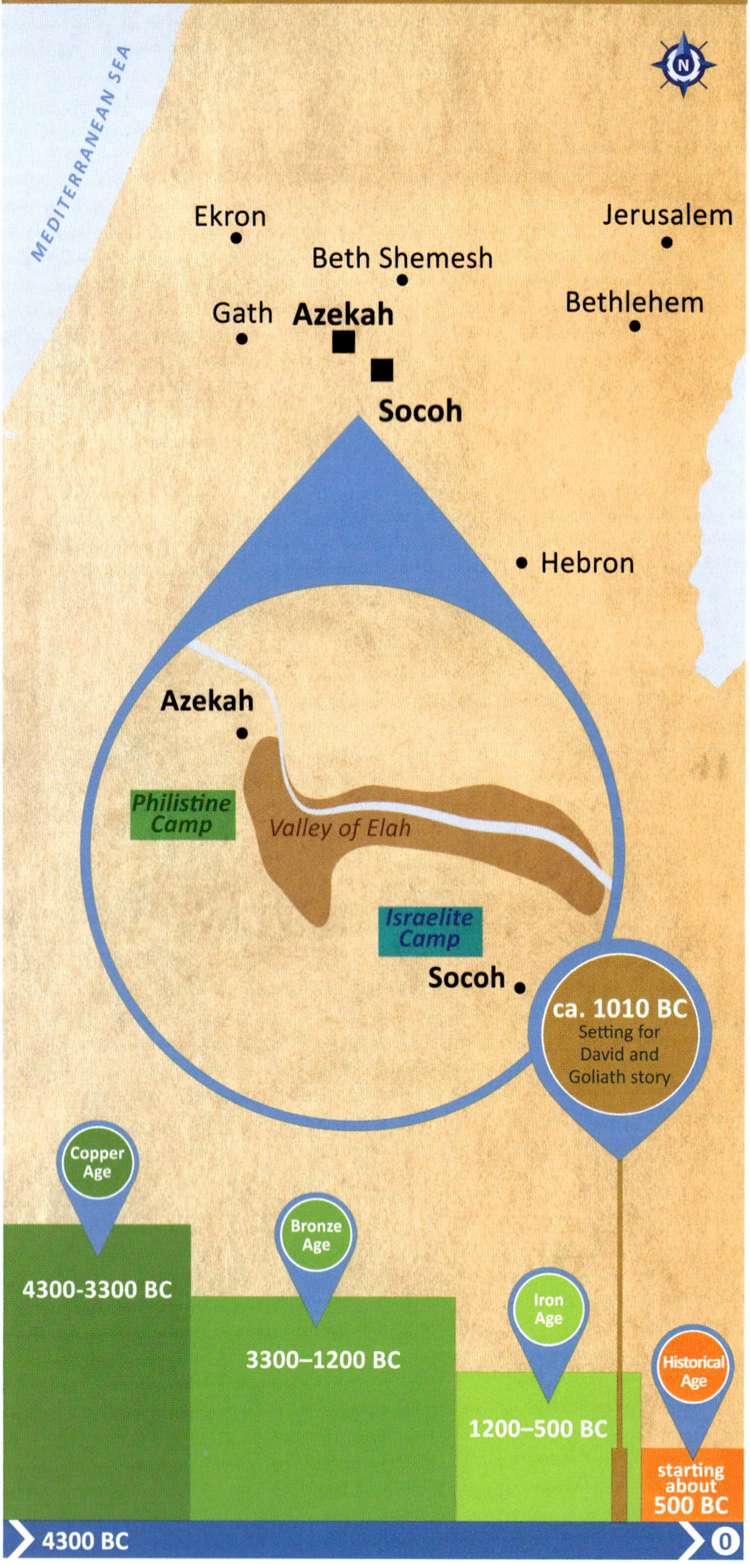

Phase 3
Mine for Clues

God's King, the People's King, or Both?

King David is anointed twice. Why? It is not enough that God wants a certain individual as king. The people must also accept him. Even though David is anointed early in his life by Samuel, he still must be anointed by the people. The king's power rests both on God's choice and the people's acceptance.

Courage versus Technology

Once Saul understands that David will not be dissuaded from fighting Goliath, the king offers his own armor to the young shepherd. David puts on the armor but quickly changes his mind and removes it, since he's not used to heavy equipment, let alone fighting in it. Instead, he relies only on his slingshot. The Bible portrays the confrontation as one between simple courage and, on the other side, obvious advantages of skill, size, and weaponry.

If a sling is used correctly, a stone can travel at 60 miles per hour and hit its target with great accuracy.

Vocabulary

> **Anoint** [verb]
to confer ceremonially a religious office by rubbing or smearing with oil

8 | King David

Intended Audience and Purpose

The two biblical books of Samuel are named after judges and the first of the prophets called to minister among Israel during the kingship period.

These two books, 1 Samuel and 2 Samuel, were originally one book in Hebrew. (The length of an ancient manuscript was often determined by the material on which it was written, and not necessarily by breaks or changes in content.) They record the deeds of Samuel, Saul, and David. Biblical writers included both heroic actions and tragic errors in judgment, apparently intending the stories to serve as cautionary tales for readers.

The Power of Choices

The story of David is one of many stories in the Bible that discuss problematic relationships between men and women. Other examples include the story of Judah's relationship with Tamar and the better-known story of Samson and Delilah. King Solomon, too, is portrayed as sinning against God in taking wives and concubines from peoples who worshiped other gods.

Biblical narratives about these characters suggest that they were up against not only external enemies but also internal challenges and temptations. Sometimes the latter could prove as formidable as the former.

The story of Joseph offers something of a contrast to the story of King David. When the wife of his master, Potiphar, attempts to seduce him, Joseph leaves her presence. He is falsely accused of attempting to seduce Potiphar's wife but eventually exonerated.

The fame of King David has been celebrated in many parts of the world. He's depicted here on a postcard in Germany from the early 20th century, in honor of the Jewish New Year.

Joseph and Potiphar's Wife, by Guido Reni, 1631. "After a time his master's wife cast her eyes on Joseph and said, 'Lie with me.' But he refused ... he left his garment in her hand and fled" Genesis 39:7-8, 12 (ESV).

King David

Phase 4
Use the Telescope

The Bible lists a line of kings descended from David, starting with King Solomon, whose signature strength is described as his immense wisdom. Solomon builds the First Temple in Jerusalem. Yet the line of kings is thought to reach far beyond Solomon: the Messiah—a promised deliverer—is predicted to descend from David. Christians have traditionally connected the Messiah prediction to the birth of Jesus. The New Testament lists Joseph and Mary (who gave birth to Jesus and raised him) as descendants of Abraham through the lineage of David.

Excavations near the Temple Mount in Jerusalem.

Summary

The two books of Samuel portray King David as a fallible human being who has many strengths but also significant weaknesses. When challenged by the prophet Nathan, David confesses his errors. But David and others are already so tied up in the consequences of his actions that they cannot be undone. Those consequences include the deaths of a soldier and a baby, infighting among his family, and the eventual breakup of his kingdom. Despite all of this, the Bible says that God forgave David. The story of David is one of both tragedy and redemption.

David is honored today not only as a masterful military leader and king, but as a poet who wrote with passion and insight about the struggles of faith. Traditionally credited for many of the psalms, the figure of David shaped the story of the Bible and shaped the history of the Jews in profound ways.

"House of David"
Are New Discoveries Still Shaping Our Understanding of the Bible?

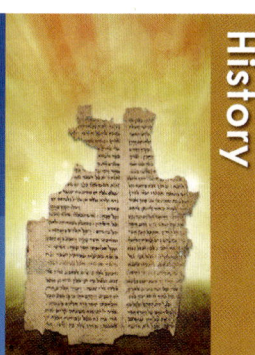

History

> "As Goliath moved closer to attack, David quickly ran out to meet him. Reaching into his shepherd's bag and taking out a stone, he hurled it with his sling and hit the Philistine in the forehead. The stone sank in, and Goliath stumbled and fell face down on the ground."
>
> 1 Samuel 17:48-49 (NLT)

David and Goliath

David is one of the Bible's most fascinating characters. Roughly three millennia later, people still read and recount the Bible's story of the young shepherd boy who kills Goliath the giant. When underdog sports teams take on favored ones, or when a small business challenges a dominant enterprise, we often describe the encounter as "David versus Goliath." But David doesn't remain a shepherd boy: The Bible says he becomes a king (2 Samuel 2). The New Testament says that David is also an ancestor of Jesus (Matthew 1).

David's Importance

David is a significant figure for people of many faiths. Traditionally, for Jews, David is seen as the one who united the tribes in a strong and cohesive kingdom ruled from Jerusalem, brought the Ark of the Covenant to Jerusalem, organized the religious worship of the people, and paved the way for the construction of the Temple. Christians see David as a foreshadowing of Jesus: a shepherd-king who is "anointed" or chosen to bring about a new kingdom. Christians also believe that Jesus was born in Bethlehem, the birthplace of David, from the same tribe as David. In medieval Europe, in the age of knights and chivalry, Christian nobility treated David as an example of a wise and pious king. In Islam, the Qur'an adds its own stories of David, some quite different from the stories of the Bible, but Muslims regard David as one of the most important prophets of God.

Where Is King David

Given David's prominent role in the biblical narrative, archaeologists have long debated why they could not find evidence of his existence outside of the Bible. Nearly 3,000 years had passed since David had supposedly walked the earth. And yet scholars couldn't find even one ancient source outside the Bible that mentioned his name.

The oldest archaeological artifact with a Bible verse found so far dates all the way back to about 600 BC. However, it doesn't mention King David. When the Dead Sea Scrolls were discovered in 1947, scholars gained access to another ancient Bible source, from before 100 BC, that included most of the hundreds of Bible verses we already knew about David. But there were still no known extrabiblical references to the great King David.

King David, Adamo Tadolini, ca. 18th-century. Column of the Immaculate Conception, Rome, Italy. King David's many talents gave artists plenty to work with. Here the artist shows him as a king looking up to the heavens while playing his lyre.

Part of the Temple Scroll that was found in Qumran Cave 11.

In 1979, archaeologists working at a site called *Ketef Hinnom*, southwest of Jerusalem's Old City, discovered two very small silver scrolls that date to about 600 BC. One includes the words of the "Priestly Blessing" found in the Book of Numbers. The scrolls, incorporated into amulets, were probably meant to bring a sense of divine protection. Even today, over two and a half millennia later, the blessing (Numbers 6:23-27) is recited at Jewish synagogues and Christian churches.

"House of David"

Tel Dan Stele.

The Famous Tel Dan Inscription

On July 21, 1993, archaeologists working at the ancient city of Dan unearthed an inscribed stone dating to around 841 BC. Another large piece of stone was found later in the same area. Though these basalt fragments displayed part of a longer inscription, one small portion stood out. The translated words read: "House of David." Finally, the biblical King David had surfaced, literally engraved in stone. It was the first evidence outside the Bible that a dynasty named after David actually existed.

Why Is This Interesting

> David is the most frequently mentioned person in the Hebrew Bible.

The sudden appearance of information from the past is nothing new. We'll see this happen again and again in our study of the Bible. We've already seen this dynamic in a chapter titled "Lost Civilizations." However, while any archaeological find can help shed light on the past, few discoveries are more important in biblical history than the first mention outside the Bible of King David.

Time Travel

The Tel Dan Inscription

Tel Dan, 841 BC

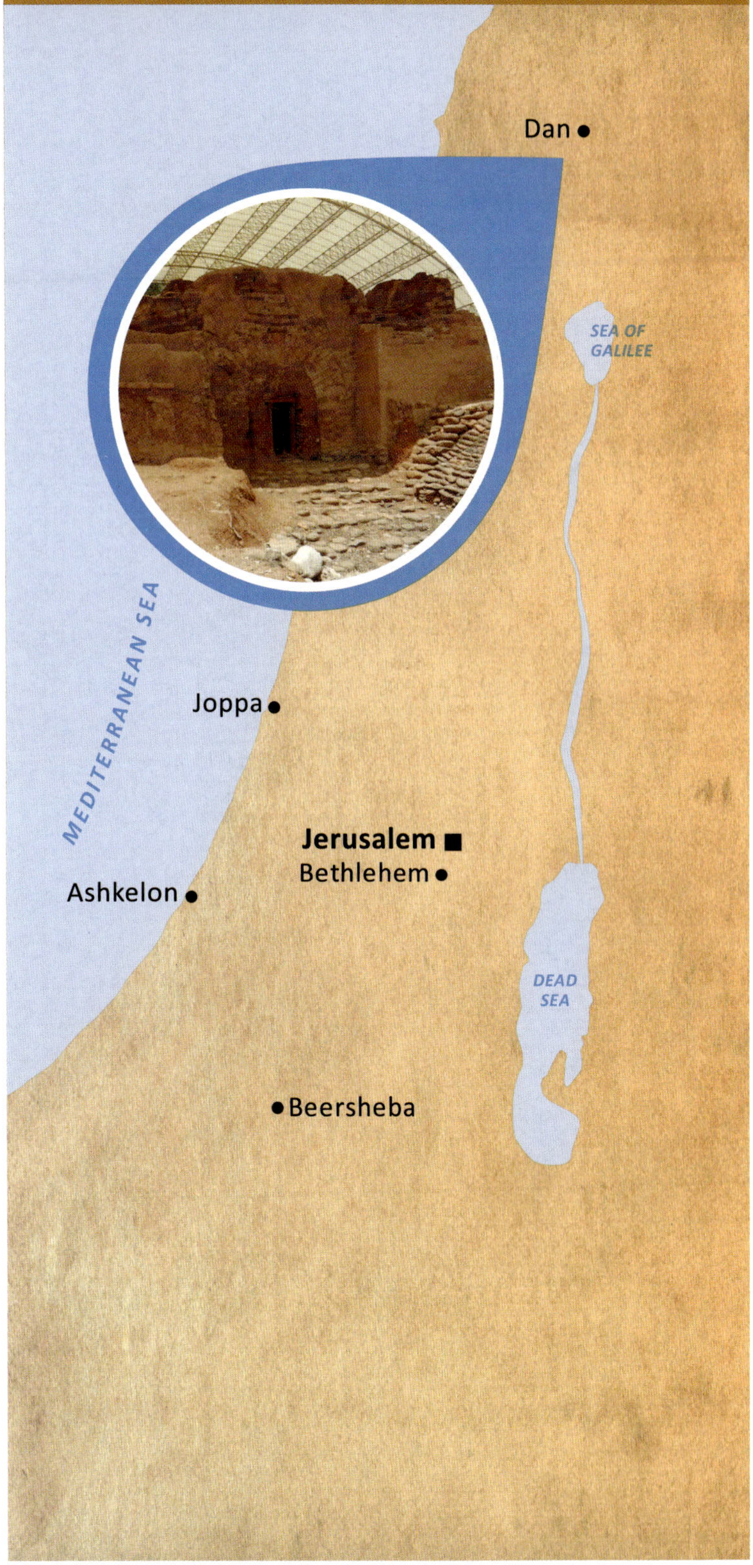

"House of David" 13

Artifacts from Biblical Times Yet to Be Discovered— If These Exist, Which One Do You Think Would Be the Most Interesting

Although various dramatic finds from biblical times have been unearthed, many artifacts described in the Bible, like other ancient sources, have never been located. If these biblical stories are factual as various groups contend, most scholars would say that these artifacts are not likely to be found. If they do exist and were discovered, this news would cause quite a sensation.

Cup from the Last Supper

The New Testament describes Jesus drinking from a cup during his "Last Supper" with the apostles before his death. Later legends arose about his "Holy Grail" and its imagined powers—and stories have been told in legends and novels. *Monty Python and the Holy Grail* (1975) and *Indiana Jones and the Last Crusade* (1989) both centered (in very different ways!) on the pursuit of the grail.

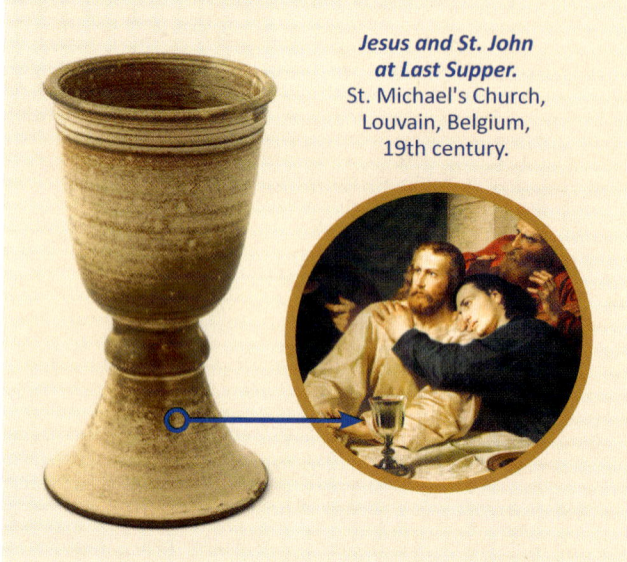

Jesus and St. John at Last Supper. St. Michael's Church, Louvain, Belgium, 19th century.

Noah's Ark

Noah builds a special boat to save his family and all the animals on the earth, two of every kind, male and female, to save them from the coming flood.

Mount Ararat
Mount Ararat (or the mountains of Ararat, in another translation) in Turkey is the place where, according to Genesis, Noah's ark came to rest after the flood.

The Ark of the Covenant

According to the Torah, the ark is used to house the stone tablets with the Law.

14 "House of David"

The Tel Dan Inscription

Judah was a kingdom in the southern part of the land of Canaan, which included Jerusalem. But this stone suggests that it was also known as the "House of David."

When archaeologists discovered the Tel Dan inscription mentioning the "House of David," it not only mentioned the Israelite king but also employed common language of that era—further evidence of its authenticity. Scholars have reconstructed the names of other kings mentioned in the Bible, too: Joram, Ahaziah son of Jehoram, and possibly Ahab (which is broken in the text).

King David Playing the Harp, Gerrit Van Honthorst, (1622). Centraal Museum, Utrecht, Netherlands.

The Irony of This Discovery

As we have seen, the first external validation of David outside of the Bible was found in the region of Dan. In the biblical account, Dan is the city where a later king, named Jeroboam, constructs a golden calf shrine and blatantly opposes the religion laid out by the biblical writers. The first discovery of King David's name appeared in a city that, in the Bible, chooses to rebel against David's legacy and his faith.

Why Does the Inscription Refer to the "House of David" and Not the "Kingdom of David"?

The City of David, from the Model of Jerusalem, Israel Museum, Jerusalem, Israel.

To answer this question, let's climb into our Time Machine and travel into the past to understand the existing family and social structure from around 3,000 years ago.

> Some Semitic people in ancient Israel thought of their government much like a family. Families in these societies were organized with the father as the head. Even adult sons would look to their father for protection and advice.

> Although many stories show women renowned for their wisdom and courage, groups of related families (called clans) typically had one man designated as their head.

> A group of related clans was called a tribe, of which again one man was usually the head. He was seen as the father of the tribe.

> When whole tribes grouped together, such as the 12 tribes of Israel, they saw the king as a kind of father figure for the entire country.

This ancient way of looking at family and government is called the "House of the Father." It helps us to understand how the actual government was viewed. We see the principle in action in 2 Samuel 3:6, which states, "During the war between the house of Saul and the house of David ..."

"House of David"

The Shishak Inscription, Temple of Amun, Karnak, Egypt. The complex of temples in Karnak, Egypt, is the largest ancient religious site in the world. The Temple of Amun is now an open-air museum.

More Names in Stone

While the discovery of the Tel Dan Inscription in 1993 was the first such find, there have been other discoveries that also refer to ancient Israel and other neighboring kings. The Tel Dan reference is largely agreed upon, but these inscriptions are still debated:

- This stele refers to disputes between ancient Israel and Moab. Scholars continue to debate whether the House of David is mentioned on the stone.

- The Shishak Inscription comes from the Temple of Amun in Karnak, Egypt. It records the military exploits of Pharoah Sheshonq I (called "Shishak" in the Bible), who appears to have invaded Israel and Judah around 925 BC, around the time of King David's grandson according to the biblical text.

The Mesha Stele, 9th century BC. Louvre, Paris.

Summary

In this chapter, we only asked our Time Machine to take us to the recent past – to experience some pivotal archaeological moments. But these amazing finds will now propel even further as we travel in the next chapter into the distant past. The study of the Bible continues. New techniques and technologies bring new information to light. In this textbook, we are mostly concerned with understanding the stories of the Bible in their context and impact. Readers will disagree on whether the stories of David are mostly accurate or mostly inaccurate. Discoveries like the Tel Dan inscription cannot tell us whether David was truly a shepherd boy or whether he actually defeated a Philistine warrior named Goliath. It can suggest, however, that behind the stories stands a historical figure. Historians and archaeologists can begin to piece together a better understanding of the setting for the dramatic David stories.

The Dead Sea Scrolls uncovered	The oldest fragment with a quotation from the Bible is found	The Tel Dan Inscription	David's name may be detected on the Mesha Stone
1947	1979	1993	1994

"House of David"

Psalms: Israel's Heart and Soul

Why Are the Psalms So Popular?

"You make springs gush forth in the valleys;
    they flow between the hills;
they give drink to every beast of the field;
    the wild donkeys quench their thirst.
Beside them the birds of the heavens dwell;
    they sing among the branches."

Psalm 104:10-12 (ESV)

The Power of Music and Song

To learn about the 20th century, you might read what historians have written. But another way to understand the soul of a people is to listen to its songs. Popular American singers such as Frank Sinatra, Nat King Cole, Billie Holiday, Elvis Presley, Bob Dylan, Aretha Franklin, Ray Charles, Johnny Cash, Tammy Wynette, Stevie Wonder, Bruce Springsteen, Whitney Houston, Gloria Estefan, Prince, Michael Jackson, and scores of others kept the beat going and monitored the pulse of the nation through good times and bad. The following has been attributed to many writers, including Scottish patriot Andrew Fletcher (1653–1716): "Give me the making of the songs of a nation, and I care not who writes its laws."

For the Israelites, the psalms chronicled their joys and despairs, their highs and lows as a people. Of the 66 books in the Bible, this book, in the opinion of many people, is the very heart and soul of the Jewish scriptures. Our name in English for this book, Psalms, comes from the Greek word psalmoi, meaning "songs sung to a harp." The Hebrew name, Tehillim, literally means "praises." Psalms first became the prayer book of the Jewish people and then later also that of Christianity.

Vocabulary

> **Chronicle** [verb], to compile in a record of events

Psalms 17

The Book of Psalms has more verses or "chapters" (songs) than any other book in the Bible. It was only later, though, that the books of the Bible were divided up according to verses and chapters. Counting by the number of words in the original, Psalms is the third longest book in the Bible, after Jeremiah and Genesis. There are 150 psalms in the version used by Protestants and Catholics. The earliest Christian monasteries made the recitation of the psalms a central part of their daily practice.

At first glance, Psalms appears to be a straightforward collection of ancient Jewish religious poetry: worship verses, plaintive mournful songs, philosophical meditations, and prayers. But a closer look reveals in many verses deep passion and soulful cries of the heart. Because the Book of Psalms frequently connects with the human condition, it is likely the most-read part of the Bible.

Many musicians point to the psalms as a source of inspiration—seeing some psalms as the first example of "the blues." How can the psalms still speak to people today, who live in a different culture? The answer may lie in their candor. The psalms display a full range of human emotion, plumbing the deepest depths of sorrow and regret and ascending to the highest peaks of joy and victory. Every human situation seems to have a corresponding psalm. The echoes of these soulful songs have reverberated in the Judeo-Christian world, and beyond.

Rice Psalter. This luxury psalter, from the 1400s, was intended for public use in a chapel, instead of private or monastic devotion. The Psalms in medieval times were almost always sung or chanted instead of simply read aloud.

How Were the Psalms Composed?

Just as American songs reflect the time of their composition—the Revolutionary War and Civil War, slavery and the struggles for racial equality, the Great Depression, the World Wars, and Vietnam—the psalms reflect the times of the Israelites. These songs likely were composed over several hundred years.

Psalm 117, the shortest one in the collection, weighs in at only two verses. It probably was written at a time of national prosperity:

> *Praise the L*ORD*, all nations!*
> *Extol him, all peoples!*
> *For great is his steadfast love toward us,*
> *and the faithfulness*
> *of the L*ORD *endures forever.*
> *Praise the L*ORD*!*
> Psalm 117 (ESV)

On the other hand, Psalm 137 was penned after the Babylonians had destroyed Jerusalem and exiled many of the Israelites:

> *By the waters of Babylon,*
> *there we sat down and wept,*
> *when we remembered Zion.*
> Psalm 137:1 (ESV)

The Book of Psalms has traditionally been associated with King David, who was nicknamed "the sweet psalmist of Israel" 2 Samuel 23:1 (ESV). The Bible portrays David, traditionally known as a songwriter, as skilled with his lyre—a hand-held harp. But as far as the biblical authors were concerned, David's main achievement was to centralize the worship of God in Jerusalem, forming the nucleus of a large choir and orchestra that would eventually sing and offer musical praises to God in the Temple (1 Chronicles 15:16-22). Many psalms are attributed to him.

The Book of Psalms is divided into five sections: chapters 1–41, 42–72, 73–89, 90–106, and 107–150.

Vocabulary

> **Plaintive** [adjective], expressing suffering or sadness

Use of Psalms and Music in Biblical Times

While we cannot reconstruct the history of individual psalms, we can trace the setting of many to the Temple in Jerusalem, the center of Jewish life. Although the Bible does not provide detailed information on how the psalms were used there, the Jewish rabbinic tradition suggests a way of using the psalms that may reflect how they were used in ancient times:

- Selected psalms were to be sung on each day of the week in public worship at the Temple. Sunday: Psalm 24, Monday: Psalm 48, Tuesday: Psalm 82, Wednesday: Psalm 94, Thursday: Psalm 81, Friday and Saturday: Psalms 92 and 93.

- Certain psalms accompanied the biblical festivals. For example, a large Levitical choir would sing Psalm 136 between 3:00 and 5:00 on the afternoon before Passover, when many lambs were sacrificed at the Temple.

- Psalms 120 to 134, called Songs of Ascent, were chanted by Jewish pilgrims as they made their way, usually on foot, up to Jerusalem three times a year to appear at the Temple for the three main biblical feasts: Passover, Pentecost, and Tabernacles.

- The Book of Psalms provides interesting hints about how music permeated the Temple. Psalm 68, for example, describes a procession led by the Ark of the Covenant and followed by singers, minstrels, and a group of young women with tambourines. Other psalms refer to trumpets, as well as stringed and wind instruments.

With the destruction of the Second Jewish Temple in Jerusalem in AD 70, such public worship came to an abrupt end. Since the words are preserved but not the melody or detailed instructions for the musicians, no one today can state with certainty how the ancient tunes sounded.

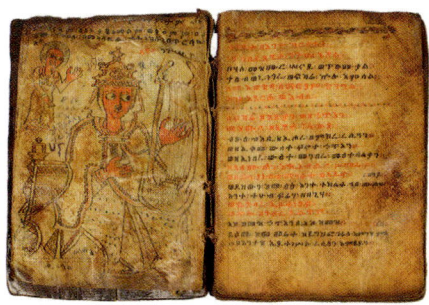

An Ethiopian psalter in Ge'ez, the prayer language of Ethiopian Christians, from the mid-19th century. Even in humbler copies of the Psalter, David is sometimes honored through the inclusion of a simple illumination featuring the king and his famous lyre.

Book of Hours, Sarum Rite. Printed by Simon Vostre, Paris, France, ca. 1512. A Book of Hours was a devotional book common in medieval times, including psalms, prayers, and monastic practices. In one of its many full-page illuminations, King David is shown playing his lyre.

The Timeless Themes of the Psalms

For many generations, the Psalms have helped Jews and Christians (and others besides) put their faith, their feelings, and even their doubts and anger at God, into words. Scholars have many ways of separating the psalms into different types, including wisdom psalms, royal psalms, psalms pleading for the destruction of enemies, and even acrostic psalms where each verse starts with the next letter in the Hebrew alphabet. The two most common types, though, are

- Psalms of petition, which appeal for God's mercy and help in times of need or danger

- Psalms of praise, affirming trust in God and offering thanks for his help

The most repeated theme in the Book of Psalms is the royal kingship of God, who is described as the all-knowing creator: "The LORD has established his throne in the heavens, and his kingdom rules over all" Psalm 103:19 (ESV).

Through the psalms, the Israelites express their longing for an ideal world, in which everyone honors and prays to God, and God will answer those prayers. The very last verse of the book reads, "Let everything that has breath praise the LORD! Praise the LORD!" Psalm 150:6 (ESV).

Psalms of Deliverance and Hope

The psalms sets forth how the Israelites (or at least the ones who wrote the psalms and guided the religious lives of the people) understood God and their relationship to him. They describe God, for instance, as a "great king over all the earth" (Psalm 47:2, ESV) who has chosen the Israelites to be his people. He delivered them from the world powers, gave them a land and united with them in a covenant of love (e.g., Psalms 105–106). God also chose David to be his royal representative on earth and anointed him to govern the people with righteousness, to bless the nation with peace and prosperity. Jerusalem was to become the earthly capital and symbol of the kingdom of God, where his people could meet with him and bring their prayers and praises.

> "As for me, I have set my King
> on Zion, my holy hill."
> I will tell of the decree:
> The LORD said to me, "You are my Son;
> today I have begotten you.
> Ask of me, and I will make the nations your heritage,
> and the ends of the earth your possession."
> Psalm 2:6-8 (ESV)

A miniature psalter from Picardy, France, ca. AD 1280-1300. During the Middle Ages most European psalters featured artistic renditions (illuminations) of David on some of the pages. Here we see him as the poet-king, with his harp, and below as a boy fighting Goliath.

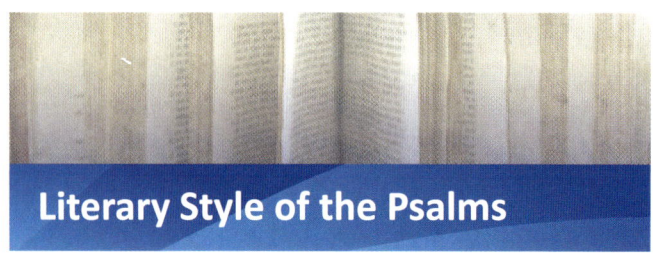

Literary Style of the Psalms

The psalms are a type of poetry. In the West, people think of poetry in terms of rhyme, rhythm, and meter. Ancient Hebrew poetry uses striking images, parallel structuring, and repetition, but it does not have rhyme. Two of the most noticeable characteristics of Hebrew poetry are metaphor and parallelism.

Use of Metaphors

A metaphor is a figure of speech that describes one thing in terms of another. The Book of Psalms includes a number of metaphors for God: God is a rock, fortress, refuge. God is also described as a deliverer, judge, creator, and king. For instance, one of the most famous psalms, Psalm 23, begins with a metaphor that expresses the psalmist's belief that God is a source of wise guidance and nurturing protection: "The LORD is my shepherd."

Parallelism

The most distinctive feature of Hebrew poetry is a two-part sentence where the second part of the line echoes or contrasts with the first, strengthening and completing the thought in the first. Another form of parallelism links two different but related thoughts, such as comparing a human father to a heavenly one. Here are some examples:

> His mischief returns upon his own head,
> and on his own skull his violence descends.
> Psalm 7:16 (ESV)

> The wicked borrows but does not pay back,
> but the righteous is generous and gives.
> Psalm 37:21 (ESV)

> As a father shows compassion to his children,
> so the LORD shows compassion
> to those who fear him.
> Psalm 103:13 (ESV)

THE BOOK OF PSALMS.

The musical instruments depicted in the Macklin Bible—harp and trumpet—introduce the Psalms as a collection of songs. The other images focus on the first two psalms, the "cover songs" in this "album." The branch and Hebrew tablets refer to the theme in the Psalms that the person who lives according to God's law will be blessed: "he is like a tree planted by streams of water" Psalm 1:3 (ESV). The two crowns, one in the clouds and one on earth with the scepter, reference the emphasis presented in Psalm 2 of Israel's king as the chosen "son" of God, the divine King.

Some Interesting Facts

- The Book of Psalms is cited more often in the New Testament than any other book from the Hebrew Bible.

- Anyone who wanted to be a bishop in the early centuries of the church was expected to be able to recite all 150 psalms from memory. Some Eastern Christian churches include a Psalm 151. Psalm 151 has also been found among the Dead Sea Scrolls, showing it was accepted among Jewish sects of the Essenes.

- Many great composers have taken the words from the Book of Psalms and fashioned music for them, ranging from Vivaldi and Handel to Mendelssohn, Liszt, and Stravinsky.

- Psalm 90 is attributed to Moses, and Psalms 72 and 127 are attributed to Solomon.

- Only 73 of the 150 psalms are attributed to David.

- When a Jew dies, the Psalms are recited over the body until the time of the burial.

- The song "40," by U2, is adapted from the words of Psalm 40.

A Brief Analysis of Psalm 23

To explore the power of these soulful songs, we will analyze the famous Psalm 23. Its poetic structure can easily be broken down into three parts.

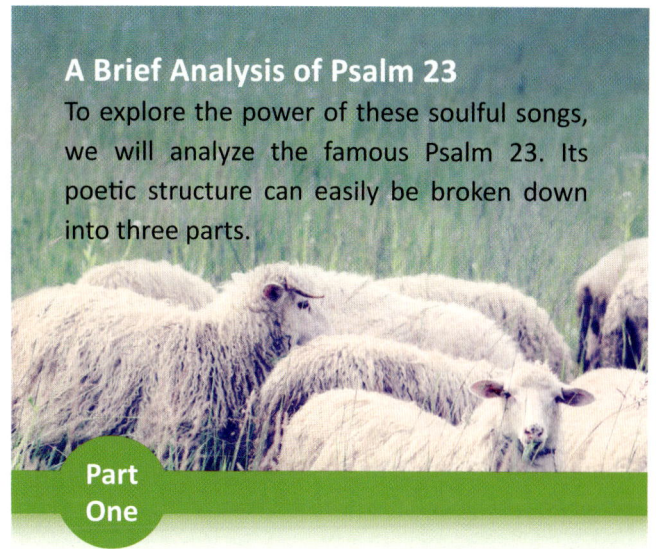

Part One

The writer presents God as a shepherd and himself as one of the sheep in God's flock. Under the care of the watchful shepherd, he's led to green meadows and quiet streams, a picture of tranquility and safety.

> *The LORD is my shepherd; I shall not want.*
> *He makes me lie down in green pastures.*
> *He leads me beside still waters.*
> *He restores my soul.*
> *He leads me in paths of righteousness*
> *for his name's sake.*
> Psalm 23:1-3 (ESV)

Part Two

The second part introduces potential danger, yet the writer remains confident. He's unafraid, for he knows the shepherd is still with him. The shepherd's special tools of the trade, his rod and staff, will protect the psalmist from harm.

> *Even though I walk through*
> *the valley of the shadow of death,*
> *I will fear no evil,*
> *for you are with me;*
> *your rod and your staff,*
> *they comfort me.*
> Psalm 23:4 (ESV)

Psalms 21

Part Three

Because the writer trusts in the shepherd's care, the potential conflict is resolved. Now the psalmist is no longer a sheep but a human guest at a banquet. His blessings are typified by an abundance of oil, and his enemies are powerless to harm him. His life overflows with goodness and mercy, and the promise of a secure future awaits him.

> You prepare a table before me
> in the presence of my enemies;
> you anoint my head with oil;
> my cup overflows.
> Surely goodness and mercy shall follow me
> all the days of my life,
> and I shall dwell in the house of the LORD forever.
> Psalm 23:5–6 (ESV)

Sheep and Shepherding

Great literature rises above time and place. Even for those of us whose only encounter with sheep might be counting them as we nod off to sleep, we can understand what the psalmist is trying to communicate. However, understanding sheep adds a bit more insight:

- Sheep are mentioned almost 200 times in the Bible, far more than any other animal, and every Israelite knew the role and value of a shepherd.

- A shepherd has to watch the sheep faithfully, caring for them 24/7/365. When the grass in one field is eaten, he has to find another.

- A proficient shepherd does not drive the flock from behind. Rather, he or she goes before the sheep and leads them. The sheep will follow if the shepherd has earned their trust.

- If given a choice, sheep normally won't drink from rapidly running water, which may startle them. They tend to prefer "still" or gently flowing water. Knowing where these water sources are is a basic element of shepherding.

- The shepherd's rod and staff are his main tools, used to navigate uneven ground, protect the flock from predators, and rescue stray lambs from thick brush.

Summary

Through its profound and poetic images, the Book of Psalms conveys some of the core struggles, fears, and hopes of the ancient Israelites. Although some of the imagery and references may be unfamiliar to the modern reader, people of very different backgrounds and cultures today find them both understandable and encouraging. The Psalms, preserved for generations in synagogues and churches around the world, have shaped classical music and even inspired some streams of modern rock.

Music

How Has the Bible Impacted Western Music Civilization?

Impact

"I will sing to the Lord, for He has triumphed gloriously; Horse and driver He has hurled into the sea."

Exodus 15:1 (NJPS)

The Sound of Music

How has the Bible influenced music? One indication of the Bible's impact on Western music is the fact that, according to one scholar, no poetry has been set to music more often than the Book of Psalms, found in the Old Testament.

Many of the 150 chapters of the Psalms are credited to David, the most famous of the Israelite kings. As a teenager and long before he rose to the throne, David was already known as a gifted musician, skilled at playing the lyre according to the Bible (1 Samuel 16:16-23).

The Book of Psalms is the most obvious place to go for references to music in the Bible, but it's hardly the only one. References to music span the entire Bible, from the early chapters of Genesis to the Book of Revelation.

Music 23

Bono
Modern Psalmist

Bono is the stage name of Paul D. Hewson (born 1960). He's the lead singer of the rock group U2. He writes almost all of U2's lyrics, frequently using religious, social, and political themes.

Bono has written about the influence of the Psalms on his songwriting.

Bono talks about the hardship David faced when he had to hide from the murderous King Saul (traditionally associated with Psalm 57). Bono says David's early songs feel like the compositions of a man facing trouble, even yelling at God. Bono refers to these psalms as early blues songs that inspired him in his writing (see Bono's introduction to *Selections from the Book of Psalms*, 1999).

The rock band U2 performs in the U.S. during a 2009 world tour.

Why the Bible?

Music played an important part in everyday life in the Ancient Near East. Evidence suggests that playing musical instruments and singing were both widespread activities. Music makes an early appearance in the Old Testament, with a man named Jubal identified as the "father" of those who play some of the ancient instruments (see Genesis 4:21). In the Book of Exodus, chapter 15, Moses and the Israelites sing after safely passing through the Red Sea. (This "Song of the Sea" is still recited today in a Jewish prayer service known as Shacharit.) The last book of the Bible refers to the song of Moses and the Israelites, sung this time by a heavenly choir (Revelation 15:3).

The Bible tells of worship in ancient Jerusalem resounding day and night with the songs of choirs and musicians. This atmosphere of song spilled over into the royal courts and often accompanied enthronements and other celebrations.

References to music—and to music in connection with other art forms, such as dancing and poetry—

The Battle Hymn of the Republic

*Mine eyes have seen the glory
of the coming of the Lord;*

*He is trampling out the vintage
where the grapes of wrath are stored;*

*He hath loosed the fateful lightning
of his terrible swift sword:*

His truth is marching on.

(Chorus)

Glory, glory, hallelujah!

Glory, glory, hallelujah!

Glory, glory, hallelujah!

His truth is marching on.

Written in 1861 by American abolitionist Julia Ward Howe, this song contains several references to biblical verses and imagery. The "grapes of wrath," for example, refer to a passage in Revelation 14. The song has had wide cultural impact, from the title of John Steinbeck's classic novel to the sermons of Martin Luther King Jr.

appear throughout the Bible. We read about elaborate musical arrangements involving large numbers of trained musicians, singers, and dancers (see, e.g., 2 Samuel 6:5; 1 Chronicles 25:1-7; 1 Kings 1:40). Even prophets, in the streets, are said to have made music with wind, string, and percussion instruments (1 Samuel 10:5). The Bible makes reference to cymbals, tambourines, lyres (a hand-held harp), lutes (a precursor to the guitar), dulcimers (a precursor to the xylophone), flutes, and trumpets.

Of course, religious ceremonies and music often go together, both in the ancient and the modern world. Some biblical passages report a close connection between forms of musical worship, ritual, and God's word. Temple sacrifice, for example, was said to involve both singing and an array of musical instruments (2 Chronicles 29:25-30).

The Old Testament encourages the people to sing and make music (e.g., Psalms 95:1; 98:1-6; and 150:1-6). The New Testament depicts Jesus and the apostles singing hymns (Mark 14:26; Acts 16:25) and encourages the early church to do the same (Colossians 3:16; Ephesians 5:18-19; James 5:13). The Book of Psalms includes instructions to the worship leader for both instrumentation and specific melodies on several psalms (see, e.g., Psalms 4:1; 8:1; 56:1; 60:1; 76:1; 88:1). Finally, the Book of Revelation features music as an important part of the heavenly courts (Revelation 5:9; 14:2-3; 15:2-4).

This striking illuminated Psalter was produced by an artist known as "Master of Jacques de Besançon" in the royal courts of Paris. It contains the Psalms, Canticles, and assorted liturgical materials. The use of these liturgical texts was greatly enhanced by the artistry. **Psalter,** France, ca. 1480–1490.

Miriam, Anselm Feurbach, 1862. Miriam, Moses's sister, led the Israelites with singing and dancing after they safely crossed the Red Sea. According to the Bible, she held a tambourine. Alte Nationalgalerie, Berlin, Germany.

Vocabulary

> **Canticle** [noun], a song with words from the Bible that is used in church services

Music

The Arch of Titus in Rome

The Arch of Titus in Rome, 15 meters tall, is the oldest surviving example of a Roman victory arch, dating from about AD 81. Depicted here is part of a famous panel from inside the arch, showing trumpets taken back to Rome in triumphal procession (probably being carried by Jewish captives). Historians believe these may be the silver trumpets that were in Jerusalem's Second Jewish Temple, destroyed by Titus in AD 70. These trumpets and other treasures from the destroyed Temple have never been found, and there is much debate over whether or not they still exist. According to the Bible, Temple music was performed with large choirs and a wide array of instruments.

According to biblical sources, Solomon's Temple (also known as the First Temple) was built in ancient Jerusalem and existed for centuries, until its destruction by Nebuchadnezzar II in 586 BC. Later, another Temple (known as the Second Temple) was erected. It lasted until the Roman army destroyed it in AD 70. The image above is a miniature version of the Second Temple and ancient Jerusalem at the Israel Museum in Jerusalem.

Music and Mourning

The destruction of the First Temple was followed by a period of sustained mourning among many Jews. Reflecting the sense of deep loss, music and singing were limited. In most Orthodox synagogues, based on long-standing traditions, Jews refrain from using musical instruments in regular services in order to honor the lost glory of Temple worship. In the centuries following the Roman destruction of the Second Temple, Jews continued to develop musical traditions within and beyond the context of the synagogue. Music remains an important part of religious and ritual life among Jews today.

Instruments of Faith

Leaders of the early Christian church, perhaps taking their cues from the Jews of the time, kept the use of musical instruments in worship to a minimum. Early Christian writers, such as Clement of Alexandria, the historian Eusebius, and John Chrysostom, explained that the people of the church themselves are "living instruments" most suited to worship. Early Christian folk music may have employed instruments outside the church, but the only substantial body of music that has survived from that era is the plainsong vocal chanting introduced through Ambrose of Milan (337–397) and Pope Gregory the Great (ca. 540–604). Throughout Christian history, new forms of spirituality—Eastern Orthodoxy, monasticism, and the Protestant Reformation, for example—often led to the development of new musical forms as well.

A stone statue of Saint John Chrysostom as found in Lichfield Cathedral, Staffordshire, England.

King Solomon
How Do You Build a Temple?

Narrative

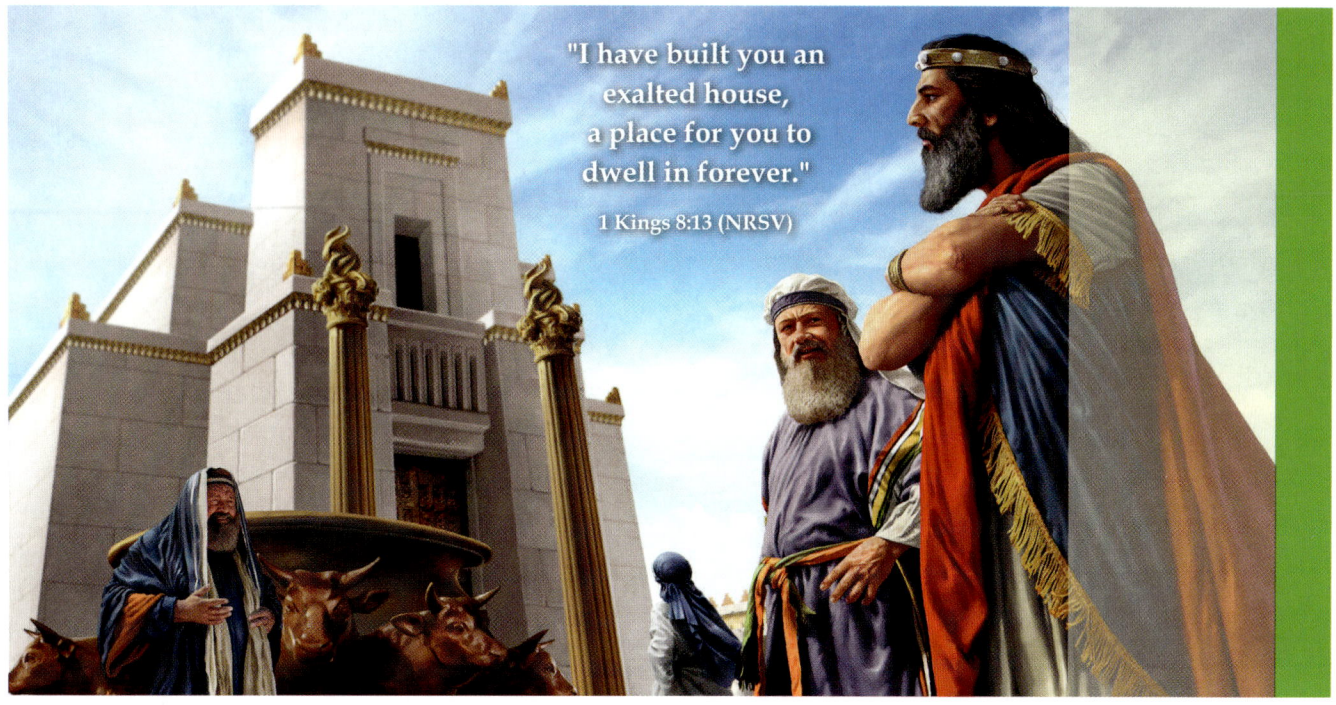

"I have built you an exalted house, a place for you to dwell in forever."
1 Kings 8:13 (NRSV)

Phase 1
Read the Story:
1 Kings 2–3; 5–6

The Story in a Nutshell

In 2 Samuel 7, David expresses his desire to create a permanent "house" for God. Is it right that the king should dwell in a palace, he asks, while the Ark of God remains in a tent? First God replies, through the prophet Nathan, that he needs no palace. But then he tells David that one of his sons will become king, and he will build the Temple. A later explanation given in the book of Chronicles says that David had shed too much blood to build the temple. His son would be a "man of peace" and well-suited to build a sacred place (1 Chronicles 22:8-10). The son who succeeds David on the throne is Solomon, whose name in Hebrew (*Shelomoh*) is derived traditionally from the word *shalom* for peace. David assembles the materials and Solomon carries out the detailed and very expensive project.

In 1 Kings 3, God appears to the new king and offers to give Solomon anything he desires. Solomon asks for an understanding heart, so that he might rule God's people justly. Pleased, God not only honors his request for wisdom but also throws in great wealth. Solomon's reputation for God-given wisdom spreads throughout Israel and beyond.

Solomon fulfills his father's wish to "build a house" for God, the glorious Temple in Jerusalem, which he dedicates with prayers, animal sacrifices, and an elaborate ceremony. God's "glory" (his presence) fills the Temple. Yet he warns Solomon that he will destroy the Temple and send the Israelites into exile if the king serves other gods (1 Kings 6-9). Later, King Nebuchadnezzar attacks Jerusalem and razes the Temple in 586 BC.

King Solomon | 31

Time Travel

King Solomon's Building Projects

Middle of the 10th century BC

The route for the transportation of wood for the construction of the Temple (from Lebanon to Joppa)

- Tyre
- Hazor
- SEA OF GALILEE
- Megiddo
- Tel Qasile
- Joppa
- Gezer
- Beth Horon
- Beth Shemesh
- **Jerusalem**
- Gaza
- Arnon River
- **Moab**
- Beersheeba
- Arad
- Zoar
- Kadesh Barnea
- Jotbathah
- Elath

MEDITERRANEAN SEA
Jordan River
DEAD SEA

Map Key:
Footpath ---
City •
Capital city ■
Scale: 1:3,000,000

Vocabulary

> **Edifice** [noun], a large and impressive building

The First and Second Jewish Temples

Construction of Solomon's Temple, also known as the First Temple, is thought to have begun in about 950 BC and to have taken fewer than ten years to complete. While no archaeological remains for the First Temple have been uncovered, the Bible gives the measurements as 90 feet long, 30 feet wide, and 45 feet high, not including some surrounding chambers. In the biblical account, the building is constructed from costly materials such as gold, bronze, and the finest imported wood. It houses the Ark of the Covenant and serves as the focus of the Jewish people's religious life for nearly four centuries, until it is destroyed by the Babylonians in 586 BC.

Decades later, after the people return from exile in the Persian Empire to Jerusalem, the building of the Second Temple is overseen by Zerubbabel (a community leader) and Jeshua (a priest). This edifice is 90 feet high and 90 feet wide, with an unknown length. The construction of the Second Temple takes more than 20 years (536–516 BC).

About 500 years later, Herod the Great greatly expanded the Second Temple. That work Herod began around 20 BC and continued for many decades, until about AD 63. The massive structure looked like a giant cube when viewed from the front, measuring 100 cubits (about 184 feet) in height and width. Behind this facade, the temple sanctuary measured 70 cubits (129 feet) wide. Many archaeological and literary records show that the Roman armies destroyed the Second Temple when they sacked Jerusalem in AD 70. For the past 19 centuries, there has been no temple in Jerusalem.

House of God, House of Gold

In the biblical narrative, Solomon spares no expense in building the Temple. The description in the text practically glimmers with gold. "So Solomon made all the things that were in the house of God: the golden altar, the tables for the bread of the Presence, the lampstands and their lamps of pure gold to burn before the inner sanctuary, as prescribed; the flowers, the lamps, and the tongs, of purest gold; the snuffers, basins, ladles, and firepans, of pure gold. As for the entrance to the temple: the inner doors to the most holy place and the doors of the nave of the temple were of gold" 2 Chronicles 4:19-22 (NRSV). Does this seem overdone?

The Temple was a statement of the Israelites' international stature, and it was central to their religious life. Even its courtyards symbolized the presence of God residing in the midst of the people. We see reflections of the power of religious belief in the expensive and beautiful buildings of the Vatican in Rome, Shwedagon Pagoda in Myanmar (Buddhist), and Prambanan Temple in Indonesia (Hindu). The ornate construction of Solomon's Temple might not seem so peculiar if we remember how important religious beliefs have been to most civilizations throughout the history of the world.

Notre Dame Cathedral, Paris, France.

Hagia Sophia, Istanbul, Turkey.

Shwedagon Pagoda, Myanmar.

Prambanan Temple, Yogyakarta, Indonesia.

A Heavenly Promise and Warning

In 1 Kings 9:4-8 (NRSV), Solomon receives a blessing from God that comes with a strong warning:

"As for you, if you will walk before me, as David your father walked, with integrity of heart and uprightness, doing according to all that I have commanded you, and keeping my statutes and my ordinances, then I will establish your royal throne over Israel forever, as I promised your father David, saying, 'There shall not fail you a successor on the throne of Israel.'

"If you turn aside from following me, you or your children, and do not keep my commandments and my statutes that I have set before you, but go and serve other gods and worship them, then I will cut Israel off from the land that I have given them; and the house that I have consecrated for my name I will cast out of my sight; and Israel will become a proverb and a taunt among all peoples. This house will become a heap of ruins; everyone passing by it will be astonished, and will hiss; and they will say, 'Why has the Lord done such a thing to this land and to this house?'"

The *Gates of Paradise*, constructed by Lorenzo Ghiberti in the 15th century on the baptistery of San Giovanni in Florence, Italy, depicts King Solomon with the queen of Sheba.

Solomon's Many Wives

Solomon's gathered a large number of wives and concubines in his royal harem, which included foreign wives, who brought their foreign gods with them. Intermarriage between royal families was widespread in the Ancient Near East and among royalty in general as a way of securing peace between nations. However, it was specifically forbidden for Israel's people and especially for Israel's rulers. In 1 Kings 11:1-8, the writer warns that marrying people from other nations will open the door to worshiping foreign gods.

Phase 2
Travel through Time

Traveling through time back to 920 BC, we arrive in the bustling trade city of Joppa on the Mediterranean coast. It's a perfect place to meet interesting people from different nations. During lunch at a local inn, we meet two spice traders from the city of Zoar, a father and son.

Arnon, aged 16, is named for a famous river in his country. Arnie, as he likes to be called, tells us about his dad's annual trips between Zoar and the big spice markets in Egypt. They left home a week ago and took the Jericho road, seeing the many layers of ruins of that ancient city. They also climbed the Mount of Olives, enjoying a panoramic view of Jerusalem.

This is Arnie's first time to Israel. Back in Zoar, Arnie's family worships Chemosh, the main Moabite god, along with several other deities that are important to their people. He's excited to see how another people worship.

"The new temple they've built is pretty impressive. Solomon, the new king, must've spared no expense. The Israelites have reserved a special area of the Temple courtyards for non-Israelites, so we were able to see and hear everything! One of the coolest things was this huge brass basin filled with water that rested on the backs of 12 bronze oxen! Everything is either decorated or covered with gold. They had just dedicated it to their god, YHWH, and they were still celebrating! The most amazing thing for me was the music and singing. A large choir was singing songs and playing instruments, and as worshipers came up to offer sacrifices they were singing, too! It felt like music filled the whole city. It sure was great to see how our neighbors worship. I can't wait to see what's next!

Temples and Sacred Space

When physical evidence is unavailable for something known only from texts, archaeologists often look for similar items for comparison. This helps them better understand and visualize the objects they're studying. In the case of Solomon's Temple, archaeologists look at other temples.

In the Bible, Solomon's Temple is described as having three sections, each holier than the last. This is called a "tripartite" ("three part") temple. While each civilization has its own type of temple or shrine, the tripartite temple is one commonly found in Syria and Canaan. The three parts can take a few different forms. The first space can be a porch, a courtyard, or a room just inside. The second space usually divides this entrance from the place where the deity rests (either a statue or object associated with or representing the deity). Finally, the third space is the holiest; that is, this space is most separated from all other spaces because the deity's presence is thought to be there. This layout creates increasing degrees of holiness as one gets closer to the deity.

Whatever civilization one explores—Egypt, Mesopotamia, Canaan, or Israel—architecture separates a deity from the surrounding inhabitants. This separation creates areas called "sacred space." These spaces are thought of as different, separate, or holier than others. A simple example helps us understand this idea. Think about how even though you live in an apartment, condo, or house—a regular type of building—that building often "feels" different than other buildings such as schools or stores. The special feeling we get from the place we live is why it's called "home." That's the idea behind creating sacred space, behind creating a "home" for our deities.

Vocabulary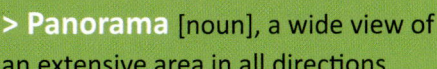

> **Panorama** [noun], a wide view of an extensive area in all directions
> **Harem** [noun], the place where a man's wives and concubines live

A replica of the **menorah** that stood in the First Temple. It is almost 6'7" in height, plated with about 65 pounds of gold. It is on display in the Jewish Quarter in Jerusalem, Israel. Property of The Temple Institute.

King Solomon (ca. 1200), Portal of Saint Anne, Notre Dame Cathedral. Paris, France.

King Solomon 35

The Throne of Solomon, ink on paper print by Ya'akov Leib Levinsohn, USA, 1890. A large colored rendition of the judgment of Solomon between two mothers who claimed to possess the same baby. An unusual portrayal of this scene (1 Kings 3:16-28). Image by the GFC Trust.

Solomon Dedicates the Temple in Jerusalem, by James Tissot, ca. 1896–1902. The Jewish Museum, New York. The powerful story of this dramatic event is described in 1 Kings 8.

Vocabulary

> **Cherubim** [noun, plural]
a specific type of angelic being

What You Would Have Seen

The Temple Courts

It's fascinating to imagine what it would have been like to visit remarkable places in ancient times. According to 1 Kings 6 and 2 Chronicles 3–4 (which both reflect opulence, but differ in actual numbers), if you had approached Solomon's Temple from the south, as an average Israelite, here is what you would have seen:

You first pass through the neighborhood of the priests. Then, after climbing a lot of steps, you come to gates of wood, overlaid with bronze. These mark the walls of the Temple area. Passing through these gates you will see that there are no permanent structures in the outer court; it's a crowded area with many worshipers. The priests are going in and out from another inner court to meet these worshipers. Many heads of families bring animals with them that are considered lawfully "fit" to sacrifice (such as sheep, calves, and doves). These animals are taken by priests to the inner court to be sacrificed there on behalf of those families. Of the approximately 600 laws in the Torah, about a third of them relate to special details involving animal sacrifices and priestly duties in the Tabernacle. The Jews believed that God had commanded sacrifices as a part of their covenant relationship.

The Bronze Altar for these sacrifices, in the inner court, is visible over a partition (wall) from the outer court. This allows everyone to see the sacrifices being offered. The altar is constructed of stones that are covered with bronze. In front of this altar, also in the inner court, sits a huge basin called the Molten Sea. It contains water for continuous personal washings and to clean up after all the messy sacrifices.

Near the entrance to the inner court you see a large choir of priests who are specially gifted singers. Music fills the air much of the time. You also hear trumpets and sometimes other instruments accompanying this all-male choir. The lyrics change depending on the day of the week. Just behind this busy inner court stands the Temple itself. According to the biblical instructions, the inside of the First Temple is 90 feet long, 30 feet wide, and 45 feet high. The courtyards make the whole complex much larger, mainly to hold all the people who come to sacrifice, worship, and watch.

Only certain appointed priests are allowed inside the actual Temple. According to the Bible, the inside walls are covered with cedar wood, displaying expert carvings of ornamentation and blooming flowers. The Temple floor is made of cypress.

The main room is called the Holy Place. Light comes from the left side of the chamber, thanks to a seven-branched Golden Lamp Stand (called the Menorah in Hebrew), burning only the purest olive oil to be found in the land. Priests trim the wicks of the Menorah and refurbish the oil so it burns constantly. The room also has a table on the right called the Table of Shew Bread, containing 12 special loaves of baked bread, representing the 12 tribes of Israel. Designated priests replace the loaves there every day with fresh ones. Directly in front, to the west, is the Golden Altar of Incense. Just behind that is another section called the Holy of Holies.

The Holy of Holies

The Holy of Holies is hidden from view. Only one person—the high priest—is allowed to go inside and only once a year for less than one hour. The Holy of Holies houses the Ark of the Covenant. Over the ark are artistic representations of two cherubim made of olive wood and covered with gold. The outstretched wings of these cherubim touch each other above the ark.

The high priest prepares himself all year spiritually, mentally, and physically to perform his main, but brief, task on the holiest day of the biblical calendar, the Day of Atonement (Yom Kippur, Leviticus 16 and 23). On that day, he alone enters this inner sanctum with a burning censer of fragrant incense in one hand and a bowl of blood from special animal sacrifices performed on that day. He then sprinkles this blood around the room and on the lid of the ark called the Mercy Seat.

The high priest does all this as the representative for the whole nation. After a special time of brief, spiritual communion with God, he emerges from the Temple, greeted by waiting multitudes of priests and Israelites outside in the courtyards. They are extremely relieved to see him come out into the daylight again, smiling and alive, a sign that God's presence will remain with his people for yet another year.

A gift from England, this bronze menorah stands outside the Israeli Parliament, the Knesset, in Jerusalem. This official State Menorah, created by Benno Elkan, contains reliefs of 30 events in Jewish history, many from the Bible. What has been called the official Bible verse of modern Israel is inscribed on it: "Not by might, nor by power, but by my Spirit, says the LORD of hosts" Zechariah 4:6 (NRSV).

Perfect Geometry

The English mathematician, scientist, and theologian Sir Isaac Newton (who developed the theory of gravity) was fascinated by the geometry of Solomon's Temple. Newton, was so impressed that he believed Solomon must have been divinely inspired to be able to construct it.

Timna Valley, about 200 miles south of Jerusalem, is the location of hundreds of copper mines, dating back to the time when Solomon is thought to have lived. Today it's a national park.

Solomon's Downfall

How could a ruler renowned for wisdom nevertheless sin against God and fall from greatness? The Book of Deuteronomy sets forth three things the king of Israel should not do (Deuteronomy 17:16-17):

- He shall not multiply horses for himself.
- He shall not multiply wives for himself who might turn his heart away from the God of Abraham, Isaac, and Jacob.
- He shall not greatly multiply for himself silver and gold.

Yet the Bible describes Solomon doing each of these three things. First Kings 10:14-25 recounts Solomon's amassing great wealth and endless amounts of gold. Verses 26-27 read: "Solomon gathered together chariots and horses; he had fourteen hundred chariots and twelve thousand horses … The king made silver as common in Jerusalem as stones" (NRSV). Finally, chapter 11 of 1 Kings claims that King Solomon loved and married many foreign women. As far as the biblical authors were concerned, all of Solomon's wisdom was of little help to him once he stopped following God's ways.

Phase 3
Mine for Clues

Learning from Nature

In the biblical account, Solomon's reputation for great wisdom spreads throughout the region. It's said that he composed 3,000 parables and 1,005 poems (1 Kings 4:32) and was one of the world's first naturalists, studying trees, animals, birds, reptiles, and fish (1 Kings 4:33). The Bible includes lessons of wisdom, attributed to Solomon, taken even from tiny creatures such as ants: "The ants are a people without strength, yet they provide their food in the summer" Proverbs 30:25 (NRSV). Not the strongest of creatures, ants are constantly planning for the future. The lazy person is warned to learn from the ant:

"Go to the ant, you lazybones;
 consider its ways, and be wise.
Without having any chief
 or officer or ruler,
it prepares its food in summer,
 and gathers its sustenance in harvest."

Proverbs 6:6-8 (NRSV)

In 1 Kings, people of all nations come to see the Temple and to hear Solomon's great wisdom. One story relates the visit of the famous queen of Sheba, who travels from Africa to witness the greatness of his realm (1 Kings 10:1-13).

Vocabulary

> **Sluggard** [noun], a lazy person

Phase 4
Use the Telescope

The Babylonians destroyed Solomon's Temple in Jerusalem in the midsummer of 586 BC. This occurred on the ninth of Av, according to the Jewish calendar. This ended what historians call the First Temple Period. The victors took many of the Jews to their land as slaves, as was typical of many conquerors in ancient history.

Seventy years later, the Second Jewish Temple was built by the exiles returning from Babylon to the ruins of Jerusalem. According to the Bible, the Second Temple was only a shadow of Solomon's grand edifice. Around 500 years later, it was refurbished and expanded dramatically by Herod "the Great," who was renowned for his cruelty but also for his architectural genius. In the New Testament, Jesus frequently worships, preaches and teaches there. He lovingly refers to the Temple as "my Father's house" (Luke 2:49).

But in AD 70, also in midsummer, on the same date that the First Temple was destroyed, on the ninth of Av (approximately the first of August), the Second Temple was leveled. This time it was done by Roman armies under General Titus, the son of Flavius, the emperor of Rome. This brutal destruction led to the great Diaspora, or dispersion of the Jewish people. Ever since that tragic day in AD 70, many Jewish people fast and pray every

Above, an artistic recreation of what the Second Temple in Jerusalem may have looked like, as viewed from the east, shortly before its destruction by Rome in AD 70.

Nothing is left from the Second Temple except for parts of a retaining wall built by Herod on the western side. The so-called Western Wall or Kotel is considered by Judaism today to be the holiest site on Earth. Thousands of Jews and many Christians gather here every day of the week to worship and pray. It's open 24 hours a day for this purpose.

year on the ninth of Av, the saddest day on the Jewish calendar. For at least the first 200 years of Christianity, many early Christians also mourned with the Jewish people on that day.

In AD 691, Muslims built a sacred memorial on the original site of the destroyed First and Second Temples, a beautifully constructed building called the Dome of the Rock. With a roof of pure gold, the Dome still stands in Jerusalem today. This Islamic structure is a reminder of the differences that commonly exist between religions all over the world, in this case between followers of the Bible and followers of the Qur'an. Both Jews and Muslims have a keen interest in this small piece of real estate. This is no surprise. According to tradition, this is the site where Abraham almost sacrificed his son Isaac (Genesis 22), where King David and King Solomon worshiped, and where both the Jewish Temples once stood.

Summary

In the biblical story, God shows his love for King David by making a promise to David and extending the covenant to his descendants forever. He allows Solomon to build the magnificent First Temple, in the heart of David's capital city, Jerusalem. In the end, however, Solomon disobeys God's commands. The Bible goes on to describe, in the centuries that followed, prophets who sought to bring the people and their rulers back to faith and obedience to the covenant. Some rulers listened, and some did not. Ultimately, Solomon's Temple is destroyed.

40 King Solomon

Hazor, Megiddo, and Gezer

What Can Archaeology Teach Us about These Biblical Cities?

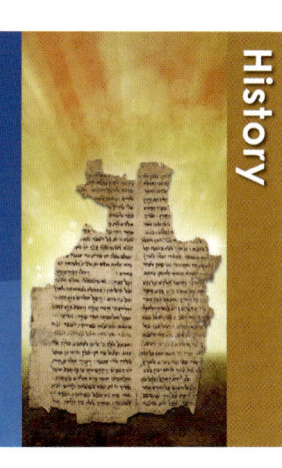

> "This was the purpose of the forced labor which Solomon imposed: It was to build the House of the LORD, his own palace ... and [to fortify] Hazor, Megiddo, and Gezer."
>
> 1 Kings 9:15 (NJPS)

Three Connected Ancient Cities

The ancient cities of Hazor, Megiddo, and Gezer may possess the key to unlocking some mysteries of the past. That, at least, has been the hope of archaeologists over recent decades. All three cities are frequently mentioned in the Bible, but their histories extend deep into antiquity. They were each thriving and strategically located centers in the land of Canaan at the time traditionally associated with the Israelites' arrival into the land. The ruins at all three sites have become a focus of modern archaeological research. The findings from the ruins of these locales have shed some light on the biblical narrative, answering some questions while raising new ones. According to 1 Kings, an ambitious building program was undertaken by King Solomon. To what extent may he have been responsible for the remains of the impressive fortifications that have been uncovered in these ancient cities?

In the 1960s, when Israeli archaeologist Yigael Yadin excavated Megiddo, he noticed that its strong fortifications and magnificent gate system were similar to those discovered in Hazor and Gezer. Based on his initial finds, Yadin concluded not only that the three cities date from Solomon's era, but that a single architect may have designed all three, using the same master plan. Other leading scholars concurred with Yadin, noting a remarkable correspondence between the biblical text (1 Kings 9:15) and the initial archaeological data.

Many archaeologists, including the well-known scholar Israel Finkelstein, now question the findings from the 1960s. In recent decades a more complicated picture has emerged. Fortifications at other sites have shown that such structures were not as distinctive as once thought. Further examination of the gates in Hazor, Megiddo, and Gezer has revealed a number of dissimilarities. Finally, new technologies used at these sites have dated the walls and gates to a later period, possibly as much as 100 to 150 years after the time in which the Bible places Solomon's reign. The conversation continues, but current evidence suggests that there was extensive construction and reconstruction in these cities from around the time of Solomon to several centuries after.

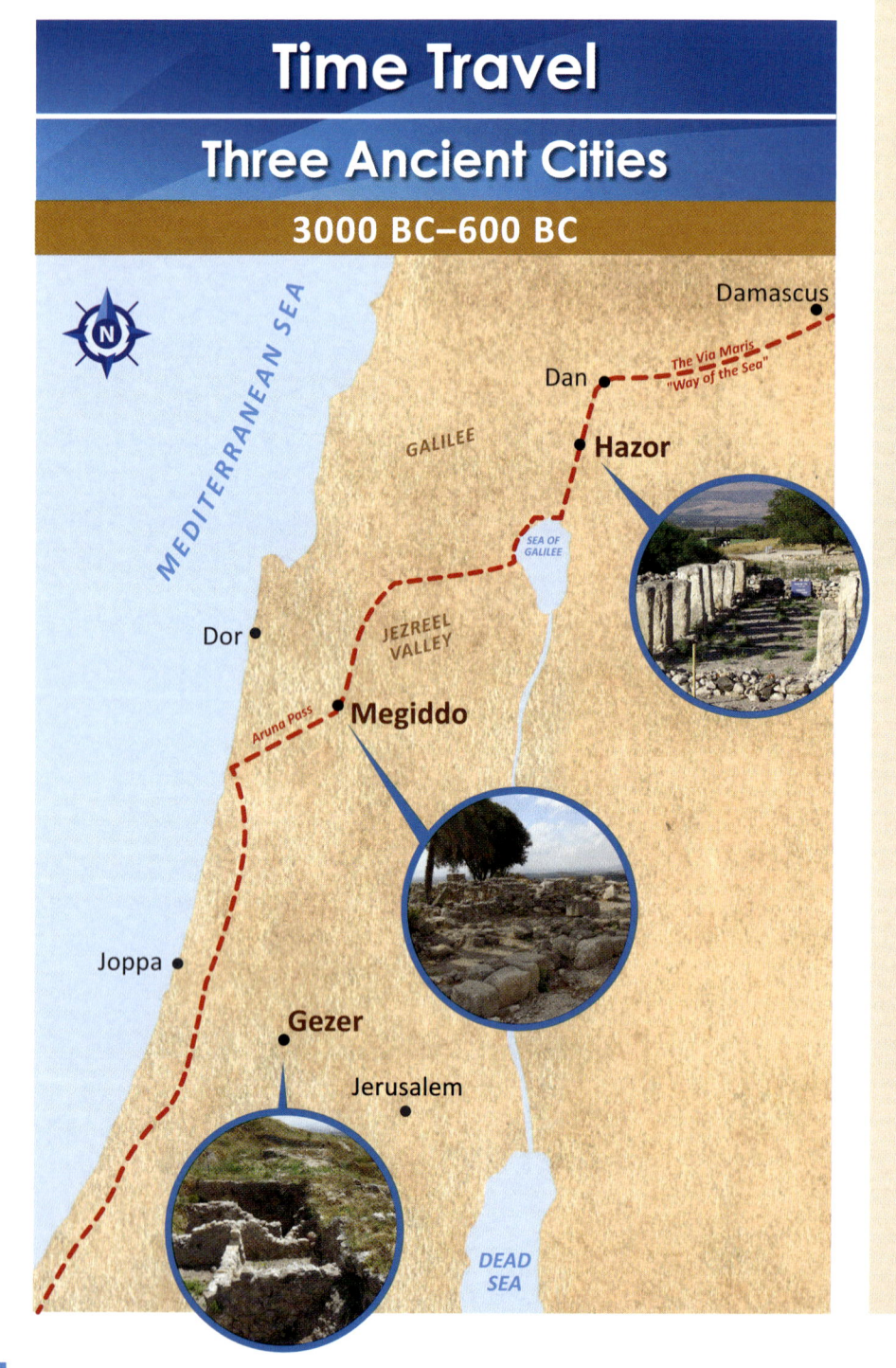

Time Travel
Three Ancient Cities
3000 BC–600 BC

International Highway

In the Ancient Near East, a major land route connected Mesopotamia and Egypt. This highway enabled traders and armies to traverse the entire region, passing through Canaanite and later Israelite territory. The city of Gezer, about 25 miles west of Jerusalem, was located east of that highway, along another road that linked the coastal area with the central hill country of Judah. North of Gezer, the cities of Megiddo and Hazor were situated along the main highway. This route was probably taken by Tiglath-pileser III when he swept down from Assyria to conquer Hazor and Galilee (2 Kings 15:29).

An extensive section of this highway extended along the Mediterranean coast. In Exodus 13:17 it was called "the way of the land of the Philistines." Much later, in Roman times, it became known as the *Via Maris* (Latin, "Way of the Sea"). In a famous passage, the prophet Isaiah had also spoken of a "way of the sea" (Hebrew, *derekh hayam*). He was probably referring to a road which marked the northern border of Israel at the time of the Assyrian conquest.

Hazor, Megiddo, and Gezer

Hazor

Hazor in Ancient Near Eastern Texts

The ancient city of Hazor lies about 12 miles north of the Sea of Galilee, in what today is called the Hula Valley. The ruins consist of two distinct sections—an upper city and a lower city. The upper city sits on a 30-acre mound approximately 130 feet above and to the south of the 170-acre lower city. At its peak, this 200-acre city would have been one of the largest in Canaan, with a population as great as 30,000. The sheer size of the upper and lower parts of the city signifies Hazor's importance, as does the mention of Hazor in several ancient texts.

At Mari, a city along the Euphrates (in modern-day Syria), documents from a royal archive dating to the 18th century BC refer to Hazor. One of these mentions that Hammurabi, the famous king of Babylon, had ambassadors residing in Hazor. This suggests there were close political ties between Hazor and Mesopotamia. Another Mari document notes the economic ties between the two places.

Many of the Amarna Letters are correspondence between local Canaanite leaders and an Egyptian pharaoh of the 14th century BC. These messages, written in Akkadian, provide further indication of Hazor's importance. Both the Akkadian documents and Joshua 11 describe Hazor as ruled by a king who not only controlled the land holdings of the city, but also administered other cities in the region.

On a clear winter day, the snowy slopes of Mount Hermon (to the north) provide a stunning backdrop for the area around ancient Hazor.

An aerial view of the upper and lower cities found at Tel Hazor. The different layers uncovered by archaeologists indicate that the city was ruled by various kings and a number of different nations during its long history.

Earliest Artifacts from Hazor's Lower City

Archaeologists have uncovered multiple artifacts of Canaanite worship in Hazor's lower city. These include a pottery mask, a bronze standard emblem depicting a snake goddess, a large stone altar with a groove for blood drainage, incense burners, and an inscribed stone decorated with a pair of hands raised toward a crescent and a disc. Some of these items date as far back as 3000 BC.

Hazor in the Bible

Archaeologists have uncovered evidence suggesting that the Canaanite city of Hazor was violently destroyed by fire. However, the city was then once again resettled and rebuilt. According to the biblical narrative, this took place when Hazor came under the control of the Israelites. The reconstruction included a palace complex and fortifications around the upper city. Excavators have also unearthed a six-chambered gate, along with long, pillared buildings and four-room houses, which are characteristic of Israelite architecture.

Megiddo

Israelite Gate: The city was rebuilt during the period of the Israelite monarchy. These are the remains of the city gate from that period. Archaeologist Yigael Yadin believed that it was built by King Solomon, but most scholars today think that it was built somewhat later, by King Jeroboam II in the eighth century BC.

This altar, found in the temple area, was used for animal sacrifice by the local population of Megiddo for around 2,000 years, from the Early Bronze Age to the Iron Age.

Megiddo—History and Warfare

The city of Megiddo is strategically situated near the western edge of the fertile Jezreel Valley. It is also close to the main regional highway. Many battles have taken place in and around the city, as armies fought to control travel through this area. One important conflict occurred during the northern military campaign of Pharaoh Thutmosis III (mid-15th century BC). As Thutmosis III approached Megiddo from the Mediterranean coast, he was faced with a strategic decision: by which way should he enter the Jezreel Valley? Only three options were available. The first two—a northern approach along the base of the Carmel mountain range, and a southern route through the Dothan Valley—both offered superior maneuverability for his large army.

But Thutmosis chose to take his troops on the third path, the main regional highway. This route runs west to east from the Mediterranean coast directly to Megiddo via Aruna. It narrows a few miles before Megiddo is reached, as it cuts through a pass in the central Carmel range. Because his enemy had positioned troops only at the northern and southern routes, the Egyptian king's tactics proved a success. After the battle, Megiddo became a vassal city of Egypt. Non-Israelite control of Megiddo in the 14th century BC is confirmed by letters found at Amarna, in which the Canaanite king of Megiddo petitioned Pharaoh for military assistance. According to the biblical account, the Israelites did not drive out the people of Megiddo when they first arrived in Canaan (Judges 1:27).

Armageddon

Megiddo is the setting for several prominent battles mentioned in the Bible. Judah's king Josiah was killed by Pharaoh Necho at Megiddo (2 Kings 23:29; 2 Chronicles 35:20-24). And Revelation 16:12-16 in the New Testament identifies Megiddo as the scene of the world's final battle, an apocalyptic event that is described as taking place at the end of days. The geographical name *Armageddon* means "Mountain (*har*) of Megiddo."

Megiddo

Earliest Artifacts from Megiddo

Archaeological finds at Megiddo include a sophisticated early Canaanite religious complex that dates as far back as 3000 BC. Megiddo's large stone altar is thought to have been in use around 2500 BC. A large collection of carved ivories, many of which reflect Egyptian influence, have been discovered in Megiddo's ruins.

Megiddo in the Bible

Although so far no clear evidence has been found that might conclusively connect King Solomon to the fortified walls of Megiddo, Hazor, and Gezer, there are other possible connections at these sites to his kingdom. Ruins of ancient buildings thought to be either stables or storehouses (see 1 Kings 9:19) are often attributed to the time of Solomon's reign. If not Solomon, then the most likely alternatives would be King Omri or his son Ahab, who ruled the northern kingdom of Israel in the ninth century BC. Both biblical and extra-biblical evidence suggest that the Omrides, the ruling descendants of Omri, expanded Israel's influence. There also seems to be further evidence of Israelite presence in Megiddo after the Omride dynasty came to an end. A jasper seal that depicts a lion in its center is inscribed with the words "Belonging to Shema servant of Jeroboam." This could refer to Jeroboam II, the eighth-century-BC king of Israel from the line of Jehu (2 Kings 14:23-29).

A Major Earthquake in the Time of Jeroboam II?

Based on geological evidence, it is estimated that a major earthquake (7.0 or greater on the Richter scale) occurs in this region on average two or three times every 1,000 years. According to Amos 1:1, a major earthquake struck the area during the time when Jeroboam was king of Israel and Uzziah king of Judah. This passage, however, probably refers to the ruler now known as King Jeroboam II and to his contemporary, King Azariah. According to the biblical record, these two kings would have reigned sometime in the first half of the eighth century BC. Yigael Yadin and other archaeologists have confirmed finding indications of "sudden destruction" at Gezer that may have been caused by a major earthquake around 760 BC. Archaeologists have found a similar pattern of destruction at Hazor during the same time period. Geologists, working independently, have found evidence in Israel that a major earthquake did shake the region in about 760 BC (plus or minus about 25 years). Was it the earthquake mentioned in Amos 1:1?

The southern stable is one of two stables in Megiddo. Evidence suggests that these were built during the period of the Israelite kings. According to the biblical narrative, King Solomon amassed chariots and horsemen and imported horses from Egypt (1 Kings 10:26-29). A large training ground is located next to the stable.

Vocabulary

> **Inscribe** [verb], to write or carve on something

> **Geology** [noun], a science that studies rocks and soil to learn about the history of the earth

> **Richter scale** [noun], a scale expressing the magnitude of a seismic disturbance (such as an earthquake)

Gezer

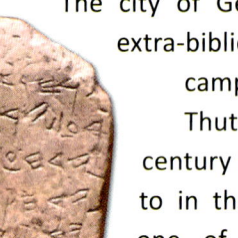

The city of Gezer is mentioned in extra-biblical records of the campaigns of Pharaoh Thutmosis III (mid-15th century BC). It is also referred to in the Amarna Letters, as one of the many strategic Canaanite cities under Egyptian control in the 14th century BC. According to the biblical story, King Horam of Gezer and his army were defeated by the Israelites at Lachish (Joshua 10:33). The Bible also narrates that the Israelites failed to drive out the Canaanite inhabitants of Gezer (Joshua 16:10), just as at Megiddo (Joshua 17:11-12).

The Gezer Calendar

Earliest Artifacts from Gezer

The most famous pre-Israelite find in Gezer is a group of eight large standing stones arranged in a line and thought to be related to Canaanite religious practices. Another discovery (from a later period) is the Gezer Calendar, dating to around the tenth century BC, which notes seasonal activities for farming. Prominent archaeologist William F. Albright, who translated it, said that the language on the inscription "is good biblical Hebrew, in a very early spelling." The calendar is of special interest to farmers working in Israel in the present day. It shows they still follow a similar pattern in the agricultural year as did their ancient predecessors.

Why Is This Interesting

The archaeological discoveries at each city and their impressive fortification systems help us to understand more about Israelite expansion in Canaan.

Gezer in the Bible

Gezer was a border town situated between the Philistines of southwest Canaan and the Israelites of the hill country to the east. The account found in 2 Samuel 5:25, which states that David drove back the Philistines as far as Gezer, may suggest that Gezer was under Philistine control during that era. According to the narrative in 1 Kings, the city then changed hands during the reign of Solomon. First, Pharaoh conquered and burned the city. He then gave it to his daughter as a wedding gift when she married King Solomon (1 Kings 9:16-17).

Why Is This Important

The archaeological record, extra-biblical texts, and biblical narrative allow us to partly reconstruct the history of the settlements at Hazor, Megiddo, and Gezer. Taken together, these sources suggest that these three cities were all major strategic centers with long and rich cultural histories.

Summary

The ancient cities of Hazor, Megiddo, and Gezer, all mentioned in the Bible, have histories that extend well back into the Canaanite period. The archaeological record and extra-biblical texts help us to reconstruct past events at these settlements. These sources show that the cities were all major strategic centers that played pivotal roles in the region. Throughout their long histories, they developed rich cultures and became the scene of dramatic events. There are still questions concerning how far archaeology confirms the stories of King Solomon and other Israelite leaders. Yet the dynamic narratives found in the Hebrew Bible help piece together the puzzle of the role played by these important cities through the centuries.

Proverbs
How Do We Make Sense of Ancient Wisdom?

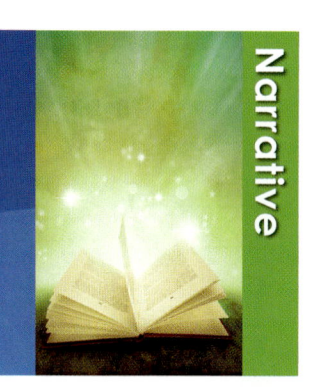

Narrative

"Go to the ant, O sluggard; consider her ways, and be wise."
Proverbs 6:6 (ESV)

Phase 1

Read the Story:
Proverbs 1; 17–18; 30–31

The Story in a Nutshell

When you think of people with wisdom, who comes to mind? Your parents or grandparents? How about a teacher or a coach? Perhaps a counselor or religious leader? It's often true that older people, those who have "been around the block," possess wisdom. We naturally turn to them for advice and encouragement in life. We assume their experiences can help inform our own decisions. Another way in which the experiences of older generations are packaged and passed down to the young is through "wise sayings" or adages, such as "Early to bed and early to rise makes a man healthy, wealthy, and wise" or "An apple a day keeps the doctor away." These are simple sayings that capture what people believe about the ways of the world and the pathways to fulfilling lives.

The ancient Book of Proverbs contains many such sayings that address everyday situations and problems. Its adages frequently contrast "wisdom" and "folly." Proverbs, the title in English, comes from the Hebrew verb *mashal*, meaning to compare. Proverbs offers a generous number of suggestions for successful living. A major theme comes early: "The fear of the LORD is the beginning of knowledge; fools despise wisdom and instruction" Proverbs 1:7 (ESV). The Hebrew word translated as "fear" in this verse can also be translated as "awe" or "deep respect."

Proverbs 47

Solomon, illustration from The Holy Bible, 1866 (engraving), by Gustave Doré, Bridgeman Art Library, Private Collection. Solomon is pictured as an old and wise king, writing his proverbs.

The Wisdom of Solomon (Juicio de Salomón), by Jusepe de Ribera, ca. 1609–1610. Galleria Borghese, Italy. The painting depicts the famous scene recorded in 1 Kings 3:16-28, in which the exceptional wisdom of the king in judgment was revealed. Two women come to him with two babies—one dead, one alive. Each woman claims to be the mother of the living child. Solomon orders the child to be cut in two, and one-half given to each mother. One mother agrees, but the other begs the king to spare the child's life and give him to the other woman. Solomon then declares that the woman who is not willing to sacrifice the life of the child is the true mother.

Phase 2
Travel through Time

Much of the book is attributed to King Solomon, although various other individuals are also named as authors. It is not surprising that Solomon became associated with wisdom literature since the Bible claims that Israel experienced its greatest growth during his reign. In the biblical narrative, Solomon seeks after wisdom (1 Kings 3:1-15), and this wisdom gives him vast knowledge, enormous wealth, and a talent for deft diplomacy and shrewd judgments.

Solomon has been associated with the wisdom literature of the Bible for thousands of years. This collection of texts in Proverbs is thought by scholars to comprise several different strands. The first strand consists of wisdom conveyed by the family or tribe. Children observed and imitated the behavior of their elders, who provided examples and instructions on wise decision-making. Another strand may have its origin in what was taught at "schools of wisdom." In these schools, the sages taught practical and court wisdom to the children of royal or noble patronage. These students were being prepared for leadership positions in the royal court in government, economics, and diplomacy. A third strand emerged from a scribal wisdom movement associated with the reign of King Hezekiah. Finally, scribes transcribed, edited, and published these collections of proverbs, including those attributed to King Solomon.

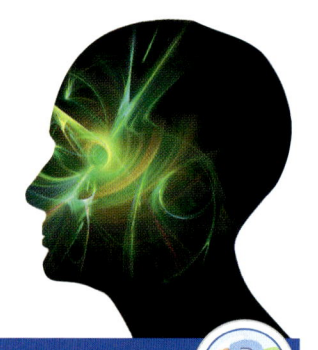

Vocabulary

> **Deft** [adjective], skillful and clever

Phase 3
Mine for Clues

Although many scholars have tried to find a unified structure to the book, it appears that the original source materials were only loosely organized. While some of these larger sections are attributed to Solomon (10:1–22:16; 25:1–29:27), several "headings" identify other sages as well. For instance, chapter 30 is said to comprise the sayings of a man named Agur son of Jakeh. Proverbs 31 is attributed to a king named Lemuel. Significantly, the book demonstrates the influence of Egyptian wisdom literature. Proverbs 22:17–24:22 resembles the *Wisdom of Amenemope*, an Egyptian text. The similarities are so striking that most scholars believe that the biblical author sometimes drew on this Egyptian wisdom tradition. A wise leader and author would have been expected to record and convey the very best of accumulated knowledge, whatever its source.

An Outline of Proverbs

1:1-7
Introduction to the book

This suggests a possible theme for Proverbs, "The fear of the LORD is the beginning of knowledge."

1:8–9:18
Prologue

A second opening section describes how wisdom is found and how foolishness and temptation interfere with this search.

10:1–22:16
The proverbs of Solomon

The proverbs attributed to Solomon consist of couplets—two lines that create a contrast or a progression.

22:17–24:22
The sayings of the wise

These sayings show a similarity between Egyptian wisdom literature (*Wisdom of Amenemope*) and biblical wisdom sayings through common ideas and language.

25:1–29:27
Proverbs compiled by Hezekiah's officials

Miscellaneous sayings are featured.

30:1-33
The sayings of Agur

Agur means "collector" in Hebrew. This portion of the book contains his collection of proverbs.

31:1-31
The sayings of King Lemuel

The first nine verses concern the responsibilities of the king. Verses 10-31 form a poem regarding the "woman of noble character" arranged as an acrostic, with each verse beginning with one of the 22 letters of the Hebrew alphabet.

"The beginning of wisdom is this: Get wisdom, and whatever you get, get insight"
Proverbs 4:7 (ESV).

Vocabulary

> **Miscellaneous** [adjective], including many things of different kinds
> **Acrostic** [noun], a poem, word puzzle, or other composition in which certain letters in each line form a word or words or an alphabetical sequence

Instructing Youth

A number of distinctive literary features characterize the book and suggest how it might have been used to teach young people, perhaps the children of royalty. Proverbs 1–8 consists of a father's advice to his sons, or a teacher's advice to his pupils. The presence of numerical sayings could be memory aids or seem to underscore the use of proverbs in training:

> "Four things on earth are small,
> but they are exceedingly wise:
> the ants are a people not strong,
> yet they provide their food in the summer;
> the rock badgers are a people not mighty,
> yet they make their homes in the cliffs;
> the locusts have no king,
> yet all of them march in rank;
> the lizard you can take in your hands,
> yet it is in kings' palaces"
>
> Proverbs 30:24-28 (ESV).

The small but wise creatures described in Proverbs 30: (from top) black worker ants preparing vegetation for their nest, rock badgers perched safely on their rocky home, locusts swarming together.

Three Kinds of Poetic Parallelism

Hebrew poetry relies extensively on a style known as parallelism, where the writer employs literary parallels to make certain points. Some scholars refer to three especially common types of parallelism found in Proverbs and other books in the Hebrew Bible.

Synonymous
When the meaning of one line is nearly the same as that of the other: "Pride goes before destruction, and a haughty spirit before a fall" Proverbs 16:18 (ESV).

Antithetical
When one line contrasts with the other, but in a way that reinforces a single point: "Whoever goes about slandering reveals secrets, but he who is trustworthy in spirit keeps a thing covered" Proverbs 11:13 (ESV).

Synthetic
When the second part of a statement completes or complements the first: "Whoever keeps his mouth and his tongue keeps himself out of trouble" Proverbs 21:23 (ESV).

Similes: We also find many similes in Proverbs. A simile is a figure of speech using the word *like* or *as* to compare one thing with another thing of a different kind. For example:
"A word fitly spoken
is like apples of gold in a setting of silver" Proverbs 25:11 (ESV).

Personification and Types

Proverbs also employs a literary technique called personification, in which abstract ideas receive human characteristics. The early chapters, for instance, describe wisdom as a beautiful woman. In chapter 8, she stands on the heights and cries out, inviting men to learn from her. Other passages use figures like "the wise woman" and "the wicked woman" to refer to types of people who could lead a young person toward prosperity or toward ruin. The first nine chapters of Proverbs continually refer to the seductive influences of an adulteress ("the wicked woman") who tempts the young man to make poor decisions (Proverbs 7:6-23; 9:13-18). By contrast, the "wise woman" preserves and protects a young man's virtue and provides sound guidance (3:13-18). These passages provide a fascinating window into the ways in which an ancient people understood men, women, and their relationships.

In one of the best-known sections of the book, 31:10-31, we see an extended description of sound judgment and practical wisdom. The passage focuses on the "woman of noble character" who works hard, provides for her family and employees, runs a successful business, plans ahead, helps the poor, anticipates needs, and uses care in her speech. The text presents these qualities as the foundation for successful living. For many generations in Jewish homes, husbands have blessed their wives at the beginning of the Sabbath with these verses.

The Macklin Bible, London, 1800. The illustration at the beginning of the Book of Proverbs shows a winged heart with the Hebrew word *da'at* ("knowledge") inscribed upon it. In the heart is an eye from which a flame travels up to a radiant cloud labeled with another Hebrew word, *chokma* ("wisdom").

Well-Known Proverbs Today

Many of the book's ancient wisdom sayings have been incorporated into common English usage.

Here are some of the better-known examples (all ESV). How many do you know?

- A soft answer turns away wrath (15:1).
- Pride goes before destruction (16:18).
- A friend loves at all times (17:17).
- A joyful heart is good medicine (17:22).
- There is a friend who sticks closer than a brother (18:24).
- Iron sharpens iron (27:17).

Phase 4
Use the Telescope

New Testament Citations

The writers of the New Testament also tapped into the wisdom of Proverbs. These writers were already familiar with this wisdom literature. It would have been natural for them to use statements from Proverbs to support the ethical teachings they wrote down.

"Better is a poor man who walks in his integrity than a rich man who is crooked in his ways"
Proverbs 28:6 (ESV).

Proverbs	The New Testament
"...for **their feet** run to evil, and they **make haste to shed blood**" (1:16).	"**Their feet are swift to shed blood**" (Romans 3:15).
"**My son, do not despise the LORD's discipline or be weary of his reproof,** for the LORD **reproves him whom he loves,** as a father the son in whom he delights" (3:11-12).	"**My son, do not regard lightly the discipline of the Lord, nor be weary when reproved by him.** For the Lord disciplines the one he loves, and chastises every son whom he receives" (Hebrews 12:5-6).
"**Toward the scorners he is scornful, but to the humble he gives favor**" (3:34).	"Therefore it says, '**God opposes the proud, but gives grace to the humble**'" (James 4:6).
"Hatred stirs up strife, but **love covers all offenses**" (10:12).	"Above all, keep loving one another earnestly, since **love covers a multitude of sins**" (1 Peter 4:8).
"**Like a dog that returns to his vomit** is a fool who repeats his folly" (26:11).	"What the true proverb says has happened to them: '**The dog returns to its own vomit**, and the sow, after washing herself, returns to wallow in the mire'" (2 Peter 2:22).

ESV translation used for all citations

Summary

The Book of Proverbs promotes what it considers wise and discerning behavior while addressing many of the challenges and tough decisions people face in their daily lives. It employs literary tools and techniques to make its teachings memorable and compelling. Although compiled in ancient times, in a very different society and culture from our own, this book has been a favorite of people the world over. Readers today still seek out wisdom in these ancient sayings.

The Song of Songs
What Does This Book Say about Love's Mysteries?

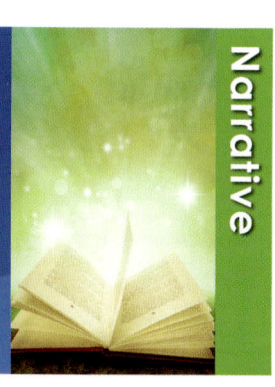

Narrative

"Many waters cannot quench love; rivers cannot sweep it away."
Song of Songs 8:7 (NIV)

Phase 1
Read the Story:
Chapters 1–8

The Song of Songs in a Nutshell

She walks in beauty, like the night
Of cloudless climes and starry skies;
And all that's best of dark and bright
Meet in her aspect and her eyes;
Thus mellowed to that tender light
Which heaven to gaudy day denies.

The opening stanza of Lord Byron's "She Walks in Beauty" gives us some of the most famous lines of romantic poetry in the English language. From Shakespeare to Byron to more modern works—whether films like *Titanic*, the novels of Nicholas Sparks, or all kinds of contemporary pop music from musicians like Taylor Swift and One Direction—our cultural traditions are awash in stories and celebrations of the joys, the beauties, and the heartaches of romantic love. Although many of us wonder whether true and lasting love really is attainable in this world, people in many cultures and all walks of life celebrate the idea. So does a particular book in the Bible.

Song of Songs is a book of love poetry. The title in Hebrew means "the very best song." Some traditions call the book Canticles, based on the Latin word for song. The book is all about love, casting it as one of the strongest of all human feelings when experienced fully.

The Song of Songs 53

While the Bible in general has much to say about God's love, Song of Songs doesn't specifically mention God. Instead, it addresses the deep human-to-human need to love and be loved. It presents Hebrew poems about love's intensity and passion, exploring the intimacy of close companionship. If you have heard that the writers of the biblical texts were prudes about romance, a closer reading of this book might challenge that viewpoint. No matter how you see these love poems, as fictional ideal or as spiritual allegory, this text delves more deeply into the mysteries of romantic love than any other book in the Bible.

The Song of Songs celebrates the delight, intimacy, and commitment of human love. Phrases such as "Love is as strong as death" and "Many waters cannot quench love" Song 8:6-7 (NIV) portray the powerful bond of love. Some scholars see a progression in the Song from the beginning of courtship (1:1–3:5), to the closeness of love's embrace (3:6–5:1), and finally to the struggle of fostering an enduring relationship (5:2–8:14). Its pages are certainly filled with lyrical (and sometimes scandalous) descriptions of physical attraction and intimacy.

The main waterfall of En Gedi (Spring of the Kid), a deep ravine in the rocky mountain cliffs above the shores of the Dead Sea in Israel. Many types of bird, plant, and animal species flourish here. The writer of the Song of Songs drew inspiration for many of his images from this lush oasis in the wilderness: "My beloved is to me a cluster of henna blossoms from the vineyards of En Gedi" Song 1:14 (NIV).

"My beloved is like a gazelle or a young stag" Song 2:9 (NIV). The Nubian ibexes pictured here are native to Israel. These sure-footed creatures are skilled at climbing and leaping on the cliffs of En Gedi, and they lend their name to this hideaway in the cleft of the mountains rising above the Dead Sea.

Phase 2
Travel through Time

Sometimes Song of Songs is called the Song (or Songs) of Solomon because it mentions the famous Israelite king seven times (1:1, 5; 3:7, 9, 11; 8:11, 12). Elsewhere in the Bible, Solomon, the son of King David, is credited with composing more than 1,000 songs and 3,000 wise sayings. The Bible claims he knew a lot about plants, animals, and farming (1 Kings 4:33). From one stylistic perspective, his authorship is not far-fetched. The Song of Songs often refers to various plant and animal species. Its lyrics create vivid images of agricultural life. The poems highlight natural settings in vineyards, orchards, and gardens. The author describes flocks and wild gazelles in detail. Nonetheless, many writings were attributed to Solomon, and there is no direct evidence of his authorship.

The lover poetically tells his beloved, "Your lips drop sweetness as the honeycomb, my bride; milk and honey are under your tongue" Song 4:11 (NIV). She is the lovely flower in the field, the most perfect rose of the Sharon Valley, and the treasured lily among the thorns (2:1-2). The natural settings of the book's passionate scenes create an intimate context for the two lovers.

The Song of Songs refers to geographical areas from Lebanon to Egypt. It mentions Damascus (7:4) as well as Mount Gilead (4:1) and Mount Hermon (4:8). It describes the wilderness refuge for natural spring water near the desolate Dead Sea, contrasting the death of the desert and salt water with the life-giving water from the springs of En Gedi (1:14).

Vocabulary

> **Lyrical** [adjective]
beautiful and imaginative
> **Allegory** [noun], a story in which a deeper level of meaning lies behind the literal meaning of the text

The Shulammite Woman

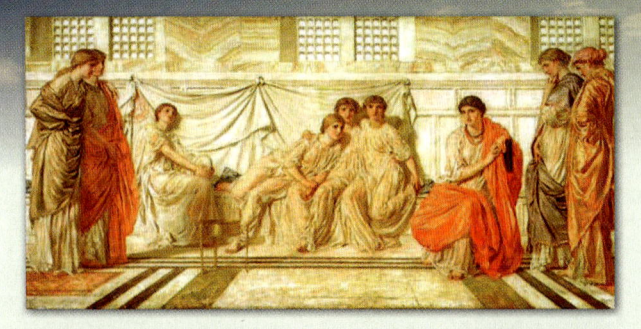

The Shulamite, Albert Joseph Moore, 1864. Walker Art Gallery, Liverpool, United Kingdom. The Shulammite woman is shown here addressing the young women of her court, perhaps the "daughters of Jerusalem" mentioned in the text. They listen with rapt attention as she speaks to them of the king, as in Song of Songs 5:10-16, where she extols the beauty of her beloved. Here delicate colors, classical poses, and rich drapery add to the dignity and beauty of the scene.

The love described in the Song of Songs is between the "king" and a Shulammite maiden (or a young woman from Shulem, see 6:13). She is a vineyard keeper with deeply tanned skin from her long hours outdoors (1:5-6). Although from a humble family, she addresses the king as "my beloved." In response, he calls her "my lover." This young Shulammite finally declares, "I belong to my beloved, and his desire is for me" Song 7:10 (NIV). The desire and longing of the two lovers for each other runs through the book.

Three voices are heard in the movement of the lyrics: (1) the bride (the Shulammite), (2) the groom (likened both to a shepherd and to a king, or possibly King Solomon), and (3) the chorus (translated in some versions as "the friends" or "the others"), who provide responses as the "daughters of Jerusalem." These friends share in the joy of Solomon and the Shulammite, both of whose names denote shalom or "peace."

The text mentions both Jerusalem and Tirzah (6:4), major cities in the north and south of the Israelite kingdom. Afterward, when Israel split into two kingdoms in around 930 BC, Samaria became the capital of the new northern kingdom.

Some interpreters suggest that Song of Songs is a treatise on love in poetic form, and the figure described is not Solomon but an idealized, fictional groom who longs for his bride, showcasing mutual love and intimacy.

Other interpreters view the book as a fictional love story to be presented as a play or performed during a wedding. The author uses words that are specially chosen to communicate passion and 50 of them do not appear anywhere else in the Bible. The poetry does not seem to follow a single pattern, and the language used may reflect an era later than that of Solomon. Debate persists on whether the book is a random collection of love songs or a series of interconnected poems.

Love's Challenges

As in every love story, the writer does not minimize the truth observed by Shakespeare in *A Midsummer Night's Dream* (Act 1, Scene 1) that "the course of true love never did run smooth." If we interpret the book as a unified narrative, then we watch as the relationship of the "king" and the Shulammite woman proceeds through courtship, commitment, separation and loss, and finally the rekindling of love. As their story unfolds, the backdrop changes continually. The settings are both urban and rural—from the king's palace and the city streets and square, to desolate mountain heights and forested wilderness, to exquisite cultivated gardens and vineyards of lush fruitfulness. And along the way, like a skilled singer-songwriter, the author uses a wealth of images that appeal to the reader's heart and senses.

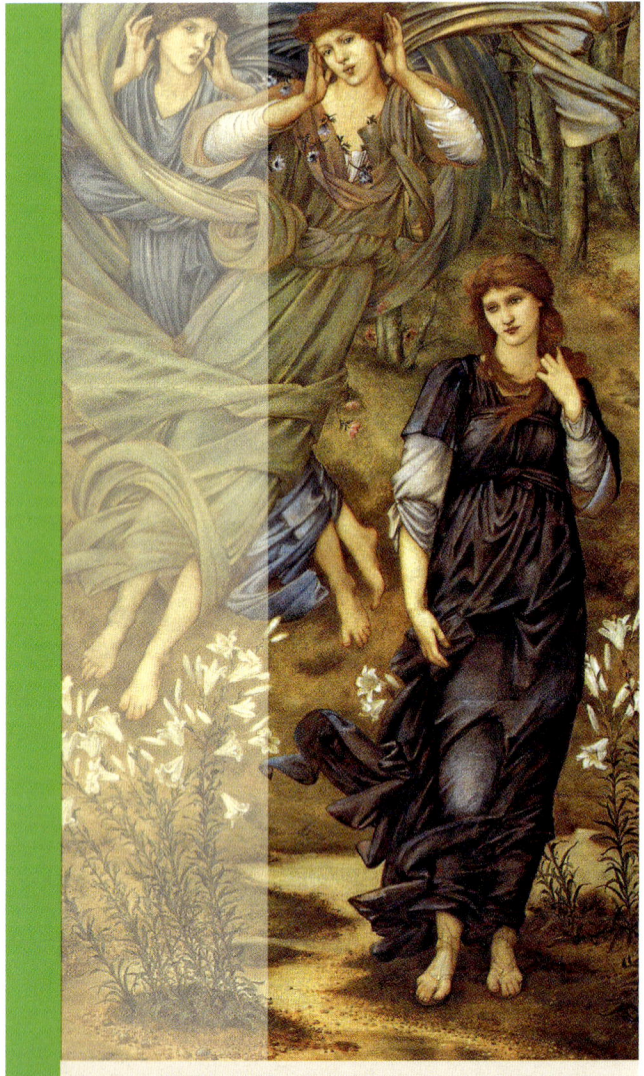

A Minstrel Playing Before Solomon, illumination for the opening verse of Song of Songs, the Rothschild *Mahzor*, manuscript on parchment. Florence, Italy, 1492. The Jewish Theological Seminary of America, New York.

In the giddy beginning of their relationship, pictures of the beauty and riches of the environment abound—the joy of spring returning after the rainy winter, the birds and flowers that symbolize the delight and abundance of life the lovers are experiencing, and the fragrance of spices that suggest the intoxication of their mutual love. The author borrows from the natural world to find ways to describe the incomparable loveliness of the beloved Shulammite. These profuse images suggest the stunning impact she has had on the king: "You have stolen my heart ... with one glance of your eyes, with one jewel of your necklace" Song 4:9 (NIV).

Yet after a period of initial delight and passion, there is a time of timidity, uncertainty, and loss. The danger of embarking on this journey of love has already been suggested by images of mountain heights and wilderness: "Come with me from Lebanon. Descend from the summit of Hermon, from the mountain haunts of leopards" Song 4:8 (NIV). The lover and his beloved are separated and suffer anguish and yearning. The beloved experiences troubled dreams and restless sleep—yet this very experience of loss causes her to recognize the value of their love and compels her to pursue it with renewed intensity.

The Song thus finally becomes a story of love found, lost, and regained. The reaffirmation of the love between the lover and beloved, with a greater degree of appreciation and commitment, brings a deep sense of peace. The triumphant assurance of steadfast love is evoked by the figure of the beloved. His love for her is like a flame of fire that cannot be quenched, even through floods of water (8:6-7). Song of Song's enthusiastic celebration of love provides one reason why this small book has appealed to so many generations since it was first written.

Sponsa de Libano (The Bride of Lebanon), Edward Burne-Jones, 1891. Walker Art Gallery, Liverpool, England. This work was inspired by a passage from the Song of Songs (4:8-11).

Phase 3
Mine for Clues

Allegorical Interpretations

Over the centuries, many religious people were uncomfortable with the book's frankly sexual depiction of two lovers intimately seeking each other. Others were inclined to read sacred texts in allegorical ways, as though the Song of Songs was really representing another kind of loving pursuit. Many people over the centuries, then, have found multiple levels of meaning in the Song of Songs.

Many Jewish scholars argued that the book is pure allegory about God's relationship with Israel. (In an allegory, each major element in the story stands for something else.) The famous Jewish sage Rabbi Akiva (ca. AD 40–137) championed the idea that the book describes God's love for Israel. Even today, rabbinic Jews read Song of Songs on Passover as a celebration of the Exodus, an image of God drawing out his bride into an everlasting relationship. Similarly, many Christian readers saw the Song of Songs as an extended metaphor describing God's love for the community of the faithful. In both these views, the detailed encounters between the lover and the beloved are literary devices illustrating the intensity of God's love for his people. This type of interpretation may have contributed to Song of Songs being accepted into the Jewish and Christian canon.

These scholars compared the book to the tradition of ancient Hebrew prophets, like Hosea, who described the relationship between God and Israel in very human terms:

> "In that day," declares the LORD,
> "you will call me 'my husband';
> you will no longer call me 'my master.'"...
> I will betroth you to me forever;
> I will betroth you in righteousness and justice,
> in love and compassion.
> I will betroth you in faithfulness,
> and you will acknowledge the LORD."
>
> Hosea 2:16, 19-20 (NIV)

Such prophets highlighted the relationship between God and his people as a covenantal relationship, like marriage, portraying God as the groom and God's people as the bride.

Still others read the book as describing the longing of a spiritual traveler on a journey into a deeper relationship with God. Such mystical approaches interpreted the story as a depiction of God's love for the soul of the individual as well as the soul's yearning for spiritual union with the divine. The seeker desires to be united with God through prayer and personal devotion. Such interpreters see the book as a love poem written to God from the heart of a mystic.

Many biblical writers and interpreters have looked at weddings and marriages as metaphors for the relationship between God and his people. Here, two survivors of Hurricane Katrina are getting married in Houston, Texas, in 2005.

The Song of Songs

Phase 4
Use the Telescope

From the Pulpit to the Bedroom

Many faith-based marriage counselors today refer to the Song of Songs as a practical guide to better intimacy between married individuals. Pastors and rabbis sometimes use this biblical book as a framework for their teaching on romance and marriage.

Whatever it was originally, whether a collection of love poems or a story of an enduring relationship or a play to be performed at weddings, the Song of Songs lives on today among those who study it for insights into love that is joyful and playful, passionate and lasting.

Two white doves are captured in a loving pose. These beautiful birds provide a recurring image in the Song. For example, in Song 4:1 the beloved tells the Shulammite that her veiled eyes are like doves. They symbolize gentleness, tenderness, and considerate love.

Vocabulary

> **Recurring** [adjective], occurring or appearing at intervals

Summary

The Song of Songs is the primary biblical text about human love. Some see it as a fictional description of two lovers whose story can inspire couples at wedding ceremonies. This view seeks to answer the question, how can a bride and groom bond with each other for a lasting life of love and companionship? Others see the Song of Songs as an allegory of God's passionate and enduring love for his people. This view says that even if people prove to be unfaithful, God's love is not conditional. Still others see this book as celebrating stages of human love, from the ardent desire of courtship, to the closeness of marriage, and to the unshakable pledge of an enduring relationship. The Song of Songs communicates desire, intimacy, and companionship in whatever interpretive framework we use. Its multidimensional descriptions of intense feeling and commitment provide insights into some of the deep mysteries of true love.

Ecclesiastes

What Is the Message of This Complex Book?

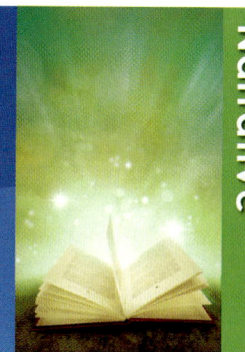

Narrative

"I know that there is nothing better for people than to be happy and to do good while they live."

Ecclesiastes 3:12 (NIV)

Phase 1

Read the Story:
Ecclesiastes 1–2; 7; 11–12

Ecclesiastes Tops the Charts

In 1965 a rock group called the Byrds released a single that topped the U.S. pop music charts for three weeks in a row: "Turn! Turn! Turn! (To Everything There Is a Season)." You can still hear the tune on radio stations that feature classic hits. While the well-known folk musician Pete Seeger wrote the lyrics, they actually originate from the King James Version of the Bible!

Like the pop hit, Ecclesiastes chapter 3 (in the King James Version) begins: "To every thing there is a season, and a time to every purpose under the heaven." Reflecting opposition to the Vietnam War, which was raging at the time, Seeger added a short personal commentary: "a time for peace, I swear it's not too late." Who would have guessed that ancient words of Hebrew wisdom would ever become a celebrated piece of pop culture so many centuries later?

Ancient Wisdom

The books of Ecclesiastes, Job, and Proverbs (and some also count Song of Songs, too) constitute the main "wisdom literature" of the Jewish scriptures, which has as its central theme the search for good judgment and understanding. Ecclesiastes describes a lifelong pursuit of wisdom but reveals that the path toward this destination is not always clear. Like this quest, the book itself is complex. Its Hebrew differs from that found in other Jewish scriptures.

Many of the statements in Ecclesiastes sound cynical or pessimistic and seem to downplay the possibility of ever experiencing joy in this life. Any wisdom truly worthy of the name, the author seems to suggest, must take into account the human experience of futility and meaninglessness, and the struggle to make sense of life and the world we inhabit. The author refers to expectations that are dashed, goals that are pursued and yet found to be ultimately unfulfilling. The lofty yet practical conclusion therefore comes almost as a surprise to many readers:

> Now all has been heard;
> here is the conclusion of the matter:
> Fear God and keep his commandments,
> for this is the duty of all mankind.
> For God will bring every deed into judgment,
> including every hidden thing,
> whether it is good or evil.
>
> Ecclesiastes 12:13-14 (NIV)

Vanitas vanitatum et omnia vanitas (Vanity of Vanities, All Is Vanity), Isaak Asknaziy, ca. 1870. The Russian painter has depicted an old and wiser King Solomon, seated upon his throne flanked by lions, sharing his hard-won wisdom with three Hebrew youths who are listening in rapt attention.

Phase 2
Travel through Time

The Book's Authorship

The writer describes himself as "the son of David, king in Jerusalem" who reigns as "king over Israel" Ecclesiastes 1:1, 12 (NIV). He then attributes mighty works to himself, similar to those of the great king Solomon (Ecclesiastes 2:3-10; 1 Kings 3–11). While this internal discussion implies that the writer is King Solomon, the book only mentions David's son, who was a king. Language scholars challenge if the Hebrew used matches Solomon's era. Conversely, later Jewish sages believe King Solomon wrote Ecclesiastes in his old age while looking back over his rich but unique life—in addition to ruling expansive geographic territories, he also had no fewer than 700 wives and 300 concubines (1 Kings 11:3).

Solomon Receiving the Queen of Sheba, Gustave Doré, Illustrated English Bible, published in 1885, Shebagart, Germany.

Phase 3
Mine for Clues

The Teacher

The Hebrew name for the book is Kohelet (literally, "the gatherer of the assembly"). Ecclesiastes, its English name, is based on similar-sounding Greek word that means "assembly gatherer." The author refers to himself as this teacher, beginning with the first verse: "The words of the teacher (*kohelet*), the son of David, king in Jerusalem."

Marriage Feast of Nastagio degli Onesti, Sandro Botticelli, ca. 1483. Private collection, Palazzo Pucci, Florence, Italy.

Enjoying Life and Remembering God

One of the main points of encouragement in Ecclesiastes is to take delight in the simple and good things life has to offer: "Go, eat your food with gladness, and drink your wine with a joyful heart ... Enjoy life with your wife, whom you love, all the days of this meaningless life" Ecclesiastes 9:7, 9 (NIV). While the dreams we chase in life may prove elusive, the author suggests, and we know our lives are fleeting and many things stand outside our control, we can still savor the everyday joys of life. The theme is expressed in the painting above (also called *The Wedding Banquet*). It depicts a marriage celebration taking place in a magnificent building. The bride and groom are seated at the head table, while brightly costumed young men carry in platters of food.

A constant theme in this book is remembering God amidst life's enjoyments, as captured in "Remember your Creator in the days of your youth" Ecclesiastes 12:1 (NIV).

The Teacher's Audience

Jesus Walks in the Portico of Solomon, James Tissot, 1886–1894. Brooklyn Museum, New York. The painting depicts an episode in the life of Jesus, recounted in the Gospel of John, chapter 10. Jesus is on a porch of the Temple in Jerusalem, named for King Solomon. He is teaching in the manner of Jewish tradition, gathering his disciples around him to hear his discourse.

Ecclesiastes provides some textual clues about the worldview and social standing of the teacher's assembly. Members of his audience likely work hard for what they have (4:8; 5:10-13). The advice to "eat, drink, and enjoy" indicates that the listeners have enough resources to meet their basic needs and more. The author implies that the audience is concerned with "gathering and storing up" 2:26 (NIV) things that should be passed on to heirs (2:18-21; 4:7-8; 5:13-17). But he also alludes to struggle and oppression in their lives (4:1; 5:8). Some audience members are guests at the royal court (8:2-4). So we can deduce that many of the teacher's listeners were well-established members of society. These listeners seem (at least in the view of Ecclesiastes's author) to be concerned with how to reconcile their comfortable material status with the Mosaic Law.

Vocabulary

> **Deduce** [verb], to form a conclusion through reason or logic

The Nature as a Symbol of Vanitas, Abraham Mignon, 1665–1679. Hessisches Landesmuseum, Darmstadt, Germany.

"Vanity of Vanities" in Art

During the 16th and 17th centuries, a genre of art known as *Vanitas* (Latin, "vanity") was popular, especially in the Netherlands. The term is drawn from the opening exclamation of Ecclesiastes, rendered in the King James Version as: "Vanity of vanities, all is vanity." Still life paintings were used to depict this theme of the futility of existence, and the pictures often featured skulls, symbolizing the certainty of death. The still life floral painting above by Dutch painter Mignon is a reflection upon this subject. It is set in a dimly lit cave with a dark pool. Plants and creatures associated with night and the underworld can be detected: a snail, insects, frogs, mushrooms, and the skeleton of a bird. Against this background, the flowers stand out with vivid life and color. As a whole, the painting conveys a sense of the transient nature of beauty and even life itself.

Vocabulary

> **Vanity** [noun], something that is empty, having no meaning or value

> **Fleeting** [adjective], lasting only for a short time

Some Key Terms

One of the most common words in Ecclesiastes is *hevel*. The primary meaning in Hebrew is "a breath, a puff of air, a vapor." We see another use of the word in Isaiah 57:13 (NIV): "The wind will carry all of them off, a mere breath (*hevel*) will blow them away." Reading that "all is *hevel*," we understand this usage to be a metaphor, a word that stands for something else. The King James Version translates it as "vanity" in 2:11; 4:4; 5:10; and 11:10. The NIV and some other versions translate it as "meaningless." It's possible that the word is an emblem for what is transitory, fleeting, or (depending on how you interpret the term) empty in life. It seems to refer to the inherent frailty and brevity of human existence.

"Under the sun," or the alternate saying "under heaven," is another frequent motif in the book. The teacher focuses on what the audience can learn about life in the world here and now (2:22; 9:4-6). Some other key words in Ecclesiastes are *toil* (*amal*), *enjoyment* (*simcha*), and *good* (*tov*).

Some Key Expressions (NIV)

1:7
"All streams flow into the sea."

1:9
"What has been will be again."

4:9
"Two are better than one."

7:1
"A good name is better than fine perfume."

9:11
"The race is not to the swift or the battle to the strong."

Possible Themes

Hebrew scholar Dr. Brad Young finds three themes running through the book. Note that others who have studied Ecclesiastes have offered other perspectives.

Death

1 The teacher views life as brief and death as the natural end of our earthly existence (1:4-11; 2:16; 12:1-7). The fragile and fleeting nature of all life reminds the teacher and his audience of the urgency to live life fully and enjoy what it offers now in light of what lies ahead (9:2-6).

God

2 The teacher sees God creating all things and playing an active role in human lives and history (3:11-15; 9:7-9). The book asserts that God is ultimately in control over human existence, but God acts in ways that are difficult or even impossible to understand (7:14; 11:1-5).

Contentment

3 The teacher asserts the importance of living in obedience to God and his word. He commends living a wise and good life before God. Readers are encouraged to eat, drink, and enjoy their God-given work (2:1-10, 24-26; 3:11-14; 5:1-20; 9:7-10; 11:8-10). To persuade his audience to embrace this message, the teacher cites his own life experiences (1:12–2:26).

Job Confessing His Presumption to God Who Answers from the Whirlwind, William Blake, ca. 1804. National Gallery of Scotland, Edinburgh. In the closing chapters of the Book of Job, God reveals the infinite wisdom with which he has created the world and its creatures, as well as the heavens. He does this by addressing a series of rhetorical questions to Job, which commences: "Where were you when I laid the earth's foundation?" Job 38:4 (NIV). After God's speech, Job is overwhelmed with a sense of the frailty and limitations of his own existence.

A Controversial Book?

Initially, some Jewish sages didn't want to include Ecclesiastes as part of the Tanakh (the Hebrew scriptures). They thought it contradicted other Hebrew scriptures and even sometimes itself! But after robust debate, the sages finally accepted Ecclesiastes into the Hebrew canon. Despite the charges of inconsistency, they believed that Ecclesiastes was closely connected to the great King Solomon, whom their scriptures hailed as "wiser than anyone else" 1 Kings 4:31 (NIV).

Yet the Bible also contrasts the wisdom of human beings with the higher wisdom of God and suggests that the will of God is often inscrutable (Psalms 104:24; 145:3; Isaiah 44:24-25; Job 12:3; 21:22; Job 38–41). The New Testament takes the same view (Romans 11:33; 1 Corinthians 1:20; 3:19; James 3:15-17). Some scholars assert that the Jewish sages accepted Ecclesiastes because it met the same basic standards required of other books that were included by Jews in the Hebrew Bible and Christians in the Old Testament and New Testament.

Phase 4
Use the Telescope

Scholars continue to debate the authorship of Ecclesiastes. The traditional author, King Solomon, is thought to have ruled in the tenth century BC, but the Book of Ecclesiastes may not have attained its current form until the third or fourth century BC. Ecclesiastes is one of the five individual scroll books that belong to the Hebrew Bible: Esther, Song of Songs, Ruth, Lamentations, and Ecclesiastes. These five scrolls came to be uniquely associated with five different biblical holy days and became part of the reading cycle accompanying the Jewish religious calendar: Purim, Passover, Shavuot (Pentecost), the Ninth of Av, and Sukkot (Tabernacles).

In traditional Judaism, the Book of Ecclesiastes is read aloud in synagogues during Sukkot. Observant Jews, whether rich or poor, keep the custom of spending eight consecutive days every autumn eating and sometimes even sleeping outdoors in temporary structures called booths or tabernacles. This custom reenacts the story in Exodus where the ancient Hebrews live in temporary dwellings as they wander in the wilderness for 40 years. This annual observance is considered by a great many Jewish commentators to be a reminder of the fleeting nature of life—one of the main messages of Ecclesiastes.

Sukkot, Moritz Daniel Oppenheim, 1880. The Jewish Museum, New York. The rabbi, wrapped in his prayer shawl, holds aloft the Torah scroll, while the smaller scroll for the festival is unrolled, to be read to the assembled worshipers.

View of an Orthodox Jewish neighborhood in Jerusalem during *Sukkot*. Small *sukkot* (booths) are built outside on the porches. Families take their meals together in these temporary structures. It's the custom to welcome with warm hospitality those who wish to join them.

Summary

Like other biblical Hebrew wisdom literature, the ancient Book of Ecclesiastes contains many proverbs and sayings. Unlike other biblical books, Ecclesiastes examines feelings of helplessness and meaninglessness. At the very least, the wise person, the author suggests, recognizes that much of human life is lost in chasing after futile endeavors that ultimately fail to satisfy. Life is filled with contradictions, the things we crave often prove unsatisfying, and (from the author's perspective) life is fleeting and passes by in a breath. According to ancient Jewish and Christian tradition, the "teacher" who relayed these insights was King Solomon, who was providing late in his life a kind of autobiographical account of his search for wisdom and meaning. Among modern scholars, another view holds that Ecclesiastes represents a collection of wisdom sayings that were gathered and committed to writing much later, perhaps in the third or fourth century BC. Whatever the case, the author recounts his experiences in seeking earthly enjoyments, including wealth, power, and romance. The book leaves it to the reader to interpret many of the book's sayings. It ends with this statement: "Fear God and keep his commandments, for this is the duty of all mankind" Ecclesiastes 12:13 (NIV).

Elijah
What Happens When Leaders Break the Law?

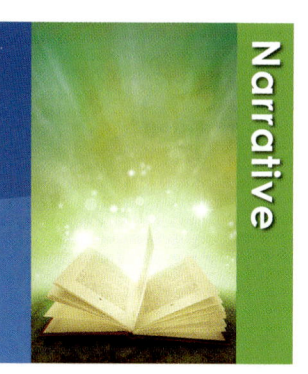

"Drink from the brook and eat what the ravens bring you, for I have commanded them to bring you food."

1 Kings 17:4 (NLT)

Phase 1

Read the Story:
1 Kings 11–12; 17–21

The Story in a Nutshell

Before America's Civil War, Abraham Lincoln (quoting from the New Testament) warned that "a house divided against itself cannot stand." An illustration of this principle occurs in the Old Testament confrontation between the prophet Elijah and the priests of Baal.

Where we pick up this story, the united monarchy established by King David has split apart. The Israelites are divided into separate kingdoms—Israel in the north and Judah in the south. Israel's king, Jeroboam, fears that his people might shift their loyalty to Judah if they travel south to worship at the Temple in Jerusalem. So Jeroboam sets up his own places of worship (at Bethel and Dan) and his own order of priests to keep his subjects in Israel. Thus begins a period of idol worship that will bring Jeroboam and his successors into constant conflict with the prophets (see 1 Kings 12:25-33).

Elijah 65

Panoramic view of the Carmel mountain range, reaching a peak elevation of about 1,800 feet.

A closer view of Mount Carmel. This part of the mountain is known as "Little Switzerland" by the locals. Over many centuries a seasonal stream, the Kelach River, has carved out a gorge from the soft limestone rocks.

Mount Carmel

Mount Carmel is normally very visible from the hills of Nazareth, which is said to be the hometown of Jesus centuries later. Nazareth is located fewer than 10 miles to the east.

Jezebel

The Bible's vivid, strongly negative description of Jezebel has made her name into an epithet for a powerful, evil woman. However, in recent years the name *Jezebel* has regained some respectability while still retaining its shock value. It is the middle name of Mick Jagger's daughter, Jade Sheena Jezebel Jagger. A popular feminist blog in the United States is called *Jezebel* and a growing number of newborn girls receive this name, despite its connotations.

The so-called Seal of Jezebel, from the Israel Museum, Jerusalem. This stone seal, 1.25 inches long, has been reliably dated to the ninth century BC and clearly belonged to a high official. The ancient Phoenician writing on the seal seems to say "property of Jezebel." Scholars still debate whether this might have been her personal seal.

One of the most spectacular clashes occurs between King Ahab and Elijah, one of Israel's great prophets. The conflict begins when King Ahab marries Jezebel, a Phoenician princess who worships Baal, the Canaanite god of storms and fertility. Queen Jezebel is an enthusiastic advocate for her faith. She makes Baal worship the major religion of the entire northern kingdom and begins killing the prophets who still worship the God of Abraham, Isaac, and Jacob (see 1 Kings 16:29-34; 18:3-4, 13).

Against this background, the writer of 1 Kings prepares us for a battle of the gods. In the story, Elijah confronts 450 prophets of Baal plus another 400 prophets of Asherah (also approved by Jezebel). The two sides gather on Mount Carmel. The God of Israel (spelled in the Hebrew text as YHWH, and often written in English as Yahweh) wins this showdown by answering Elijah's prayer with fire from heaven (1 Kings 18).

After this dramatic demonstration, Elijah prompts the spectators to seize the prophets of Baal and kill all 450 of them (18:10). But after Jezebel threatens to do the same to him, Elijah flees to a cave at Mount Horeb, which the Bible identifies as another name for Mount Sinai, where Moses and the Israelites had once witnessed God speaking atop the mountain through clouds and thunder, earthquakes and fire. Elijah's encounter with God is very different. He's presented with a great wind, an earthquake, and fire, yet he senses God's presence in none of these. Instead, God's presence comes to him through the "sound" of absolute silence (the Hebrew text is sometimes translated "a still, small voice").

Vocabulary

> **Divine** [adjective], relating to or coming from God
> **Epithet** [noun], a word or phrase used to describe a person or thing

Phase 2
Travel through Time

Wouldn't you love to be able to go back in time to prevent a historical disaster? More than one novel or movie has employed this idea.

In the biblical disaster stories, you could go back and warn King Solomon, "You might want to reconsider those hundreds of wives who worship other gods, or you'll find yourself in serious trouble." According to the Book of Kings, it isn't the people Solomon rules over that mess things up. Solomon makes most of the mess himself.

Solomon's desire to maintain peaceful relations with the nearby nations, at least in the Bible's telling of the story, leads him to marry members of various foreign royal families. Solomon's desire to please his growing harem causes him to build monuments and places of worship for their foreign gods. Solomon does this even though the Israelites have been warned against it.

But neither Solomon nor the people of Israel follow these instructions. After Solomon completes his reign over Israel, the trouble begins. The once-united kingdom is divided between north and south.

Rehoboam follows his father, Solomon, as the rightful king. In 1 Kings, Jeroboam speaks out on behalf of the people of Israel, and asks Solomon's son to lighten the burden of high taxes and forced labor. Rehoboam makes a disastrous decision. Instead of listening to his older, wiser advisers, Rehoboam listens to the younger ones, who encourage him to take a hard line: "My father laid heavy burdens on you, but I'm going to make them even heavier! My father beat you with whips, but I will beat you with scorpions!" 1 Kings 12:14-15 (NLT). So the king pays no attention to the people.

As a result, the 10 northern tribes revolt and choose Jeroboam, who is not from David's family, to be their king. Rehoboam is left with only the tribes of Judah and Benjamin.

Among the seemingly impossible stories of the Bible, the description of Elijah ascending into heaven has been one of the most intriguing. The image here was taken from the 1800 Macklin Bible.

Elijah tells his student Elisha that if he will be an eyewitness to his dramatic departure from earth he will receive a "double portion" of Elijah's powerful prophetic spirit (2 Kings 2:9-11). The Bible tells that he does see the departure and goes on to perform many more miracles than Elijah. Elisha keeps the mantle (cape) left behind by Elijah, as seen in the illustration above.

The Warning at Solomon's Dedication of the Temple

"If you or your descendants abandon me and disobey the commands and decrees I have given you, and if you serve and worship other gods, then I will uproot Israel from this land that I have given them. I will reject this Temple that I have made holy to honor my name. I will make Israel an object of mockery and ridicule among the nations" 1 Kings 9:6-7 (NLT).

The Divided Kingdoms: A Brief History

The northern kingdom, Israel, lasts from about 930 to 722 BC (about 208 years), ruled by 19 kings. Two Assyrian rulers, Shalmaneser V and Sargon II, defeat Hoshea, the last of Israel's kings, in 722 BC (see 2 Kings 17–18).

The 10 northern tribes become known as the "10 lost tribes of Israel" because they are scattered in other countries after the destruction of Samaria, the capital, by the Assyrians. Their descendants have become virtually impossible to verify (though many theories abound).

The southern kingdom, Judah, and its 20 monarchs last considerably longer, from Rehoboam in about 930 BC to Zedekiah in 586 BC (approximately 344 years). The end comes when Nebuchadnezzar, king of Babylon, overthrows Jerusalem and destroys Solomon's Temple, carrying many of the people into exile. The people would not return from their exile, according to the Bible, for 70 years.

The larger and wealthier northern kingdom comes to be known as Israel. The southern kingdom becomes known as Judah (from which the words Jew and Judaism come), meaning "praise."

Thus the united kingdom becomes a divided kingdom, a state of affairs that will last for two centuries.

According to the Bible, because the kings and people of Israel continue to worship gods other than the God of Israel and fail to keep the terms of his covenant, the prophets speak out against them with increasing frequency.

What's at Stake

Elijah is one of several prophets (along with Elisha, Amos, Hosea, Micah, and Isaiah) mentioned in the Bible during the divided kingdom who warn the Israelites that they should return to YHWH (God). Elijah's work comes at a crucial time in Israel's history: Queen Jezebel is trying to wipe out the worship of YHWH.

Prophets

Abraham and Moses are among the first figures in the Bible who are called prophets, followed by Samuel (who is also the last of the judges). A prophet was to serve as a messenger for God, often delivering unpopular warnings. Prophets often began their speeches with, "Thus says the LORD ... " Some, like Elijah, seem to have traveled with few if any people—perhaps just a servant (19:2). Even so, some kings, such as Ahab, keep court prophets as well. Prophets often are unwelcome, resisted, and sometimes even persecuted by the powerful political leaders and by the masses they speak against. Those called to be prophets sometimes shrink from this difficult, thankless job.

"Then Elijah brought him down from the upper room and gave him to his mother. 'Look!' he said. 'Your son is alive!'" 1 Kings 17:23 (NLT).
Elijah Resuscitating the Son of the Widow of Sarepta, Louis Hersent. Musée des Beaux-Arts, Angers, France.

Vocabulary

> **Crucial** [adjective], vitally important

Phase 3
Mine for Clues

Ignoring God's Decrees

The story of King Ahab begins with the mention of another "sin" perpetrated during his time. "Then he set up an Asherah pole. He did more to provoke the anger of the LORD, the God of Israel, than any of the other kings before him.

"It was during his reign that Hiel, a man from Bethel, rebuilt Jericho. When he laid its foundations, it cost him the life of his oldest son, Abiram. And when he completed it and set up its gates, it cost him the life of his youngest son, Segub." The Bible says this all happened "according to the message from the LORD concerning Jericho spoken by Joshua son of Nun" 1 Kings 16:33-34 (NLT).

What's so bad about rebuilding Jericho? In the Book of Joshua, Jericho is the first city conquered by the Israelites as they enter the land. After the walls fall, the Israelites are warned not to rebuild the city (Joshua 6:26). Jericho is to remain eternally in shambles as a symbol of God's judgment. The biblical author suggests that allowing Hiel to rebuild the city demonstrates King Ahab's disregard for this biblical caution.

This statue marks the traditional location on Mount Carmel where Elijah faced off against the prophets of Baal. The statue stands outside the Carmelite Monastery, a Roman Catholic order that was founded before the year AD 1200. It's a popular tourist destination.

Elijah, Elisha, and Biblical Symbolism

Fire is a major motif in the exploits of Elijah. A divine fire comes upon Mount Carmel in response to his prayer (1 Kings 18:38). King Ahaziah, Ahab's son, twice sends messengers to Elijah demanding that he appear before the king. Twice Elijah has the messengers devoured by a divine fire (2 Kings 1:10, 12). At the end of the Elijah story, he ascends in a whirlwind to heaven, taken up by a chariot of fire led by horses of fire (2 Kings 2:11). Elijah is a most zealous prophet, intolerant of faithlessness and uncompromising against idolatry. With Elijah gone, Elisha takes up his mantle and assumes the prophetic task. Elisha will conduct his prophetic mission by miracles involving water, not fire.

Elijah's War against Baal Worship

Baal was a popular regional god of rain, thunder, fertility, and agriculture. In the biblical account, Elijah wages an ongoing struggle against Baal worship in Israel. This may explain why one of Elijah's first official duties as a prophet is to proclaim a terrible drought that will last for about three years. Through this drastic action, the biblical author implies, Elijah shows the people that it's not Baal, the supposed rain god, who is in charge; rather it is the God of Israel who controls the weather. According to the Bible, the long drought comes to a dramatic and sudden end after the clash on Mount Carmel in 1 Kings 18. Elijah's very name reinforces this message. His name in Hebrew, *Eliyahu*, means, "My God is the LORD (YHWH)."

Elijah's Story Told in Art

Der Spiegel menschlicher Behältnis, German translation of the *Mirror of Human Salvation*, Southern Germany, likely Regensburg, ca. 1450-1460.

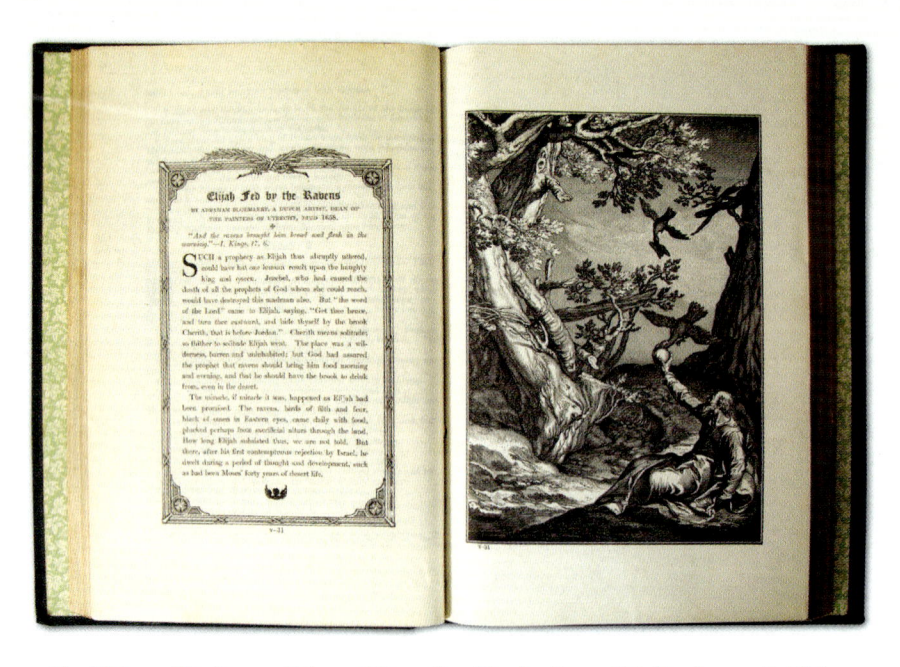

The Bible and Its Story – Volume I. Compiler: Charles Horne & Julius Bewer. Publisher: Auxiliary Educational League, New York, 1915.

Phase 4
Use the Telescope

The Law Applies to Everyone

In 1 Kings 21, after 22 years of ruling the northern kingdom, King Ahab sees the vineyards of his neighbor Naboth near his palace at Megiddo in the Jezreel Valley and wants to turn them into his own personal vegetable garden. Naboth refuses to surrender his land, a prized possession in his family for many generations, for any price.

Not happy with getting no for an answer, King Ahab sulks around his palace. He stops eating. Queen Jezebel soon finds out why and insists that he, the king, should seize whatever his heart desires. To make this happen, the queen organizes against Naboth. Some false witnesses claim they heard Naboth curse both the God of Israel and the king, leading to Naboth's execution for blasphemy against God.

After this apparent travesty of justice, King Ahab swoops in and grabs the vineyard. This might appear to be the end of the story, but in the Bible's account, Elijah confronts the king and asks pointedly, "Have you murdered and also inherited?"—in other words, do you really think that after you have silenced this poor man through murder you can now just walk in and steal his property like nothing has ever happened?

Next, Elijah prophesies doom to Ahab and Jezebel because of their corrupt ways. Elijah's reprimand is both severe and insulting, yet the king does not dare to punish him for his sharp words. King Ahab understands that he did a terrible wrong and dramatically repents.

The biblical author conveys a lesson about human and divine authority. Kings who rule in Israel do not have absolute authority. The Israelites believed that kings, like everyone else, were subject to the laws of their God because those laws represent a higher authority. Therefore King Ahab cannot simply follow his whims.

The Widow of Zarephath

One of the most remarkable parts of the Elijah story concerns a non-Jewish widow who lives outside of Israel in the Phoenician town of Zarephath. Elijah flees from Ahab to a hiding place east of the Jordan River. God sends him to the town and when Elijah asks the widow for bread to eat, she replies that she does not even have enough to feed herself and her son. Elijah promises that God will provide for her miraculously, and his promise comes true. Later, when the woman's son dies, Elijah takes her son upstairs and prays for him. The Bible relates a peculiar detail: Elijah "stretched himself out over the child three times and cried out to the LORD, 'O LORD my God, please let this child's life return to him.' The LORD heard Elijah's prayer, and the life of the child returned, and he revived!" 1 Kings 17:21-22 (NLT).

It's the first example in the Bible of a dead person restored to life. The widow of Zarephath sees it as a powerful demonstration of divine authority. She says, "Now I know for sure that you are a man of God, and that the LORD truly speaks through you" 1 Kings 17:24 (NLT).

Jezebel and Ahab Met by Elijah, Frederic Leighton, ca. 1863. Scarborough Art Gallery, Scarborough, England.

Top: Looking east toward Mount Tabor from the Arab village of Daburiyya, population about 10,000 (2010 census). This village is in the territory that was assigned in Bible times to the Israelite tribe of Isaachar. Tabor has an elevation of about 1,800 feet. Nazareth is located just a few miles away. Bottom: A view of snow-covered Mount Hermon on a sunny day in early spring. Mount Hermon is located in the far northeast corner of modern Israel, straddling the border between the nations of Israel and Syria. It rises to a height of more than 10,000 feet in Syria but even on the Israel side, seen here, it reaches an elevation of 7,200 feet. A three-month ski season there attracts tens of thousands of people from all over Israel during an average winter. The Jordan River is partly fed by the melting snows of Mount Hermon.

Elijah and Moses in the New Testament

Elijah and Moses feature in the New Testament Gospels of Matthew, Mark, and Luke. They appear in the story known as the Transfiguration (see, e.g., Matthew 17:1-12), traditionally believed to be located on either Mount Tabor (near Nazareth) or Mount Hermon (about 50 miles to the northeast).

The return of Elijah is prophesied in Malachi 4:5 as happening "before the great and dreadful day of the LORD arrives" (NLT). In Luke, an angel foretells that John the Baptist (whom the gospels describe as a precursor to Jesus) will live "with the spirit and power of Elijah" Luke 1:17 (NLT). In the Gospel of Matthew, later in the timeline of the life and ministry of Jesus, Jesus says that John the Baptist was the Elijah who was foretold in Malachi (Matthew 11:14). Such was the stature of the prophet Elijah that, even in the time of Jesus, he loomed large in the imagination and religious life of the people.

Summary

Elijah is one of the great prophets of the Bible. He's represented as a messenger without compromise. Elijah believes in the righteousness of his message and confronts those he considers corrupt rulers and false prophets. Although greatly outnumbered, and at times discouraged, he is ready to pay for his mission with his own life. The "war" that Elijah fights is a battle over his absolute belief that there is only one true God in Israel. He declares, "I have zealously served the LORD God Almighty" 1 Kings 19:10 (NLT). According to 2 Kings, Elijah never dies. He ascends into heaven in a fiery chariot, led by horses of fire.

The authors of the New Testament write that both Elijah and Moses, the two greatest prophets of the Tanakh (the Old Testament), meet with Jesus and his three closest apostles on the mount where Jesus is transfigured (e.g., Matthew 17:1-13). Jesus declares that John the Baptist, his cousin and forerunner, has come in the spirit and power of Elijah. Many Christians believe that John the Baptist was at least the partial fulfillment of Malachi's prophecy.

In the light of Malachi 4:1-5, Jews hold that Elijah will one day return to herald the coming of the Messiah. Many Jewish stories tell of a mysterious guest (Elijah) who appears at times to help the poor. The Passover Seder is a special family meal held each spring to remember the events of the Book of Exodus. Jewish families leave the prophet a glass of wine ("Elijah's cup") and stand together as they open the door for *Eliyahu Ha-Navee*, Elijah the Prophet.

Sennacherib's Assault

What Happens when the Mighty Assyrian Army Confronts Jerusalem?

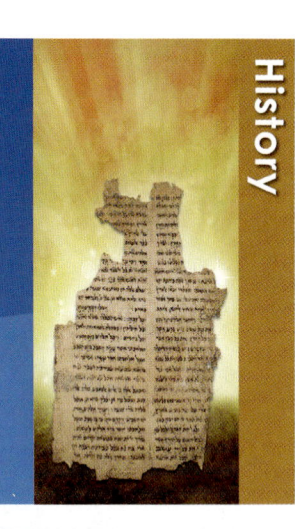

"Sennacherib king of Assyria came up against all the fortified cities of Judah and took them."

2 Kings 18:13 (NKJV)

The Rise of the Assyrians

While King Ahaz ruled from Jerusalem over the southern kingdom of Judah, the northern kingdom of Israel was experiencing dramatic changes. The Assyrian Empire, in its quest to claim the road to Egypt, encountered the kingdoms of Israel and Judah. Starting in 738 BC, at Judah's invitation the Assyrians began sporadic but aggressive attacks on the militarily weaker northern areas of Canaan, now populated by the Israelites.

Vocabulary

> **Sporadic** [adjective]
occurring in irregular instances

The Divided Israelite Kingdom

When we pick up the biblical story, Israel, already smaller than many other territories, is even more vulnerable because it no longer belongs to a unified nation under a strong ruler. For almost 200 years, Israel in the north and Judah in the south have been divided. Israel is also vulnerable, in the view of the biblical authors, because it has abandoned its covenant responsibilities and lost the favor and protection of God. The worship of other gods continues in both kingdoms. But the southern kingdom, where the Temple is located and the priesthood is headquartered, keeps closer to the Jewish people's spiritual heritage. According to the biblical authors, the northern kingdom has strayed far from the covenant and stands alone before much larger nations.

Time Travel

The Kingdoms of Israel and Judah

ca. 700 BC

Tribes of Israel

JUDAH	ISRAEL	
Judah	Dan	Asher
Benjamin	Ephraim	Naphtali
(Levi)	Manasseh	Gad
	Issachar	Reuben
	Zebulun	(Levi)
	Simeon	

From the original 12 tribes of Israel there are two special cases: Joseph and Levi. Joseph came to be represented by his sons Ephraim and Manasseh (also called the two half tribes). Levi, as the priestly tribe, was given no inheritance of its own and was cared for by all the other tribes that it religiously represented and served.

Assyrian Dealings in the Promised Land (722–701 BC)

In 722 BC, King Sargon II of Assyria makes his move, conquering the northern kingdom, including its capital, Samaria, and takes a large part of its population into exile. The southern kingdom stays out of the conflict and lives to fight another day. The fight will come much sooner, however, than anyone in Judah could wish.

In 701 BC, after a series of rebellions throughout his empire, King Sennacherib of Assyria (son of Sargon II) assembles a huge army to extinguish the flames of resistance. Following early victories over Babylon and Egypt, Assyria turns its gaze to the rebellious cities of Israel's southern kingdom (Judah) under King Hezekiah. The smaller cities of Judah fall like dominoes at Sennacherib's feet. After an extremely brutal conquest, he soon establishes his headquarters in the city of Lachish, second only to Jerusalem as the most important fortified city of Judah. From there he sets out to capture the jewel of the crown, Jerusalem. If Jerusalem were to fall, all of Judah would belong to Assyria, including the Temple's treasures. King Hezekiah, Judah's ruler, now watches in terror as the Assyrian army draws closer and closer to his city. Will Jerusalem be defeated, like Samaria before it?

A stone relief from the walls of a palace in Nineveh, created about 700 BC. It depicts Sennacherib's assault on one of the cities of Judah using a siege machine and siege tower. On display in the British Museum.

Sennacherib's Encounter with Jerusalem: The Bible's View

The people inside Jerusalem have been dreading this day for months. Now as Judah's soldiers peer out from atop the walls, they view a terrifying display of military might gathering outside. A large portion of the Assyrian army has come from Lachish and barricaded the roads to Jerusalem. A group of Assyrian officials approaches the wall, and one of them delivers a speech to the people and officials of Jerusalem. In this speech he asks, "In whom do you trust?" Egypt? Themselves? Even their own god, Yahweh? He gives a reason why trust in each one is foolish, and ends his speech with a final question, "Who among all the gods... have delivered their countries...that the LORD should deliver Jerusalem?" (2 Kings 18:35, NKJV)

King Hezekiah, after hearing the speech, tears his clothes in anguish. The prophet Isaiah, however, replies that God will save Jerusalem, "For I [God] will defend this city, to save it For My own sake and for My servant David's sake" (2 Kings 19:34, NKJV). That night, in the biblical account, the angel of the LORD kills 185,000 Assyrians. Jerusalem is saved.

The biblical narrative credits the angel of the LORD with the slaughter of the Assyrians. Some interpreters have offered theories, such as a plague or virus that spread through the Assyrian camp and devastated their ranks. Unlike Lachish, no mass graves have been discovered. The Bible does say that Sennacherib, in addition to losing so many troops, heard rumors of trouble brewing at home and hurried back. Whatever might have happened, in the biblical narrative, Sennacherib abandons the field, on the verge of what seemed to be the eminent conquest of Jerusalem, and with it the key stronghold of Judah. The Assyrian army returns to Nineveh. Jerusalem is spared. The kingdom of Judah survives.

Sennacherib Prism (Taylor Prism) 686 BC. British Museum, London, England.

Sennacherib's Prism

Later on, however, King Sennacherib boasted of his great military feats in the southern part of Israel (Judah), giving the impression of almost total victory. He oversaw production of three six-sided prisms inscribed with accounts that contained this proud claim. The object is called the Taylor Prism. Archaeologists discovered it in the 1800s in the ruins of ancient Nineveh. Yet neither the biblical account (2 Kings 18:13-37) nor any archaeological digs since have confirmed Sennacherib's subtle suggestion of dominating Jerusalem during that era. How should we understand this?

Vocabulary

> **Feat** [noun]
an act notable especially for courage

A small part of a replica of the *Lachish Relief*, 700–681 BC, located at the Israel Museum, Jerusalem, Israel. Assyrian soldiers are depicted carrying off spoils from Lachish, a key city of Judah, while Jewish prisoners who survived the brutal assault take their belongings with them into exile.

Sennacherib's Return from Jerusalem: His View

When he returned to Nineveh, Sennacherib boasted about his military achievements. He described the many cities he conquered. For Jerusalem, however, his claim is slightly different. He says that he trapped Hezekiah, the king of Judah, "like a bird in a cage."

He never claims to have conquered the city outright, but he does say that King Hezekiah was terrified and was forced to accept a humiliating tribute, stripping the gold from the Temple doors and doorposts, sending great quantities of jewels and gold, "all kinds of valuable treasures," and his daughters and musicians. This is more than the Bible itself claims that Hezekiah paid as tribute.

If Sennacherib had destroyed Jerusalem as the Assyrian army had done to so many other cities, we would expect to find evidence in the stones of the ancient city. The archaeological record suggests that Jerusalem continued to flourish for another 100 years, until King Nebuchadnezzar and the Babylonians conquered the city in 587–586 BC. Whatever the details, Jerusalem still stood, and Sennacherib did not break the back of the Jewish people.

Some of the walls of the ancient city of Lachish, seen here, have been excavated by archaeologists. Tel Lachish, about 40 miles southwest of Jerusalem, is one of Israel's major historical sites.

Vocabulary

> **Relief** [noun], a sculptural technique by which figures project out from their background

> **Insinuation** [noun], a usually demeaning remark made in an indirect way

Why Is This Important

If Sennacherib had taken Jerusalem, and treated Jerusalem like all the other cities he conquered, then he would have leveled the city and taken its inhabitants into slavery. If that scenario had played out, the historical consequences would have been dramatic. History is filled with tribes and nations that disappeared when they were defeated. So it's possible, if Sennacherib had sacked Jerusalem and enslaved its people, that there would be no Jews, and no Bible, today. An unwanted outcome of this, however, was that later leaders considered Jerusalem invincible.

Why Is This Interesting

Abundant archaeological evidence attests to the Assyrian military campaign against Judah in 701 BC, corroborating many of Sennacherib's claims. For example, at Lachish, archaeologists have found royal seals—the Lachish Seals—from the time of Hezekiah, that were used to mark and secure the contents of huge vessels of wheat, oil, and wine stored at Lachish, possibly to be used to withstand a lengthy siege by an invading army. Other indisputable artifacts have also been uncovered at Lachish that provide proof of the attack, such as loads of sling stones to hurl against the enemy. The spectacular and very detailed Lachish Relief on the walls of Sennacherib's palace in Nineveh, discovered in the 1800s and now displayed in the British Museum, are a vivid reminder of the brutality of the Assyrian conquest. The graphic images on the Lachish Relief show how brutal the Assyrians were to oathbreakers and illustrate the fear of the Israelites. And we have already mentioned the Assyrian prisms, our third major source of historical information. The evidence for the destruction of Lachish and the Assyrian campaign in Judah is strong. It establishes that the Sennacherib described in the Bible existed and conquered the cities of Judah in rapid succession, with the help of a large army.

Biblical Narratives in Other Sources

The Sennacherib Prism is a strong example of how historians look at the Bible as well as extra-biblical writings and archaeological evidence to piece together a fuller picture of what happened in ancient Israel. When it comes to the "stories" of Sennacherib and the "stones" of Jerusalem and Lachish, numerous points of agreement with the Bible allow for a fairly detailed reconstruction of this particular Assyrian campaign.

We find agreement, for instance, on the conquest of Lachish, on a reference to 30 talents of gold and Jerusalem's treasures going off to Nineveh as tribute, and other small details. This kind of agreement from multiple independent sources gives historians confidence that we do indeed possess some knowledge of what happened so long ago.

It's also an example of how what is unstated can be just as important as what is stated. Sennacherib's boast that he trapped King Hezekiah "like a bird in a cage" adds evidence that Hezekiah existed and that Sennacherib, for whatever reason, was not able to kill the "bird."

King Hezekiah Displays His Treasure, Vicente López y Portaña, 1789. Museo de Bellas Artes, Valencia, Spain.

Hezekiah's Tunnel

The Bible mentions Hezekiah's water tunnel at the end of its account of Hezekiah's reign. A tunnel that many consider the very same tunnel that Hezekiah constructed has become a favorite tourist stop in Jerusalem. An inscription inside the tunnel, the shape of the letters, and an analysis of organic material on the walls, all point to the time of Hezekiah's reign. During a siege, the tunnel would have served to bring water to the inhabitants of Jerusalem within the city walls and to enable them to survive even a long siege. Modern engineers consider it an amazing accomplishment for its time.

Copy of the Shiloah inscription from the eighth century BC that was found in the Hezekiah tunnel. The inscription records the day the diggers joined the two halves of the tunnel. The original Shiloah (Siloam) inscription is kept in the Archaeological Museum, Istanbul, Turkey.

Water flows throughout the year in this tunnel underneath Jerusalem known as Hezekiah's tunnel. Visitors by the thousands still wade through this underground aqueduct, which is 550 yards long.

Historical Half-Truths and Their Implications, *The Da Vinci Code*

It's not only ancient kings like Sennacherib who like to make exaggerated claims. Not long ago, Dan Brown's *The Da Vinci Code* became a runaway global best seller. Unlike the prism, this is not a primary source but a popular book that makes claims about such sources. Doubleday, the book's publisher, claims it is "the bestselling adult novel of all time within a one-year period." In Brown's tale, a riveting mixture of historical truths and half truths, Leonardo da Vinci assumes the role of the protector of the real "truth" about Jesus, using his creative genius to keep the alleged message alive for generations.

A feature movie followed, and this fictional account got people asking questions about the "real story" behind the Bible. Yet the book was packaged and sold to the public not merely as a work of fiction, but as a new insight into history based on actual historical authorities. The problem only grew worse when Brown made the same misleading claims in media interviews and on websites. A flurry of scholarly books and articles quickly showed that the "evidence" for the author's claims fell apart on further examination. These scholars pointed out that many of this highly entertaining book's key historical claims and insinuations are completely fabricated and even contradicted by the historical evidence.

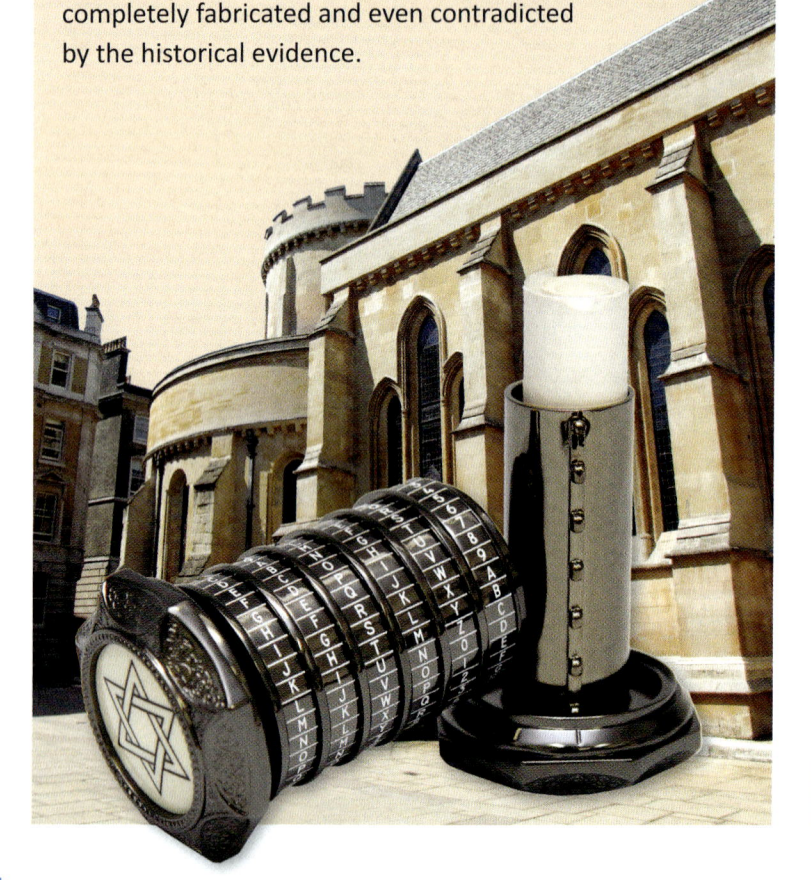

The Question of Historical Accuracy

As with Sennacherib's famous prism, the controversial best seller *The Da Vinci Code* raised questions about the Bible's historical accuracy. Author Dan Brown's claims were quickly debunked. All sources that claim to present knowledge of the ancient world, including the Bible and the Sennacherib Prism and modern best sellers, are subject to careful scrutiny.

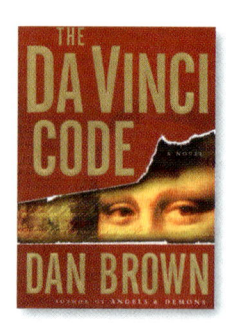

Summary

In an age when vast quantities of information are delivered on demand online, it's important to ask whether the information we're receiving is reliable. When it comes to ancient sources, there is a justified skepticism. Can we know anything about what happened so long ago and so far away? Cases like the siege of Sennacherib demonstrate how multiple pieces of information can come together to reveal a relatively confident picture of what happened in ancient times. Taking the stories in the Bible alongside stories we find elsewhere, together with the evidence we find in archaeology, we see interesting variations and important points of agreement. The Bible, in this instance, is an important historical source. It describes a dramatic encounter long ago that could have wiped out the Jewish people. Yet Jerusalem endured, and the Jews survived to write their stories and pass them on to later generations.

Vocabulary

> **Debunk** [verb], to expose as false

King Josiah's Reform

How Was Jerusalem Renewed As Israel's Center of Worship?

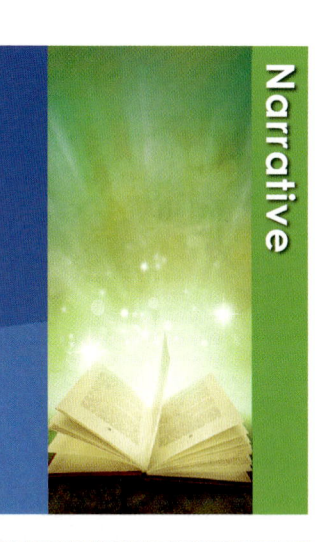

Narrative

"Josiah removed all the shrines of the high places that were in the towns of Samaria, which kings of Israel had made, provoking the LORD to anger."

2 Kings 23:19 (NRSV)

Phase 1

Read the Story:
2 Kings 22:1–23:30

The Story in a Nutshell

The kingship of Josiah follows a long series of kings who are described either as doing "what was right in the sight of the LORD" (mentioned 10 times in 1–2 Kings) or "what was evil in the sight of the LORD" (mentioned 31 times in 1–2 Kings, NRSV). In this part of the Bible, "evil" is typically defined as idolatry and as worship at shrines, altars, and "high places" atop hills or mountains rather than at the Temple in Jerusalem. Monarchs of the northern kingdom, beginning with Jeroboam I (who set up rival altars to the Temple), are consistently condemned for their idolatry. The strongest criticism, however, is reserved for Manasseh, who becomes king of the southern kingdom at age 12 and rules for 55 years. Manasseh introduces idolatry by building altars to the "host of heaven" and erecting a carved image of the goddess Asherah in the Temple. The Bible also says that Manasseh reestablishes altars to Ba'al, the Canaanite god, and introduces other prohibited religious practices (2 Kings 21). Amon, who rules for two years after his father, Manasseh, also worships idols.

Josiah's Discovery

According to 2 Kings, Josiah becomes king at the age of eight, following the assassination of his father, Amon. Eighteen years later, King Josiah decides to renovate the Temple, which has been neglected. Josiah appoints several servants to oversee the work and gives them money to buy building materials and to hire builders and artists. During the renovation, Hilkiah the high priest discovers a "Book of Law" in the Temple. The scribe Shaphan reads the book and brings it to King Josiah, who has Shaphan read it to him. Josiah reacts with sorrow, tearing his clothing in distress. He commands his servants to "inquire of the Lord for me, for the people, and for all Judah concerning the words of this book that has been found; for great is the wrath of the Lord that is kindled against us, because our ancestors did not obey the words of this book, to do according to all that is written concerning us" 2 Kings 22:13 (NRSV). Josiah believes that he and his people have not fulfilled what is written in the Book of Law. Huldah the prophetess predicts the destruction of Judah, so Josiah launches a comprehensive program of religious reform. As part of the plan, Josiah gathers the people and reads the Book of Law to them. (We will discuss the Book of Law further below.) The people recommit themselves to following the covenant and celebrate Passover, one of the most important religious festivals (2 Kings 23).

Josiah's Reforms

Josiah's reforms are intended to eliminate idolatry and to centralize worship in Jerusalem. His reforms include the following:

- The Temple is cleared of idols.
- Competing altars near Jerusalem and in the Judean hills are destroyed.
- The northern center of worship built earlier by Jeroboam at Bethel is destroyed.
- The priests of the competing shrines and altars are removed.
- The altars and temples located in the region of Samaria (the capital of the former kingdom of Israel) are destroyed.

The Bible characterizes Josiah as follows: "Before him there was no king like him, who turned to the Lord with all his heart, with all his soul, and with all his might, according to all the law of Moses; nor did any like him arise after him" 2 Kings 23:25 (NRSV). Even David and Solomon do not get this kind of praise in the Bible!

Tragically, Josiah dies in the prime of his life, after ruling for 31 years. Pharaoh Necho, the king of Egypt, is on his way to Assyria, and Josiah goes out to meet him. A battle ensues and Josiah is fatally wounded. Josiah is buried in the royal tombs in Jerusalem and is greatly mourned by the people
(2 Chronicles 35:20-27).

An altar uncovered at Tel Dan, in northern Israel. The construction of the complex is attributed to Jeroboam son of Nebat, who also founds a ritual area at Bethel. Archaeological excavations indicate that this ritual space was expanded and renovated in the days of Jeroboam II (the son of Jehoash) in the eighth century BC.

Statuette of King Necho, ca. 610–595 BC. Brooklyn Museum, Charles Edwin Wilbour Fund, New York.

Phase 2
Travel through Time

According to the Bible, prior to the building of the Temple, in Jerusalem, the Israelites and their predecessors worship God in various places. The patriarchs, for example, build altars and worship God at Hebron, Beersheba, and Bethel. During their wanderings in the desert, the Israelites' center of worship is the Tabernacle, which they carry from place to place. Among other things, the Tabernacle houses the golden Menorah, the Altar, and the Ark of the Covenant. When Joshua leads the Israelites into Canaan, the Tabernacle is set up in Shiloh (Joshua 18:1), but God is also worshiped in Gilgal, Shechem, and elsewhere.

Due to the presence of the Tabernacle, Shiloh enjoys a special status for many years (1 Samuel 1–3), but it is not the only legitimate place of worship. The Israelites also worship at "high places" and altars throughout the land. Samuel the prophet builds an altar in Ramah where he lives (1 Samuel 7:17).

The Book of 1 Kings claims that centralized worship begins with the building of the Temple in Jerusalem. King Solomon's prayers during the Temple consecration express the hope that all of Israel, and even Gentiles, will pray at or toward the Temple. A few years after Solomon's death, however, the kingdom splits in two. Jeroboam, leader of the northern kingdom of Israel, establishes places of worship at Bethel and Dan. These compete with Solomon's Temple in Jerusalem (in the southern kingdom of Judah). While the Bible depicts Jeroboam's actions as idolatry, the Israelites in the northern kingdom consider the temples at Bethel and Dan to be legitimate.

According to Deuteronomy, centralized group worship is required once the people enter the land of Israel. Once the Temple was established in Jerusalem, sacrifices were only to be offered there. Jerusalem is referred to many times as "the place" or "the city" that the Lord has chosen (1 Kings 8:44, 48; 11:32, 36; 14:21; 2 Kings 23:27).

Moses with His Rod and His Brazen Serpent, engraving by John Hall after Benjamin West, 1793. Wellcome Library, London, England.

The Bronze Serpent

According to Numbers 21, when the Israelites complain about a shortage of food and water, God sends snakes that kill many people. To stop the plague of snakes, "Moses made a serpent of bronze, and put it upon a pole; and whenever a serpent bit someone, that person would look at the serpent of bronze and live" Numbers 21:9 (NRSV). Later the bronze serpent is kept in the Temple. As the centuries pass, however, the bronze snake becomes an object of veneration. King Hezekiah later destroys it (2 Kings 18:4) as he seeks to purify Judah from idolatry. Even so, Hezekiah's son Manasseh reintroduces idolatry.

As a result of Josiah's reforms, Jerusalem becomes the only legitimate place of worship, a status that is maintained throughout the Second Temple period. The New Testament describes Jesus and his followers, including the apostle Paul, as acknowledging the importance of the Temple in Jerusalem. Essentially, from the time of Josiah until today, the Jewish people, whether living in Israel or in the Diaspora, have acknowledged the special status of Jerusalem. During prayers Jews customarily face Jerusalem, a practice said to be initiated by King Solomon (1 Kings 8:44-52).

Vocabulary

> **Veneration** [noun], respect inspired by the dignity

A cylinder of Nabonidus (ruled 555–539 BC) found in the sun temple in the city of Sippar (modern-day Iraq). The cylinder tells the story of the building of a temple to the god of the moon in Haran and the building of a temple to the god of the sun in Sippar. Inset: The stele (a stone slab or column) of Nabonidus, the last Babylonian king.

Altar to the god Aten, in Tell el-Amarna, Egypt. Inset: A relief showing Akhenaten with his wife Nefertiti and their children. Above them is the sun disk, Aten. Relief from ca. 1350 BC. The Neues Museum, Berlin, Germany.

Vocabulary

> **Henotheism** [noun], the worship of one god without denying the existence of other gods

Phase 3
Mine for Clues

Religious Transitions in the Ancient Near East

Archaeological findings indicate that changes and disruptions in patterns of worship occurred not only in Judah, but also in other locations in the Ancient Near East. These changes were often fiercely opposed by the priests who held power. Consider the examples of the Babylonian king Nabonidus and the Egyptian king Akhenaten.

Nabonidus was the son of a priestess in the Temple of Sin, the Babylonian god of the moon. When Nabonidus came to power, the main Babylonian god was Marduk. Nabonidus tried to shift the focus of Babylonian worship to the moon god, Sin, but met fierce resistance from the priests and followers of Marduk. When Cyrus, the king of Persia, invaded Babylon, he likely ended the reign of Belshazzar, the regent ruler mentioned often in the book of Daniel, while Nabonidus the king was away. In Babylon the followers of Marduk saw Cyrus as a savior who had come to restore the worship of Marduk to its former glory. Nabonidus, who had lost popular support, also lost the kingdom, and Cyrus took over the largest and strongest empire in the Ancient Near East.

Prior to Akhenaten, who ruled Egypt in the 14th century BC, each city had its own gods, with Amon as the main god. The priests of Amon, who were dispersed throughout Egypt, had accumulated great power and political influence. Akhenaten sought to break up their power and, according to some historians, established strong henotheistic or monotheistic worship of the sun disk, Aten. Akhenaten shut down the temples of Amon and the other gods and exiled or executed their priests. Not surprisingly, Akhenaten's acts created intense resentment. Following his death, the priests of Amon and their supporters abolished Akhenaten's religious policies and Tutankhamun, the king who succeeded Akhenaten, was named after the god Amon.

King Josiah's Reform

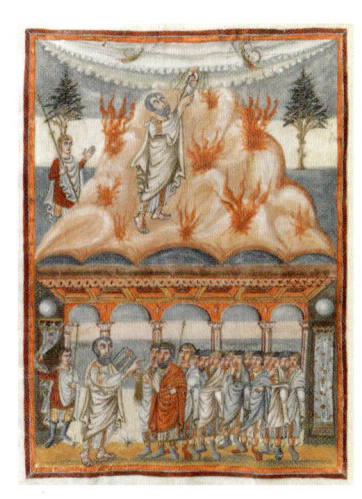

Moses Receiving the Tablets of Law and
Moses Addressing Aaron and the Israelites
Moutier-Grandval Bible (Add MS 10546), ca. 834-843.
The British Library, London. The British Library Board.

Which Book Does Josiah Find?

Since Josiah's reforms show significant parallels with the Book of Deuteronomy, scholars have labored to understand the relationship between Deuteronomy and the "Book of Law" described in 2 Kings. Are they more or less the same texts? Are the reforms undertaken in order to carry out the laws stated in Deuteronomy? Or does Deuteronomy reflect reforms previously enacted by Josiah? Scholars continue to debate these questions. Whatever the case, the idea of centralized worship is a leading theme in Deuteronomy as well as in 1–2 Kings (and 1–2 Chronicles).

Archaeological Findings

At Tel Arad in Israel, archaeologists found ruins of temple from the First Temple period. It includes a hall, a "holy of holies" area (the most sacred part of any temple), altars, and stone monuments. This temple was destroyed in the seventh century BC, a time period that roughly correlates with the settings for the stories of Hezekiah and Josiah. Elsewhere, in Tel Beer Sheva (Beersheba), archaeologists have discovered an altar with four elevated corners. The structure had been dismantled and used to build the walls of the city. The temples at Tel Arad and Tel Beer Sheva may be the kinds of temples that Josiah orders destroyed in the story in 2 Kings.

An altar found at Tel Arad in Israel that was likely used for sacrifices. The altar was built with unfinished stones because of the prohibition against building an altar using hewn stones: "But if you make for me an altar of stone, do not build it of hewn stones; for if you use a chisel upon it you profane it" Exodus 20:25 (NRSV).

Tel Beersheba, Israel.
Inset: Restored altar with four elevated corner stones, known as horns. These are the kinds of altars that are destroyed in the Josiah story.

King Josiah's Reform

Phase 4
Use the Telescope

Jerusalem's special status in the Bible and in Judaism was achieved over many years, but Josiah's reforms very likely played a central role in the process. King David establishes his capital in Jerusalem, and Solomon builds the Temple there. Even after the division of the kingdom, Jerusalem serves as the capital of the southern kingdom of Judah, although the people of the northern kingdom of Israel do not go there to worship. The city's status begins to change during Hezekiah's rule, after the northern kingdom is destroyed by the Assyrians in 722 BC. Many refugees from the north fill the streets of Jerusalem, and the city expands. While Hezekiah tries to centralize worship there, King Josiah completes the task by eliminating worship in other locations.

Jerusalem is today a city that attracts visitors, tourists, and worshipers from all three Abrahamic religions—Judaism, Christianity, and Islam.

Summary

Josiah, who becomes king of Judah as a child, eventually transforms Jerusalem into the exclusive place of Israelite worship. He does so by implementing broad and comprehensive religious reforms. Jerusalem's special status was maintained during the Babylonian exile and the Second Temple period. The city serves not only as the spiritual center of Judaism, but also as the launching point for the new faith founded by Jesus and his followers. In time, Jerusalem becomes a destination for Christian pilgrims and, centuries later, also becomes one of the three holiest cities for Muslims.

Prophets of a Future Hope

What Role and Purpose Did the Prophets Serve?

Narrative

"I spoke to the prophets, gave them many visions and told parables through them."
Hosea 12:10 (NIV)

Phase 1

Read the Story:
Jeremiah 23:1-8; 30-33; Isaiah 2; 9:1-7; Micah 4:1–5:7; Zechariah 9:9-17; Jonah 1–4

The Story in a Nutshell

The Old Testament prophets are best known for their predictions of doom. But the prophets also carried a message of hope for the families of Israel:

"'They will come and shout for joy on the heights of Zion;
  they will rejoice in the bounty of the Lord—
the grain, the new wine and the olive oil,
  the young of the flocks and herds.
They will be like a well-watered garden,
  and they will sorrow no more'" Jeremiah 31:12 (NIV).

While many of these prophecies of hope relate to satisfying immediate needs and desires (being delivered from captivity, returning home, rebuilding Jerusalem and the Temple), others look further into the future. Some point to the coming of a great leader, who will redeem Israel and restore it to an age of perfection.

Vocabulary

> **Zion** [noun], another name for Jerusalem

Majors and Minors

According to the Christian division of the books of the Old Testament, there are four Major Prophets in the Bible:

- Isaiah
- Jeremiah
- Ezekiel
- Daniel

In the Jewish tradition, Daniel is not listed among the prophets. He appears in the last section of the Hebrew scriptures, called the Writings. Some scholars conclude that Daniel must have been written later than the other prophets' books, while others insist that Daniel belongs among the prophetic writings. The other prophetic books, "the Twelve," are considered Minor Prophets: Hosea, Joel, Amos, Obadiah, Jonah, Micah, Nahum, Habakkuk, Zephaniah, Haggai, Zechariah, and Malachi.

The terms *major* and *minor* in no way denote level of importance. Instead, they reflect the length of the prophetic books. The Major Prophets are the longest prophetic books while the Minor Prophets are shorter. Jeremiah, one of the Major Prophets, has been divided into more than 1,300 verses. Obadiah, one of the Minor Prophets, has been divided into 21.

THE BOOK OF THE PROPHET ISAIAH.

Opening page of the Book of Isaiah from the Macklin Bible, 1800.

Vocabulary

> **Denote** [transitive verb], to mean something

Prophets of Hope

References to the redemption of Israel are scattered throughout the Old Testament. Often they express the longing for a great military and political leader like King David. Following are some passages in the Hebrew Bible associated with this future leader:

- "'The days are coming,' declares the LORD, 'when I will raise up for David a righteous Branch, a King who will reign wisely
and do what is just and right in the land.
In his days Judah will be saved
and Israel will live in safety.
This is the name by which he will be called:
The LORD Our Righteous Savior'"
Jeremiah 23:5-6 (NIV).

- "'In that day [declares the LORD] "I will restore David's fallen shelter—I will repair its broken walls and restore its ruins—and will rebuild it as it used to be'" Amos 9:11 (NIV).

- "'The Redeemer will come to Zion, to those in Jacob who repent of their sins,' declares the LORD" Isaiah 59:20 (NIV).

- "For to us a child is born,
to us a son is given,
and the government will be on his shoulders.
And he will be called
Wonderful Counselor, Mighty God,
Everlasting Father, Prince of Peace"
Isaiah 9:6 (NIV).

- "The LORD will be king over the whole earth. On that day there will be one LORD, and his name the only name ...
"[Jerusalem] will be inhabited; never again will it be destroyed. Jerusalem will be secure" Zechariah 14:9, 11 (NIV).

Phase 2
Travel through Time

Who Were the Prophets?

Traveling back to ancient Israel, we meet a small band of people walking down the road together. They all share a unique appearance, from their clothing and hairstyles to the instruments some are carrying. But the biggest difference is the special passion visible on their faces. This passion—they say for God and for righteousness—sets them apart from their fellow Israelites. The rest of society calls them prophets. Prophets claim to have a message from God. Often the message applies to the present or the near future, including some harsh condemnations for actions. Sometimes it's for distant generations. Whatever the timing of the message, the role of a biblical prophet is to deliver the words of God—words of warning, words of comfort, or words of instruction. The warnings often address social issues that are still relevant today, such as the mistreatment of the vulnerable, the oppression of the poor, or the abuses and injustices of the powerful. They also encourage the people of Israel to keep the Mosaic Covenant and their obligations to God.

According to the Bible's account, several of these prophets are also the leaders of their people, such as Abraham, Moses, and Deborah. In the biblical books about the monarchy, we see that Israel often considers its prophets as messengers for God. In the Bible's account of Ezekiel's call to prophecy, he is told by God: "You must speak my words to them, whether they listen or fail to listen, for they are rebellious" Ezekiel 2:7 (NIV).

We find some additional clues about what a prophet is:

- A man or woman of God. Hebrew prophetesses include Miriam (Moses' sister), Hulda, and Deborah (the judge)
- A seer or visionary (one who has visions that convey the prophecy, Numbers 12:6)
- A watchman for the people (Hosea 9:8)

The prophet *Ezekiel*, statue by Carlo Chelli (1859), located at the base of the Column of the Immaculate Conception in Rome, Italy.

Vocabulary

> **Visions** [noun]
an experience of seeing and even hearing something or someone; maybe in a trance or dream state

Prophets of a Future Hope

The God of All Nations

The Bible repeatedly says that the God of Israel will one day be known throughout the world. This theme begins with the promises to Abraham in Genesis that he will be the father of many nations and ultimately all nations will be "blessed" through him. Several of the major and minor prophets further develop this theme.

- "Many peoples and powerful nations will come to Jerusalem to seek the LORD Almighty and to entreat him" Zechariah 8:22 (NIV).
- "My house will be called a house of prayer for all nations" Isaiah 56:7 (NIV).
- "'My name will be great among the nations, from where the sun rises to where it sets. In every place incense and pure offerings will be brought to me, because my name will be great among the nations,' says the LORD Almighty" Malachi 1:11 (NIV).

One annual event seems to perpetuate visibly this belief in God of All Nations. The Jerusalem March is a traditional parade through the streets of Jerusalem held every year at the end of summer during the biblical holiday called the Feast of Tabernacles (*Sukkot* in Hebrew). Starting in 1980 thousands of Christians from more than 50 nations have joined the Jewish people in this annual celebration. This display of Jewish-Christian relations is organized in part by the ICEJ (International Christian Embassy Jerusalem).

Prophetic Acts of Drama

Prophets communicate mostly through words, but sometimes, in the biblical stories, they engage in something more like performance art. They convey their messages in dramatic and unexpected ways, hoping to cause the people to pay attention to the message they believe God has given them. According to the Bible stories:

- Jeremiah smashes a clay jar in front of the elders and priests to illustrate how God will smash the nation of Judah beyond repair if the people turn from God (Jeremiah 19).
- Jeremiah wears an oxen yoke on his neck to demonstrate how God will put the Israelites under the heavy yoke of the Babylonian King Nebuchadnezzar (Jeremiah 27).
- Hosea marries Gomer, a prostitute, and has children with her, in order to illustrate God's love for his unfaithful people (Hosea 1:2-3).
- Isaiah warns of the Assyrian captivity of the Egyptians and Ethiopians by walking about stripped down and barefoot for three years (Isaiah 20).
- Ezekiel lies on his side for over a year to warn of the coming siege of Jerusalem (Ezekiel 4).

But we also discover that not everyone who claims to be a prophet in ancient Israel is accepted as one. Some prophets (the biblical authors viewed them as "false" prophets) claimed to speak for other gods. Other prophets were criticized for telling the rulers what they wanted to hear, rather than condemning their excesses and injustices. The Law of Moses, however, warns about false prophets. "But a prophet who presumes to speak in my name anything I have not commanded, or a prophet who speaks in the name of other gods, is to be put to death" Deuteronomy 18:20 (NIV).

Vocabulary

> **Lucrative** [adjective], producing wealth
> **Yoke** [noun], a bar that is attached to the necks of two work animals (such as oxen) allowing them to pull a plow

Prophets of a Future Hope

Phase 3
Mine for Clues

Different Styles for Different Prophets

According to these biblical writers, does God change his way of speaking? If that were so, however, why would the books of the prophets use such different writing styles? Does God change his way of speaking? Later Jewish interpreters have argued that no two prophets prophesy in the same way. In other words these interpreters claimed that each prophet exercises a role in formulating the prophecy so that God's message is given expression in different ways through different people. The prophecies of Isaiah are rich with the language and metaphors of city life, while the prophecies of Amos use rural images. In the Book of Amos, the prophet lives in a small town bordering on the desert. This would explain why, when Amos criticizes rich people for their gluttony and exploitation of the poor, he calls them fat cows (Amos 4:1), language that might fit Amos's background and profession as a herdsman. According to the Bible, prophets are not simply recorders of God's message; they are great orators who move the people with their beautiful language.

Reining In the Royals

The English historian Lord Acton once famously said: "Power tends to corrupt, and absolute power corrupts absolutely." In the ancient world, the monarchy usually wielded significant power. Western democracies developed systems to balance powers so that no single faction could gain absolute power. These include parliaments that offset royal power or different branches of government—executive, legislative, and judicial—that keep each other in check. In the Bible's telling, ancient Israel has its own check on the power of the king: the biblical prophets are expected to hold the kings accountable for their actions, often in moral and religious obedience areas.

The prophet *Isaiah*, statue by Salvatore Revelli (1859), situated at the base of the Column of the Immaculate Conception in Rome, Italy.

U.S. Supreme Court building in Washington, D.C.

U.S. Capitol building in Washington, D.C. The American government has, since its creation, operated as a constitutional democracy based on a system of checks and balances. The three parts of the government that help maintain this balance are the Executive Branch (the president and his administration), the Legislative Branch (the House of Representatives and the Senate), and the Judicial Branch (the Supreme Court). All three branches are accountable to one another. Many nations find ways to balance powers against one another. The Hebrew Bible represents more than one political structure, but prophets persisted in their influence on leaders' moral and occasionally political decisions—or their consequences.

Prophets of a Future Hope

A reconstruction using original bricks of the Ishtar Gate of ancient Babylon on display at the Pergamon Museum in Berlin, Germany. It was first constructed in 575 BC by order of King Nebuchadnezzar II.

Assyrian relief (865 BC) taken from the ruins of the Palace of Nimrod in the ancient Assyrian capital of Calah (Genesis 10:8-12), on display in the British Museum, London, England. The great empires that held sway over the Ancient Near East appear to have interacted with Israel, including the Egyptians, Assyrians, Babylonians, Persians, and Romans. They are all mentioned frequently in the Bible. The Bible portrays the prophets of Israel sometimes describing or even predicting their rise and fall.

In the biblical picture, the prophets embody loyalty to God and the covenant rather than fidelity to the king. They spurn wealth and social status. This allows them to take a much-needed critical perspective on the politics of the day. They interact extensively with Israel's kings, mostly criticizing them for their wrongful deeds but also, at times, encouraging them when they do right.

Prophets of Doom and of Hope

Prophets cannot be typecast. Some prophesy doom while others deliver words of hope. In the Book of Jeremiah, he prophesies about the destruction of Jerusalem, but also about the city's rebuilding and future greatness. He prophesies the fall of the king but also the rise of a new king from the House of David. This reflects Jeremiah's mission: "'See, today I appoint you over nations and kingdoms to uproot and tear down, to destroy and overthrow, to build and to plant'" Jeremiah 1:10 (NIV). Jeremiah predicts both destruction and renewal, punishment and deliverance.

Prophets and Anti-Imperialism

Prophets in the biblical narrative not only challenge the people for their wrongdoing and their oppression of the weak (especially of strangers, widows, and orphans), they also speak judgment against the empires that oppress them for their excesses and their oppression of smaller nations. Isaiah writes of the fall of the Assyrian Empire: "When the LORD has finished all his work against Mount Zion and Jerusalem, he will say, 'I will punish the king of Assyria for the willful pride of his heart and the haughty look in his eyes'" Isaiah 10:12 (NIV). This is explained as punishment for Assyria's brutal subjugation of other peoples. The prophet delivers messages for various nations about the abuse of power and impending judgments. People today who condemn abuses of power, injustices against the poor, and the excesses of "empire" sometimes find inspiration in the writings of the ancient prophets who thundered against oppression in their time.

Jonah and the Whale, by Dutch artist Pieter Lastman, 1621. Museum Kunstpalast, Düsseldorf, Germany.

Jonah, the Reluctant Prophet

The prophet Jonah being swallowed by a "whale" of a fish is one of the best-known stories in the Hebrew Bible.

The dramatic story begins when God commands Jonah to go to the city of Nineveh, the capital of Assyria, with a message that God will destroy it. The Assyrians were powerful enemies of Israel, and Jonah wants God to destroy them. Fearing that they will repent, and God will forgive them and spare them from destruction, Jonah resists the order to go to Nineveh.

So the rebellious Jonah boards a ship bound in the opposite direction, for Tarshish. Jonah doesn't get far. Instead, a storm strikes, and Jonah understands the storm is from God. He tells the men aboard the ship that they should throw him overboard in order to save their lives. The Bible says he is swallowed by a large fish, where he spends three miserable, slimy days and nights.

In the belly of this large fish (not necessarily a whale), the desperate Jonah recites scriptures that ask for mercy. What response does he get to his prayers? According to the story, God hears Jonah's pleas and causes the fish to vomit the reluctant prophet onto dry land.

Finally, Jonah goes to Nineveh and delivers his warning message from God: "Forty more days and Nineveh will be overthrown" Jonah 3:4 (NIV). That's it—Jonah's whole message.

Much to Jonah's disappointment, the story relates that the people of Nineveh turn from their wrongdoing and repent. The ruler of Nineveh issues an edict: "Do not let people or animals, herds or flocks, taste anything; do not let them eat or drink. But let people and animals be covered with sackcloth. Let everyone call urgently on God. Let them give up their evil ways and their violence. Who knows? God may yet relent and with compassion turn from his fierce anger so that we will not perish" Jonah 3:7-9 (NIV).

The malcontent Jonah is so anxious to see Nineveh go up in flames that he actually builds a booth outside the city and waited to see what would happen (Jonah 4:5).

When God responds with mercy and spares the city, this seems "very wrong" to Jonah (4:1). The prophet is so upset that for the second time in the story he is ready to die. Throwing words from the Torah back at God, Jonah explains why he was reluctant to go to Nineveh, "I knew that you are a gracious and compassionate God, slow to anger and abounding in love, a God who relents from sending calamity" Jonah 4:2 (NIV).

The biblical writer wants to show that the one who delivered Israel from bondage in Egypt and from captivity in Babylon is ready to offer deliverance to anyone who turns away from evil and toward God. This is why the Book of Jonah has been read for centuries in Jewish synagogues worldwide on the Day of Atonement (Yom Kippur), the most solemn Jewish holiday of the year.

Prophets of a Future Hope

Phase 4
Use the Telescope

When we hear the word *prophet*, we often think of someone who foretells the future. Yet the biblical prophet is someone who, it is claimed, simply speaks the message of God. Sometimes that message is about the injustices of the present. Sometimes the prophets simply bring a message of impending judgment and destruction. And sometimes, indeed, the prophet's message seems to predict the future.

There are many ways that modern readers have understood these "predictions." If the prophecy is very specific, and the prophet seems to foretell something that does indeed take place, then some scholars conclude that the "prophecy" must have been written "after" the event it claims to predict. If we were to read an article that "predicted" a terrorist attack on September 11, 2001, for instance, then we might conclude that the author of the article predicted the future. Or that the author is falsely claiming to have predicted the event.

This is an ongoing conversation in the world of biblical scholarship. Many Jewish and Christian scholars, who believe it is possible that God could give prophets glimpses into the future, examine the evidence and believe that the books of the prophets sometimes predict future events. Many other scholars do not believe in supernatural things such as prophecies or divine inspiration; they examine the evidence and conclude that books such as Daniel were written after the events they claim to foretell.

Other scholars are less concerned about their actual historical origin, and suggest that the books of the biblical prophets speak to universal themes of humankind and society. In this view, the prophets are not predicting the future but explaining that certain kinds of behavior will always lead to chaos and destruction, and other kinds of behavior will always lead to order and life, justice and peace. While this may not suffice for all the "predictions" in the Bible, it provides another way of understanding prophecy as rooted in a keen insight into humankind, society, and the natural order of things.

From the perspective of many Jews and Christians, there are biblical prophecies that have been fulfilled. Yet there are also many, they would say, that still point to a future hope. The books of the prophets also speak of an age of peace, such as in these words from Isaiah:

"He will judge between the nations
   and will settle disputes for many people.
They will beat their swords into plowshares
   and their spears into pruning hooks.
Nation will not take up sword against nation,
   nor will they train for war anymore"
Isaiah 2:4 (NIV).

Many Jews and Christians call this a verse of "messianic hope." For Jews, it points toward a hopeful vision for humanity. For Christians, it points toward the life and biblical account of Jesus of Nazareth. In both cases, the biblical prophets evoke hope in the future. The writings of the biblical prophets have also served as an inspiration to many social movements throughout the world.

Summary

The biblical prophets provide some of the most colorful characters and some of the most memorable stories in the Bible. The prophets are viewed as messengers from God, bringing messages of hope in times of trouble and messages of judgment in times of sin and injustice. Scholars continue to debate the origins of these prophecies and the historical nature of the prophets themselves. The prophets also spoke to countless social issues, such as the oppression of the weak by the powerful, or the neglect of the poor by the rich. These writings continue to shape social dialogue today, along with their continuous role for religious belief.

Job
What Does the Bible Say to the Suffering?

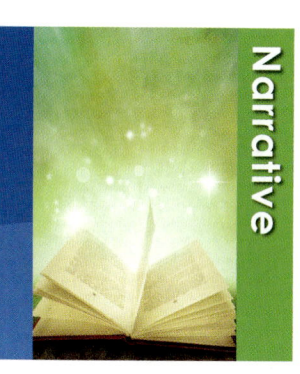

Narrative

> "No one said a word to Job, for they saw that his suffering was too great for words."
>
> Job 2:13 (NLT)

Phase 1

Read the Story:
Job 1–3; 4:1-8; 6–7; 29–31; 38–42

The Story in a Nutshell

At the center of the Book of Job is the story of a "blameless and just" man who is made to endure all kinds of suffering. He loses his children and everything he owns. Then he loses his health, developing painful sores from the top of his head to the soles of his feet. In his complaints, Job provides graphic descriptions of his agony: "My body is covered with maggots and scabs. My skin breaks open, oozing with pus" Job 7:5 (NLT). He has terrifying nightmares. Things are so bad that he prefers death to life: "I hate my life and don't want to go on living. Oh, leave me alone for my few remaining days" Job 7:16 (NLT).

Job's friends sit silently and mourn with him for seven days. Then, taking turns to speak, they argue that such an extraordinary series of painful events must mean that God is angry with Job. Surely he has done something, they suggest, to anger God. Throughout the book, Job maintains his integrity, insists that he's done nothing to deserve this torment, and demands that God explain himself. When God speaks at last, he does not answer Job's accusations so much as he delivers a series of questions that Job cannot answer. God asks Job where he was when the earth was made, or when God divided night from day and set the boundaries of the sea. God never explains why he permitted Job to suffer so terribly, but he points to the smallness of Job's perspective and his ignorance about the ways of God and the mysteries of the world.

Vocabulary

> **Integrity** [noun]
adherence to moral and ethical ideals, honesty

Job 93

Job Rebuked by His Friends, William Blake, 1805. Morgan Library and Museum, New York.

With Friends like These …

The Hebrew Bible does not refer to "Satan" (*Ha-Satan* in Hebrew means "the Accuser") very often. One of the very few books of the Old Testament that clearly refers to Satan, and the book that describes him at much greater length than anywhere else in the Bible, is the Book of Job. In Job, Satan appears before God along with other "members of the heavenly court" Job 1:6 (NLT). In keeping with his name, the Accuser acts like a prosecuting attorney, claiming that Job is only faithful to God because it earns him divine rewards. This puts the celestial contest in action, as Satan sets out to prove that Job will curse God if his blessings are stripped away.

This angelic being becomes known by many other names in later Jewish tradition (Belial, Sammael) and is well-known in the New Testament as the Devil (*diabolos*, the Greek translation of Satan), the Evil One, the Adversary, and the ruler of a host of rebellious angelic beings (Matthew 25:41). The Gospels describe Jesus being personally tempted by Satan (Matthew 4; Mark 1; Luke 4), and in the Gospel of John Jesus calls him the "father of lies" and a "murderer from the beginning" John 8:44 (NLT). Because of this designation, and because he is often described with the imagery of a serpent and dragon (see Revelation 12), many Bible interpreters assert that it was this angelic adversary who originally tempted Adam and Eve in the form of a serpent in the Garden of Eden.

Job is chastened and humbled. Here is Job's final answer to the host of questions God asked:

"I know that you can do anything,
  and no one can stop you.
You asked, 'Who is this that questions my wisdom with such ignorance?'
  It is I—and I was talking about things I knew nothing about,
  things far too wonderful for me.
You said, 'Listen and I will speak!
  I have some questions for you,
  and you must answer them.'
I had only heard about you before,
  but now I have seen you with my own eyes.
I take back everything I said,
  and I sit in dust and ashes to show my repentance" Job 42:2-6 (NLT).

Finally, at the end of the story, God vindicates Job and restores everything he possessed. The Bible says in Job 42:10, "When Job prayed for his friends, the LORD restored his fortunes" (NLT). His wealth is restored and his family reestablished. Once his tests are over, God blesses Job with even more than he had before. Job goes on to live a long, blessed life.

What's at Stake

The Book of Job grapples with deep human questions. The Hebrews believed that God is loving and just. How, then, should they understand it when terrible suffering falls upon people who do not seem to deserve it?

Vocabulary

> **Chasten** [verb]
to correct by punishment or suffering
> **Grapple** [verb]
to seize something firmly; to wrestle with

Phase 2
Travel through Time

Job is the only story in the Bible that tells us almost nothing about when or where the story is supposed to have taken place. The Book of Job is categorized by Bible scholars as Wisdom Literature, like Psalms and Proverbs.

What we do know is that the Book of Job is an exceptional work of Hebrew poetry, and it appears to concern someone who is not an Israelite. There is no reference to the Torah, a temple, or a priesthood—no way for Job to learn more about the ways of God. It wrestles with universal human questions, but Job does not draw on the specific resources of the Jewish tradition.

Some scholars have suggested that the story is a vivid parable, a fictional tale to teach us real-life lessons. The later rabbinic-type parables of Jesus in the New Testament, such as the prodigal son and the good Samaritan stories, possess a similar style. It's difficult to tell whether they are recounting morality tales (parables) or attempting to describe real events. Job is mentioned elsewhere in the Bible, which suggests that he was, in the storytelling of the time, characterized as a well-known figure with a reputation for integrity and wealth (see Ezekiel 14:14 and James 5:11).

Fountain of Job in the Hinnom Valley, near Jerusalem, by David Roberts, 1841. Library of Congress, Washington, D.C. David Roberts was a Scottish painter who toured the Near East, 1838–1840. His paintings give us a glimpse at how the Ancient Near East may have looked at that time.

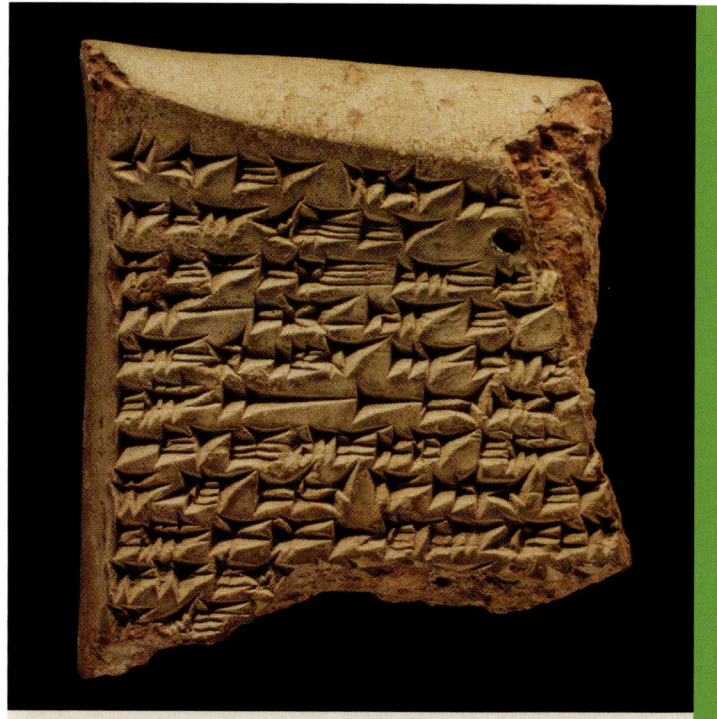

Ludlul bēl nēmeqi - Let Me Praise the Lord of Wisdom. A cuneiform tablet inscribed with this ancient Mesopotamian poem, in Akkadian, that has a similar theme as the biblical story of Job. 930-604 BC. British Museum, London. Copyright The Trustees of the British Museum. All rights reserved.

Job 95

Sitting for Seven Days

The friends of the suffering Job are actually the most helpful when they keep their mouths shut and simply grieve with him. This is what they do for the first seven days of their visit. Rather than talking about what is happening to their friend, they sit nearby and quietly sympathize with him. Judaism would later adopt a similar seven-day period of mourning as a tradition for family and close friends. Called the shivah, it begins right after the funeral.

One of the ancient customs of Jewish mourning is the withdrawal for seven days to the sanctuary of the home following the death of a family member. During this period of "sitting shivah," mourners do not take part in joyous events or go on long trips.

Why Do Bad Things Happen to Good People?

Job's story has been a matter of heated debate among rabbis, theologians, and philosophers ever since it was written. Philosophers today like to discuss "the problem of evil," which asks whether a good and all-powerful God would permit evil. The ancient question, addressed in Job, is slightly different: Why do bad things happen to good people, and why are the wicked so often unpunished? Job's friends represent a "retributive" view in which all suffering is punishment from God. The Book of Job himself represents a more complex view, one in which the actions of God are often mysterious. The book also addresses how people act in the midst of hardships, and whether human beings have the perspective and the right to question the actions of God.

Phase 3
Mine for Clues

Great Patience and Great Faith

There is a saying that a long-suffering person has "the patience of Job." What Job exhibits during his time of great trouble is more than patience, however. He also shows tremendous faith.

Job ignores the advice of his distressed wife, who tells him, "Are you still trying to maintain your integrity? Curse God and die" Job 2:9 (NLT). Instead, Job declares later in the story, "God might kill me, but I have no other hope" Job 13:15 (NLT). The story seems to caution people who are trying to understand suffering—theirs or others'—not to assume or assign reasons for the suffering. The great patience of Job could be understood as demonstrating great faith.

Fantastical Beasts

The Book of Job describes two magnificent and mysterious creatures: Behemoth, a land giant (chapter 40), and Leviathan (chapter 41), a sea monster. These may refer to ordinary animals (some scholars suggest a hippo and a crocodile) or to massive primeval creatures, but the stylized poetic portrayal is common in Ancient Near Eastern mythology—imaginative scenes that make a serious, real-world point. Leviathan represents the primordial forces of chaos and disorder that must be controlled or overcome to create a world of peace and order (cf. Psalm 74:14). In Job 40 and 41, God claims that for him these fearsome monsters present no problem whatsoever. He even describes himself domesticating Behemoth (40:24) and treating Leviathan as his pet and plaything (41:5). One of the points of the book seems to be: Since Job cannot overcome Leviathan, how can he hope to win the argument with God who controls Leviathan? Leviathan, or the sea dragon, appears elsewhere in the Bible as a symbol of opposition that God will ultimately destroy (Isaiah 27:1; Revelation 20:2).

Job's Story Told in Art

Job, Nathan Rapoport, 1968. Yad Vashem, Jerusalem, Israel.

Job, Léon Bonnat, 1880. Musée Bonnat-Helleu, Bayonne, France.

In this image Job is depicted as bereft of all clothing and hope, in despair of life itself, crying out plaintively toward the heavens.

A statue of Job is featured in Israel at the Yad Vashem, the world center for Holocaust studies founding in 1953. The name *Yad Vashem* is based on a passage from the Book of Isaiah, "I will give them ... a memorial and a name ... It will never disappear!" Isaiah 56:5 (NLT). The Holocaust is the name given to the Nazi campaign of systematic extermination in World War II, which resulted in the murder of 6 million Jews, including 1.5 million Jewish children. The Israelis find Job's story a fitting symbol of Jewish suffering through the centuries, especially during the Holocaust. Job's story is a fitting symbol, in microcosm, of all that the Jewish people have suffered and endured as a whole, especially during the Holocaust.

Job and His Friends, Ilya Repin, 1869. The State Russian Museum, St. Petersburg.

In this painting, Job and his wife sit on ashes, in relative darkness and gloom, visited by friends who are in the same shadowy space. The brighter illuminated hills in the background may indicate the better future still ahead, of which Job and company are all still oblivious.

Statue of *Job*, Dallas Anderson, 1983. The Crystal Cathedral, Garden Grove, California.

Phase 4
Use the Telescope

Over the centuries, Job has inspired novels, plays, songs, poems, and pieces of artwork far too numerous to list. The musical and movie *Fiddler on the Roof*, based on the stories of Sholem Aleichem, draws much of its inspiration from the Book of Job. The following conversation reflects the judgmental view of Job's friends:

> **Tevye:** Yes, but if Perchik did nothing wrong, he wouldn't be in trouble.
> **Hodel:** Oh Papa, how can you say that? What wrongs did Joseph do, and Abraham, and Moses? And they had troubles.

In his book *The First Dissident: The Book of Job in Today's Politics* (1992), the late William Safire, an American journalist and presidential speechwriter, gave his own unique take on this difficult story: "If the Book of Job reaches across two and a half millennia to teach anything…it is this: Human beings are sure to wander in ignorance and to fall into error, and it is better—more righteous in the eyes of God—for them to react by questioning rather than accepting. Confronted with inexplicable injustice, it is better to be irate than resigned."

Summary

The Book of Job is a remarkable work of Ancient Near Eastern literature. While the main character, Job himself, may not be an Israelite, the story reflects deeply Hebrew convictions about God and his relationship to humankind. The book gives the reader a "view from above," a glimpse of the heavenly court and the hidden reason behind what happens to Job, but God never actually gives Job an explanation.

Job refuses to curse God for what has happened to him. God, he says, is still his only hope. The book ends with soaring descriptions of the power and authority of God, with Job's humble response, and with the restoration of Job's wealth and family.

Esther

How Did a Young Woman Come to Be Remembered as a Savior of Her People?

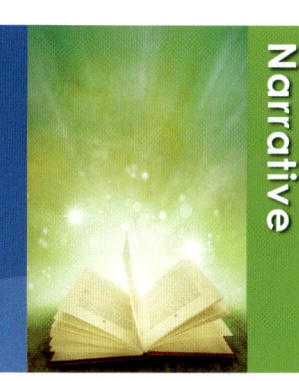

Narrative

"'The adversary and enemy,' replied Esther, 'is this evil Haman!'"
Esther 7:6 (NJPS)

Phase 1

Read the Story:
Esther 1–10

The Story in a Nutshell

In the Book of Esther, the Feast of Purim is not just any meal. It symbolizes deliverance from the threat of total annihilation. Today Jews worldwide still celebrate Purim at the end of each winter. The deliverance is also recorded earlier in the book. Queen Esther, a Jew whose race was unknown to her husband, king of Persia, risks her life to reveal the plot of Haman, the king's vizier.

Persia

The ancient Persian Empire rose to power in the 6th century BC, overpowering the Babylonians, centered in what is modern Iran. Within fewer than 100 years, it became the largest empire the world had ever seen stretching from Egypt to modern Turkey and over to India.

Cyrus the Great, Darius, and Xerxes were key Persian rulers; Xerxes (featured in the popular 2006 movie *300*) tried to push the empire into Greece in 480 BC. Persia was held together by an elaborate road system and a common administrative language (Imperial Aramaic). Alexander the Great began to conquer Persia in 334 BC.

Queen Vashti. Painting by Ann Manry Kenyon, 2012. Vashti was replaced as queen because she refused to be paraded in front of the king's friends.

Strong Women

On the last day of the long feast, King Ahasuerus (thought by many historians to be Xerxes) summons his lovely wife, Queen Vashti, who has been presiding over her own feast for the women. The king wants to show off her beauty in the dining hall, which is filled with men celebrating. Vashti refuses to come. The furious king asks his advisers what to do about Vashti's disobedience. One of them answers: Since Vashti's refusal might encourage women throughout the kingdom to disrespect their husbands, the king should banish and replace her with someone else who is "more worthy than she" Esther 1:19 (NJPS). The king and his officials like this plan. A kingdomwide beauty contest begins. After months of searching, Esther, recognized for her extraordinary beauty, becomes the new queen. Unknown to almost everyone, including Ahasuerus, Esther is Jewish.

When the Jewish people are put in danger, Esther seeks out Mordecai, her elder cousin, for advice. He suggests that she became queen "for just such a crisis" Esther 4:14 (NJPS). Mordecai tells Esther that she may be in a position to save her people from destruction.

The Mordecai-Haman Conflict

As the story continues, Mordecai, Esther's well-known Jewish cousin, refuses to bow down to Haman, a royal official promoted by Ahasuerus. Furious, Haman seeks permission from the king to kill all the Jews in the empire. Ahasuerus agrees, and when he issues his decree that all the Jews are to be slaughtered on a single day, the Jews fast and mourn.

Esther enters the king's presence uninvited, potentially a capital crime in that culture. This is a high-risk move. The king might choose to side with Haman, his hand-picked official, and he is within his rights (according to the traditions of the time) to have Esther executed. She understands the risk and is willing to sacrifice herself to save her people. Queen Esther, having won the king's favor, organizes two banquets to save her people and vanquish their nemesis, Haman. Esther not only asks the king to do what is right. She appeals to him on the basis of his finding favor for her. She has kept her Jewish identity a secret, but now she reveals it and pleads on behalf of her people. Finally, she identifies Haman as "the adversary and enemy" Esther 7:6 (NJPS). The king believes her, and Haman dies on the gallows he had prepared for Mordecai.

The Celebration

The Book of Esther records one last banquet: the first Feast of Purim, a day of grateful celebration for the Jews' deliverance through the courage of Mordecai and Queen Esther.

The book ends as Mordecai rises to a position second only to the king. This development echoes Joseph's rise in Pharaoh's administration (Genesis 41:37-45).

Vocabulary

> **Fast** [verb], to abstain from food
> **Decree** [noun], an official order

Phase 2
Travel through Time

Picture yourself walking in the fifth century BC in the city of Susa—a capital city of a great empire in Mesopotamia. A large Jewish community lives here. They also must have had a commitment to preserve the teachings of the Torah, likely involving regular gatherings that became the synagogues. By the time they return to Jerusalem a system ensues. Some scholars believe that Jews even then, as they do now, would have prayed facing Jerusalem. By outward appearances, this is a thriving and wealthy community, but just a few decades earlier, in 586 BC, they had been deported from Jerusalem. When the southern kingdom of Judah fell to Babylon, their Temple was destroyed. The Temple, built by King Solomon, was the center of Jewish religious life. Without it many of the Jews felt that God himself had abandoned them.

The Context of Esther

The biblical narrative seems to place Esther in an era in regional history replete with dominant kings. If she indeed lived in the fifth century BC, it was the time of the Achaemenid dynasty started by Darius I, and included Xerxes I and Artaxerxes I among others. The sequence of fifth-century Persian kings continued the Achaemenid dynasty started by Cyrus the Great, and included Darius I, Xerxes I, Artaxerxes I, and others.

Standard of Cyrus the Great.

Archaeological ruins of an ancient fortress in Susa (sometimes rendered Shushan), in modern-day Iran.

According to tradition, the tomb of Queen Esther is located in Hamadan, Iran. An Iranian Jewish woman is pictured here, 2008, praying at Queen Esther's tomb.

Vocabulary

> **Nemesis** [noun], a determined enemy, one's opponent and archrival

Esther 101

Illustrated Scroll of Esther Handwritten in Hebrew. Ink and pigment on parchment, Ferrara, Italy, ca. 1615. The Gross Family Collection, Tel Aviv. (Photo credit: Ardon Bar-Hama).

Vocabulary

> **Foreshadow** [verb], to signal or warn about a future or upcoming event by indicating it in advance

Hard to Be Away from Home

Another chapter in this textbook, which describes the rebuilding of Jerusalem and the Temple under Zerubbabel (in the books of Ezra and Nehemiah), explores who these enemies are back in the Jewish homeland. The story of Esther is about an enemy who plans the complete destruction of the Jews who remain in the Persian Empire.

From Orphan to Queen

According to the story, Esther is raised by her cousin, Mordecai, after the death of her parents. He becomes like a father to her, and she rises all the way to become the queen of the most powerful empire on earth.

Two Bad Bit Players

The stories of the Bible often describe bit players who are champions of the people. Esther 2:19-23, however, describes two bit players who are bad. The sinister plot of Bigthan and Teresh to kill the king never really has a chance. It is, however, the first small step in a journey that foreshadows and finally results in Mordecai rising in rank in Persia.

Depiction of Bigthan and Teresh by the French illustrator Antoine Caron (1521–1599). Munich Culture Institute, Munich, Germany.

102 Esther

Phase 3
Mine for Clues

The Book of Esther tells a story about a political struggle where the Jews in Persia may be wiped out entirely. The survival of the people depends on the high-stakes showdown between two formidable rivals, Mordecai and Haman.

If we mine the text carefully, we find the family backgrounds of Mordecai and Haman. Mordecai is said to be the son of Yair, son of Shimei, son of Kish (Esther 2:5). Two of these names are associated with the tribe of Benjamin, and specifically with King Saul. Ancient Jewish interpreters say that the Bible, in this way, is implying that Mordecai and his cousin Esther are descendants of King Saul.

Their nemesis, Haman, is described as the son of Hammedatha the "Agagite." This description resonates with the name Agag, king of the Amalekites. In the biblical narrative, the Amalekites are rejected by God on account of their wicked ways. God commands King Saul to destroy them. However, Saul fails by keeping King Agag alive (1 Samuel 15:9).

The Book of Esther thus depicts the life and death contest between Mordecai/Esther and Haman as a kind of rerun of the fateful struggle between Saul and Agag, king of the Amalekites.

Illustrated Scroll of Esther in an ornamental case, handwritten in Hebrew. Ink on parchment, in silver, with garnets and turquoise. Israel, 1900s.

The Feast of Purim

The Jewish people celebrate the annual Feast of Purim, which usually falls during the month of March. Like Hanukkah, Purim celebrates deliverance. Some of its traditions include:

- Fasting for a whole day just before Purim to identify with the fast by Queen Esther before she goes in to see the king.
- Reading aloud the Scroll of Esther on the evening and day of Purim.
- Noisemaking to drown out Haman's name whenever it comes up during the reading of the Scroll of Esther. The idea is to eradicate even the memory of this villain.
- A festive meal on Purim afternoon as a reminder of the lavish banquets.
- Sending special food baskets to friends and neighbors, based on Esther 9:22.
- Dressing up and masquerading in costumes. This is the one Jewish holiday on which rabbis permit men and women to dress in clothes of the opposite sex. This adds a sort of carnival atmosphere.
- Creating comical plays based on ironic twists, similar to the plot twists in Esther.

Esther 103

Phase 4
Use the Telescope

Dr. Albert Einstein (1879–1955). Like any race, the Jews long history includes various prominent figures. Perhaps few since the time of Esther have made an impact as important as Albert Einstein's. This German-born Jewish scientist won the Nobel Prize in Physics in 1921.

From Hebrews to Israelites to Jews

The Jewish people were originally called Hebrews by others. This designation first appears in Genesis 14:13 to describe Abraham, who is a foreigner and outsider.

After Abraham's grandson is renamed, from Jacob to Israel, the Hebrews begin to be called the children of Jacob, or the children of Israel, or more simply, the Israelites.

The word *Jew* (in Hebrew, *Yehudi*) is related to the name Judah, one of Jacob's 12 sons. In Hebrew, the name Judah literally means "God be praised." Judah is the founder of one of the 12 tribes of Israel. From this tribe comes Israel's greatest monarch, King David.

The term *Jew* appears throughout the Book of Esther as a title for Mordecai and his people (Esther 10:3, 3:6, 4:14). At some point, after returning from the Babylonian exile, the term *Jew* began to be used for all the people of Israel, no matter what tribe they may have been from. The term was applied to all of the people taken from Israel and brought to Babylon, or scattered around the ancient world. From this we eventually get the word *Judaism*, referring to the religion and culture of the descendants of Abraham, Isaac, and Jacob.

The term *Jews* is found in the books of Ezra, Nehemiah, and Daniel. In the Book of Esther, the word sets up points of tension and drama for Mordecai, Esther, and their people in their confrontation with enemies seeking their destruction.

There appears to be an intensity that characterizes many among them, and whether this is reflective of their historical journey as a people is only one possibility of what has transpired. Nonetheless, while Jews account for only 0.2 percent of the global population, they account for 22 percent of Nobel Prizes.

Dr. Jonas Salk (1914–1995) Jewish American medical researcher and virologist. In the 1950s, the crippling disease of polio was the most frightening health problem of the postwar era. Many people lived in dread of contracting this terrible illness until Salk came out with his "miracle vaccine" in 1957, which stopped the scourge of polio.

Summary

In the Book of Esther, the fate of an entire people, in the largest empire the world had ever seen, hangs in the balance. A wise man named Mordecai acts shrewdly in a time of trial and is elevated to the highest office in the land, besides the king himself. But the story memorably focuses on a young woman, Esther, and her extraordinary courage. As the story is told, her beauty gave her a position of influence, and Esther risked her life to save her people. The story is remembered every time that Purim is celebrated.

The Bible tells many stories of powerful men. Esther is one story of a powerful young woman who used her power to help her people at a critical moment.

Daniel
Stories of Fortitude
How Does One Live While in Exile?

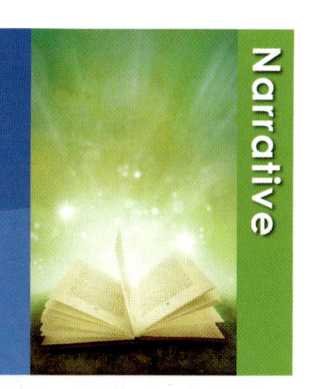

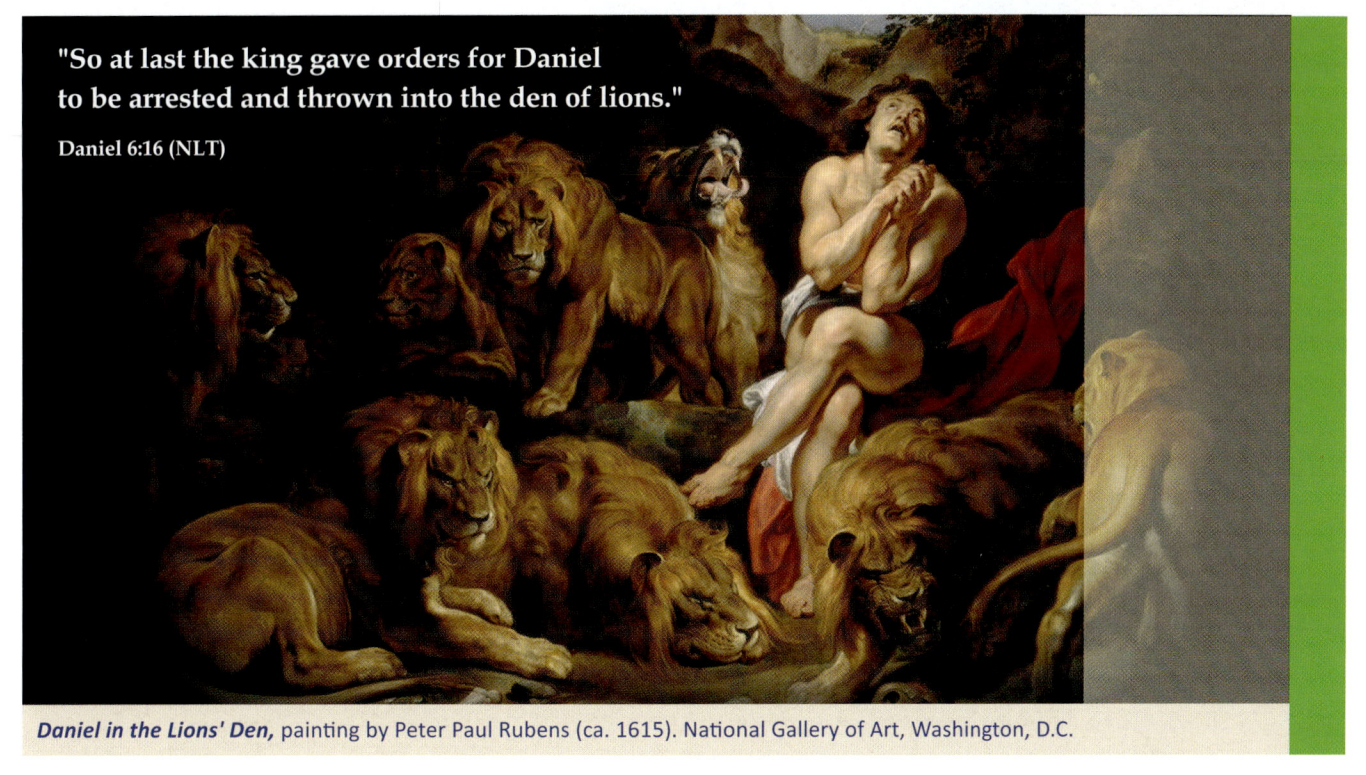

> "So at last the king gave orders for Daniel to be arrested and thrown into the den of lions."
> Daniel 6:16 (NLT)

Daniel in the Lions' Den, painting by Peter Paul Rubens (ca. 1615). National Gallery of Art, Washington, D.C.

Phase 1

Read the Story:

Daniel 1:1-7; 2–6

The Story in a Nutshell

The Book of Daniel begins with the fall of Judah to Babylon, which occurs in stages. According to the Bible, Daniel is part of the first wave of captives; they are taken to Babylon, some 500 miles away. Historians place the first wave of exile/deportation to Babylon around 600 BC, shortly before Jerusalem and the Temple are thought to have been destroyed. In the Bible's account, Daniel spends about 70 years there, enduring the whole period of Jewish captivity, and becomes a respected prophet and leader. Already as a teenager, Daniel gains the attention of Babylonian officials. How does this happen?

The victorious king, Nebuchadnezzar, orders his chief of staff to select a group of young Israelite men to train in the language and literature of the Babylonians. They are to:

- Descend from royal lineage
- Have no physical defects
- Be handsome
- Be well-educated and intelligent
- Be versed in every branch of wisdom
- Be competent to serve in the king's palace

Several Jewish youths meet these qualifications, including Daniel. They study together for three years and then are appointed to the king's court—reflective of known practices in antiquity with foreigners.

Daniel Interprets the Dream of King Nebuchadnezzar and Wins His Favor, Grant Romney Clawson.

Interpreting Dreams

The Book of Daniel says that soon after becoming king, Nebuchadnezzar has dreams that trouble him. He wants to know what they mean. So he challenges his entire court of wise men and astrologers to recount the dream and its interpretation (Daniel 2:5). They respond that the task is impossible. The king decrees that they all be executed. According to the Bible, the meaning of the king's dream is revealed to Daniel in a vision. Daniel is brought to the king and tells the king both the dream and its meaning. Astonished at Daniel's words, the king rewards him by making him ruler over all of Babylon. At Daniel's request, three of his friends also receive important positions of leadership.

Vocabulary

> **Ration** [noun]
a fixed portion of food

> **Kosher** [adjective]
permissible to eat according to Jewish law

Royal Rations

They receive a daily royal ration of Babylonian food and wine. While others might be flattered by this treatment, it represents a problem for them. The food menu conflicts with Jewish dietary laws, and partaking of it would violate their covenant with God. Daniel therefore asks the palace master to provide him and his Jewish companions a much simpler diet of water and vegetables. Afraid that he will lose his head if his charges lose weight, the palace master objects. So Daniel proposes a test. Daniel and his companions will eat their kosher diet for ten days. Then the palace master can compare them with the non-Jewish men eating all the rich royal rations. If Daniel and his friends are healthy, they can continue with their special diet; if not, they must go back to the royal rations. Reluctantly, the palace master agrees. Ten days later, Daniel and his friends pass the test. From that point forward, they are allowed to eat as they choose without interference. At the end of their educational and training period, the Bible tells us that the king finds the young men ten times better than all the magicians and enchanters in his kingdom.

Customers buy kosher food at the U.S. Open tennis tournament in New York. To be certified as kosher the food must conform to all the regulations of Jewish dietary laws known collectively as *kashruth*. The regulations include no pork, shrimp, lobster, or crabs—all prohibited in the Old Testament—plus some other more traditional restrictions added later, such as keeping meat and dairy separate.

Things Heat Up

Soon Daniel and his friends face another test. The king has an enormous golden image made, and he requires everyone to bow down and worship it. Those who refuse will be thrown into a blazing furnace. Daniel's three Jewish friends—Shadrach, Meshach, and Abednego—refuse to comply with the order, since doing so would violate one of the basic commitments of their faith. Generations before Daniel's time, according to the Bible, the Ten Commandments given to Moses included strict rules on this topic. "You must not have any other god but me. You must not make for yourself an idol of any kind, or an image of anything in the heavens or on the earth or in the sea. You must not bow down to them or worship them" Deuteronomy 5:7-9 (NLT). Shadrach, Meshach, and Abednego are not afraid of the consequences of their actions: "If we are thrown into the blazing furnace," they tell the king, "the God whom we serve is able to save us. He will rescue us from your power, Your Majesty. But even if he doesn't, we want to make it clear to you, Your Majesty, that we will never serve your gods or worship the gold statue you have set up" Daniel 3:17-18 (NLT). Furious, Nebuchadnezzar has the furnace heated seven times hotter than normal and orders his soldiers to throw the young men into the fire.

The Fiery Furnace

The king then notices four people in the fire, all walking unharmed. (He marvels that the fourth looks like a divine being.) Nebuchadnezzar calls the three men out of the furnace. According to the Bible, "The fire had not touched them. Not a hair on their heads was singed, and their clothing was not scorched. They didn't even smell of smoke!" Daniel 3:27 (NLT). Convinced of the power of their God, the king says, "There is no other god who can rescue like this!" Daniel 3:29 (NLT). Nebuchadnezzar orders that no one in the empire may speak against this God, under penalty of death.

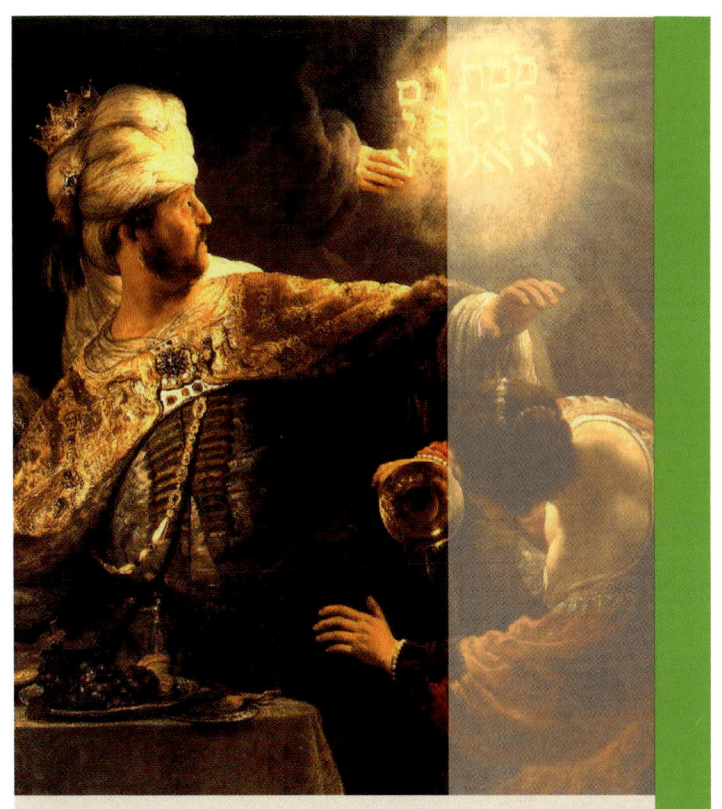

Belshazzar's Feast. Oil on canvas painting by Rembrandt ca. 1636.

The Writing on the Wall

Years later, a king named Belshazzar is sitting on the throne. As the Bible tells the story, during a royal feast, a drunken Belshazzar brings out vessels looted from the Temple in Jerusalem, items considered sacred by the Jewish people. The king lets the bawdy crowd drink from the vessels as they flaunt and praise their Babylonian deities. Suddenly, they see fingers of a human hand writing on one of the palace walls. Again, no one can interpret what is written, so Daniel, by now an old man, is summoned. He tells King Belshazzar that his haughty behavior is offensive to the God of Israel. The writing on the wall spells out a message no king wants to hear: "This is what these words mean," Daniel tells him: "*Mene* means 'numbered'—God has numbered the days of your reign and has brought it to an end. *Tekel* means 'weighed'—you have been weighed on the balances and have not measured up. *Parsin* means 'divided'—your kingdom has been divided and given to the Medes and Persians" Daniel 5:26-28 (NLT). In the biblical account, that night Belshazzar is killed, and a leader named Darius the Mede takes over.

Daniel in the Lions' Den

The next episode in the story of Daniel's life takes place under King Darius the Mede. An edict goes forth commanding all citizens to worship Darius. Daniel refuses and continues praying to the God of Israel. As punishment, he is thrown into a den of lions, even though Darius vainly tries to save him. Daniel's enemies, who had set him up for this, correctly remind the king that according to the "law of the Medes and the Persians" (6:15) his own royal decrees cannot be changed or revoked.

What kind of lion would Daniel have encountered? The Persian lion, also known today as the Asiatic lion, at one time roamed freely throughout the Ancient Near East, including present-day Israel. Today, however, these "biblical lions" are almost extinct. Only about 200 still exist in the wild, all of them confined to a small forested region of western India.

As the story goes on, Daniel survives his night with the lions unscathed. In the morning, he informs the nervous king that God had shut their mouths. After releasing Daniel, the king arrests Daniel's enemies and family members, and throws them to the lions. They are all devoured instantly. Then, according to the Bible, Darius issues a royal decree that everyone is to respect the God of Daniel.

Daniel's Answer to the King, painting by Briton Rivière, 1890. Manchester Art Gallery. Daniel was thrown into a den of hungry lions for praying to God, thus disobeying a royal decree designed by his enemies especially to ensnare him. The Bible says the Lord sent an angel to shut the mouths of the hungry cats so they could not harm him.

Daniel in the Lions' Den, a statue on the western portal of the Church of Saint Trophime in Arles, France. There has been a church on this site since the 400s. This statue and the present church date from the 1100s.

Life in Exile & Diaspora

Several collections of cuneiform texts from Mesopotamia mention Jews in exile. While the Assyrians typically deported and scattered people they conquered, the Babylonians tended to keep people groups together. The Babylonians provided them land to work, and then imposed taxes or mandatory periods of service. This raised revenue for the empire. Documents from these exiled communities include rental contracts, grain and date deliveries, tax collections, and more. Records from Babylon show rations being provided to the exiled king of Judah, Jehoiachin.

Jewish family taking their belongings into exile, from a replica of the Lachish Relief, 700–681 BC, Israel Museum, Jerusalem, Israel.

Phase 2
Travel through Time

Longing for Jerusalem

According to the biblical text, some four centuries after David establishes Jerusalem as the capital of Israel, Jerusalem falls to the Babylonians, and it falls hard. Zedekiah, the last person in history to sit on David's throne, is warned by the prophet Jeremiah not to resist the invading Babylonians. But Zedekiah listens instead to his advisers, who are counting on the support of Egypt. After Zedekiah and his forces hold out in the walled city of Jerusalem for 18 months, the city finally falls around 586 BC. Because of the king's lengthy (and ultimately futile) resistance, Zedekiah's sons are killed before his eyes, his officers are executed, and he is blinded and taken in chains to Babylon. Then the Babylonian commander destroys the Temple, the royal palace, and the homes of all the prominent citizens. The Temple furnishings and treasures are carried back to Babylon.

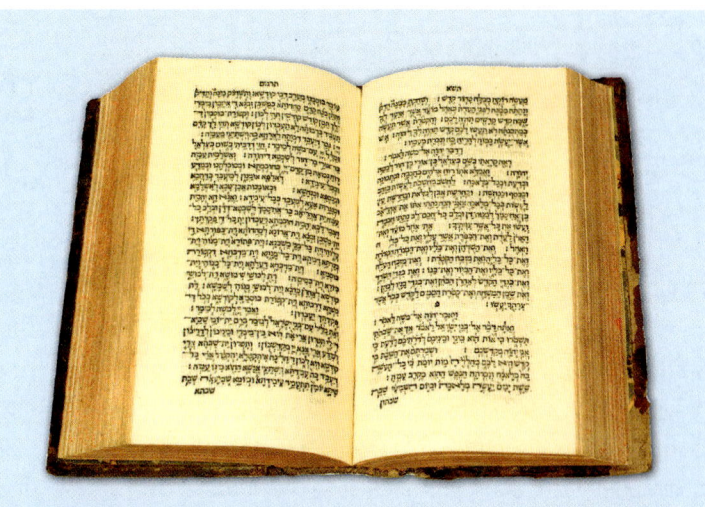

Daniel Bomberg Bible containing Pentateuch with Aramaic translation.

Aramaic

About half of Daniel (2:4–7:28) is written in Aramaic rather than Hebrew, the main language of the Old Testament (the two languages are closely related). Aramaic originally was spoken by the Arameans, who resided in northwestern Mesopotamia. Over time, Aramaic spread and became the second-most-used language of the Assyrian and Babylonian empires, and the administrative language of the Persian Empire.

Daniel and the Three Kings

Traveling back through time, we meet the Jewish people in a foreign land. Their deep sorrow and burning passion to return home to Jerusalem influences their faith and culture for generations to come.

One striking part of the story of Daniel and his fellow exiles is their ability to attain influential positions in foreign kingdoms. The Book of Daniel emphasizes the power of God in the diaspora, outside of Canaan, particularly with three powerful rulers:

Daniel 4 ends with King Nebuchadnezzar lifting his eyes to the heavens and proclaiming Daniel's God to be supreme.

Daniel 5 relates the story of another ruler, King Belshazzar. Yet even when Daniel gives this king the terrible news that "God has numbered the days of your reign and has brought it to an end" (Daniel 5:25, NLT), the king does not harm him.

Daniel 6 Though he was forced to cast Daniel into a den of lions, King Darius was overjoyed to find Daniel alive the next day, ordered him released, and decreed that "in every part of my kingdom people must fear and reverence the God of Daniel" (6:26, NIV).

Phase 3
Mine for Clues

What's in a Name?

The Book of Daniel has some of the most memorable names in the Bible: Shadrach, Meshach, Abednego, and Nebuchadnezzar. You probably wouldn't give your baby one of those names today. But neither did the mothers of the first three. Daniel and his friends were assigned new Babylonian names by the chief of the Babylonian officers: "Daniel was called Belteshazzar. Hananiah was called Shadrach. Mishael was called Meshach. Azariah was called Abednego" Daniel 1:7 (NLT). Their Jewish names carried a reference to the God of Israel. Names ending in "el" stand for Elohim (God) and names ending in "yah" are a testimony to Yahweh (YHWH).

The big challenge facing Daniel and his fellow Jewish exiles in the great Babylonian Empire is that of retaining their faith and identity. A primary component of your identity is your name. With changes in one's life or circumstances often came a change in name. As foreigners assimilating in Babylon, they receive Babylonian names.

The name Daniel remains popular for boys and also girls (in the form of Danielle). This Hebrew name means "God is my judge." Though some vestiges of Hebrew remained, most abandoned it for Aramaic. Although biblical Hebrew was well preserved in ancient texts, most remarkably the Dead Sea Scrolls, it wasn't until the 1930s and the establishment of Israel in 1948 that it began to be reintroduced as a common language.

Phase 4
Use the Telescope

Apocalyptic Literature

Much of the Hebrew Bible tells the stories of the ancient Israelites. An important thread in those stories is the covenants made between God and the patriarchs, prophets, and kings. Some elements of those covenants pertain to past or present times, others to the future. Full of dreams and visions, the Book of Daniel challenges the Jewish people to look forward. It is a major biblical example of what scholars call apocalyptic (or revelatory) literature.

Apocalyptic literature deals with hidden knowledge and, within the context of the Bible, often relates to the future. Today people tend to associate the word *apocalyptic* with ideas—often frightening ideas—about the end of the world. However, Daniel's "apocalypse" provides a sense of hope, a revelation of better things to come.

Some apocalyptic literature envisions a time when the power of evil will be broken, and the purposes of God for humanity and the cosmos are worked out.

Vocabulary

> **Assimilate** [verb]
to absorb one culture into another, so the original is hardly recognizable and no longer unique

Summary

While exiled to a foreign land, Daniel and his companions are portrayed as steadfastly choosing to live according to their faith in God, even in the face of almost certain death. The Bible claims that the young Jews are saved from a fiery furnace. It portrays Daniel at a later stage walking out of a den of hungry lions without a scratch. These examples encouraged the diaspora Jewish communities to have faith in the present and hope for the future.

Coming Home from Babylon

How Do You Rebuild in the Face of Opposition?

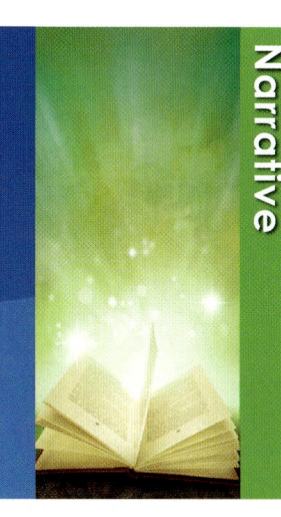

"Come, let us rebuild the wall of Jerusalem and suffer no more disgrace."
Nehemiah 2:17 (NJPS)

Phase 1

Read the Story:
Haggai 1–2; Ezra 1, 3; Nehemiah 2–4, 8

The Story in a Nutshell

After spending about 70 years in Babylonian exile, the Bible says, the Israelites are finally allowed to return to their homeland. They are eager to rebuild Jerusalem, and especially the Temple, which the Babylonians destroyed decades earlier. They begin the reconstruction effort but face opposition from people who have settled in the area while the Jews had been in exile. Eventually the rebuilding project grinds to a complete halt. The prophet Haggai tells the Jews that God is calling on the people to complete the Temple. Zerubbabel, a local governor, leads the renewal project until the Temple is finished. The city's walls, however, remain in ruins.

Decades later, two Hebrew men named Ezra (a scribe and priest) and Nehemiah (a high official in the Persian court) return to Jerusalem from exile. Nehemiah leads the people in rebuilding the walls of Jerusalem in just 52 days (Nehemiah 6:15). Ezra reads the "Book of the Law of Moses" to the people, who recommit themselves to the God of Israel.

Vocabulary

> **Exile** [noun], the state of being banished from one's own country, often for political reasons

The walls that today surround the Old City of Jerusalem were built in the early 1500s by the Ottoman ruler Suleiman the Magnificent. Over the past 4,000 years, Jerusalem has been destroyed and rebuilt more than 20 times. Some of the stones in the current wall date to previous destructions of the city from more than 2,000 years ago.

Coming Back from Babylon

Despite their struggles, the Jews have many reasons to be grateful. Compared to the 400 years of the Hebrews living in Egypt, as told in the Book of Exodus, the Babylonian captivity is relatively brief; they begin to return home after about 50 to 60 years (often associated with the prophecy in Jeremiah of 70 years). The Persians, who by this point have taken over Babylon, help the Jews to settle back in their homeland. The Bible indicates that the Jews returning from exile, in contrast to earlier generations, do not take up the worship of other gods. Many of them reclaim the land they had once occupied. This process will take time and the efforts of various leaders over a few generations. The main leaders include:

- **Zerubbabel**, who leads the first group of returning Jews back from Babylon to rebuild the Temple
- **Ezra**, who teaches the Book of the Law of Moses
- **Nehemiah**, who rebuilds the city walls of Jerusalem

The Arch of Titus in Rome was built shortly after the Romans destroyed Jerusalem in AD 70. They built the arch to commemorate their victory over the city. This relief from the arch shows Roman soldiers, wearing victory wreaths, carting off treasures from the Second Temple, including the Golden Lampstand, the Table of Showbread, and silver trumpets.

Lost Along the Way

The fate of the Ark of the Covenant is unclear. It may have been stolen or lost when the First Temple was destroyed in ca. 586 BC. It was likely not present in the Second Temple.

Evidence suggests a Golden Lampstand (menorah) was among the objects in the Second Temple. The Arch of Titus, a famous architectural landmark, clearly portrays the Temple's Golden Menorah being hauled off to Rome after the Second Temple was razed by Titus and the Roman army in AD 70. Also pictured on the arch are Jewish captives, who would serve as slaves in the Roman Empire.

Phase 2
Travel through Time

According to most scholars, the return from Babylonian exile comes chronologically at the end of the Old Testament narrative. What else do we know about the Jews during this period? The evidence suggests that:
- Babylon has been overthrown by the Persians.
- Many Jews return from Babylonian exile.
- The Temple in Jerusalem is rebuilt.
- The Jews face no immediate enemies.

Among the significant changes that emerge from this period are the following: the Jews no longer live in one central place, and they develop new forms of religious worship.

No Longer Together in One Place

Prior to the Babylonian captivity, according to the Bible, the Israelites generally lived together as a single group, first in Egypt and later in Canaan. After Babylon destroys Jerusalem, it is mostly the leaders and the upper class who go into exile around 586 BC. The rest of the people stay behind in Canaan. "But some of the poorest in the land were left by the chief of the guards, to be vinedressers and field hands" 2 Kings 25:12 (NJPS).

Now, about 50 years later, King Cyrus of Persia conquers the Babylonians and then grants the Jews permission to return home. However, that's easier said than done. During their time in Babylon, the Jews have settled down, built homes, established livelihoods, and raised families. Most of the current generation was born in Babylon, not Canaan. So despite receiving permission to return, most of the Jews choose to remain in Babylon. Even those who do return do so gradually, over a period of years and not all at once.

Another factor is the changing population of Canaan. The Jews who had remained in Canaan throughout the period of exile now live alongside various groups of non-Jews. Some of the inhabitants do not want to see the Temple and other structures rebuilt. In fact, the Bible says, the threat against those involved in rebuilding became so great that Nehemiah requires his workers to do their work with one hand while holding a weapon in the other (Nehemiah 4:15-18).

For the first time in their history, the Jewish people are scattered and living in different areas, with permanent settlements both inside and outside the original areas of settlement in Canaan. (Being dispersed instead of in one place is called the diaspora.) From this point on, their identity is no longer defined by being gathered in one, or even two, locations.

Vocabulary

> **Diaspora** [noun]
a scattered population originating from one place

Time Travel | The Return from Babylon | Near East, 500–400 BC

- Jewish communities in exile
- Nehemiah's route from Shushan
- Ezra and Nehemiah return to Jerusalem from Babylon (ca. 460–425 BC)
- Earlier route of returns from exile (ca. 540–515 BC)

Coming Home from Babylon

Synagogue

The practice of meeting for study and worship (which began in Babylon) eventually led to the creation of the synagogue. Josephus, the first-century Jewish historian, mentions synagogues in the cities of Dora, Caesarea, Nazareth, and Capernaum. The Babylonian Talmud, written several centuries later, says that there were 394 synagogues in Jerusalem alone in AD 70, the year the city was destroyed by the Romans. Today many synagogues are also used as schools and community centers.

Baram, in the Galilee region, was established as a small Jewish village in ca. 500 BC. After the destruction of Jerusalem in AD 70, the population grew, and the town became a center for Jewish learning. The townspeople built two synagogues. The gates of the larger one, dating from about AD 250, are seen here, facing south toward Jerusalem.

New Centers for Worship and Study

Before the Babylonian Exile, the Israelites had places to worship God and perform required sacrifices. These included the Tabernacle, the Temple, and lesser-known temporary structures. But they faced new questions after returning from exile and finding the Temple in ruins. Where should they perform sacrifices? How should they worship God? Does the covenant still hold?

According to the Bible, the prophet Ezekiel predicts the destruction of Jerusalem and the Temple (Ezekiel 24; 33). But he assures his fellow Jews that God's covenant of love is unbreakable (Ezekiel 16:59-60; 36). Ezekiel shares his visions of them eventually returning to the Promised Land and rebuilding the Temple (Ezekiel 40–48).

After Solomon built the Temple in Jerusalem, the Israelites increasingly offered sacrifices only there. When absent from the Temple, they orient themselves physically toward Jerusalem during prayer. The prayers they compose in exile will eventually be brought back to Israel. Later, especially after the Second Temple is destroyed in the first century AD, important schools of biblical study will spring up among the Jews in Babylon.

While Jerusalem remains the indispensable spiritual center, for practical reasons the worship of God and the study of scripture now take place wherever the Jewish people find themselves.

Jewish students studying the Talmud at a Beit Midrash (study center or, literally, a "house of learning").

Phase 3
Mine for Clues

According to the book that bears his name, Nehemiah was the "cupbearer" for King Artaxerxes. This may sound like a waiter at a restaurant, but in the courts of the Ancient Near East it was a title of great respect. The cupbearer served the royal family at table. When the rulers feared palace intrigues and plots against their lives, however, the cupbearer made certain that their drinks were unpoisoned, even sampling the wine before serving it. If the wine was poisoned, the cupbearer's death would serve to warn the king.

Only the most respected, principled, and trustworthy individuals were given the task. Cupbearers risked their lives for those they served, and they were well rewarded for their services. Nehemiah was apparently wealthy, and the king cared enough for him to grant him his wish. He is one of many figures in the stories of the Hebrew Bible who attained an exalted title in foreign courts. In the Bible authors' view, God often works by raising up individuals of extraordinary character and talent into positions of authority among the empires. The first such story is that of Joseph in the courts of Egypt, but later stories include Daniel and his friends in Babylon, Esther and Mordecai, Ezra, and Nehemiah. To the ancient Jews, whether living in Israel or scattered across far-flung empires, these stories conveyed that God was still engaged in their history, still working to fulfill their covenant.

From Abraham to the Second Temple

As we approach the end of the Old Testament, let's review the biblical account of the journeys and dwelling places of successive generations of Israelites.

- At 75, Abraham sets out from Haran with God's promise to make his descendants a great nation.
- Abraham and Sarah arrive in Canaan. In old age, they produce a son, Isaac.
- Isaac's son, Jacob, has 12 boys. One of them, Joseph, provides for the family in Egypt when famine strikes.
- The Israelites (descendants of Jacob, also called Israel) escape from Egyptian slavery during the Exodus.
- Led by Moses, and then Joshua, the Israelites return to Canaan and conquer their enemies.
- During the period of the judges, leaders ("judges") rescue the Israelites from their enemies.
- Under King David and King Solomon, Israel becomes a great nation, establishes Jerusalem as its capital, and builds the First Temple.
- The northern kingdom (Israel) falls to Assyria in 722 BC. Prophets blame the people for breaking the covenant and worshiping other gods. The people of Israel are scattered throughout the vast Assyrian empire.
- Similarly, the southern kingdom (Judah, and its capital, Jerusalem) falls to the Babylonians around 586 BC; again idolatry is the named cause. The people are taken captive and exiled to Babylon. While in exile the Jewish communities stay closer together, which helps them retain a strong Jewish identity.
- The Persians, under King Cyrus, defeat Judah's Babylonian captors in 538 BC.
- Soon Cyrus allows the Judeans to start return to their homeland. They begin to build the Second Temple.

Coming Home from Babylon

Nehemiah: Man of Prayer

The Book of Nehemiah portrays prayer not only as a way to praise God and confess one's failings, but also to learn about and carry out God's wishes. The Book of Nehemiah has nine prayers in only 13 chapters, including the longest prayer in the Bible (9:5-38). The prayer rehearses interactions between the Israelites, their enemies, and God, and ends with a commitment to renew the covenant. The first prayer in the book begins with thanks for God's unbreakable bond of love: "O LORD, God of Heaven, great and awesome God, who stays faithful to His covenant with those who love Him and keep His commandments! Let Your ear be attentive and Your eyes open to receive the prayer of Your servant that I am praying to You now" Nehemiah 1:5-6 (NJPS).

King Cyrus

Isaiah 44:28 and 45:1, 13 portray King Cyrus of Persia as an instrument and messiah directed by God. Cyrus conquers the Babylonians and allows the Jews to go home and rebuild their Temple. Cyrus, who founded an empire that lasted for two centuries, becomes a friendly deliverer for the Jewish people in exile. Unlike other conquerors, Cyrus does not relocate conquered peoples.

The Mausoleum (tomb) of Cyrus the Great of Persia (ca. 600–530 BC) located near the city of Shiraz, in modern-day Iran.

Ezra

In the biblical account, the Persians appoint Ezra, a contemporary of the prophet Haggai, to take responsibility for the Jews' religious affairs. Back in Jerusalem, he reads the Book of the Law of Moses and receives a promise from the leaders of Judah to uphold it.

Nehemiah

Later, Nehemiah arrives to lead the rebuilding of Jerusalem's walls. But his greatest achievement is creating an administrative structure for Judah and Jerusalem.

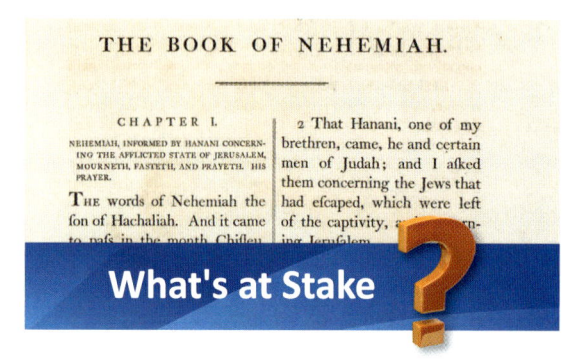

What's at Stake

Following the many ups and downs the Israelites have experienced over the generations, the Book of Nehemiah portrays them at the dawn of a new era. But as they begin to rebuild Jerusalem, their homes, and their lives, Nehemiah reminds the people of the need to remain obedient to God: "Be mindful of the promise You gave to Your servant Moses: 'If you are unfaithful, I will scatter you among the peoples; but if you turn back to Me, faithfully keep My commandments, even if your dispersed are at the ends of the earth, I will gather them from there and bring them to the place where I have chosen to establish My name'" Nehemiah 1:8-9 (NJPS).

Vocabulary

> **Administrative** [adjective]
relating to the process of managing or organizing

> **Contemporary** [noun]
someone living about the same time as someone else

Coming Home from Babylon

Phase 4
Use the Telescope

Biblical Departures and Returns

In the overarching story of the Hebrew Bible and the Christian New Testament, the Israelites (called Jews toward the end of the Old Testament period) make two eventful journeys from the area known at different times as Canaan or Israel. The Hebrew Bible records two returns, and many consider the modern immigration of Jews after the Holocaust a third return. In the first journey, around 70 people—Jacob, 11 of his 12 sons, and their families—move from Canaan to Egypt during a time of severe famine. One of Jacob's sons, Joseph, has become a political leader in Egypt. After Joseph's death, new pharaohs are fearful of the growing number of Israelites. The Israelites are enslaved until, centuries later, the prophet Moses leads them out of Egyptian bondage and towards Canaan. By then, the Bible says, the little band of 70 Israelites has become a large people. Joshua leads them into Canaan after Moses dies.

The second journey is a forced evacuation by a foreign power. This takes place in the sixth century BC when the Babylonians destroy Jerusalem and the First Temple. Not everyone is exiled to Babylon, and many eventually stay in Babylon instead of returning. Those who do return meet stiff opposition as they slowly rebuild the Temple and the city of Jerusalem.

The Second Temple stands for about 600 years until it too is destroyed in AD 70 by the Romans. This event leads to a broad dispersion of Jews into many regions and countries. Throughout the following centuries, Jews often become integrated into local societies while also maintaining a distinct identity, religion, and culture. In some places they flourish. In many others they suffer intense persecution. Throughout that long period, the role of history and tradition—including ancestral stories from the Bible—remains strong.

Biblical Departures and Returns

Israel in Egypt, Edward Poynter, 1867. Guildhall Art Gallery, London. In response to a famine, some Israelites follow Abraham's great-grandson Joseph, son of Jacob, into Egypt. By biblical accounts it would be placed ca. 1700 BC.

The Flight of the Prisoners, James Tissot, 1902. Jewish Museum, New York City. Jewish residents who survived the destruction of their holy city and Temple are taken as prisoners from Jerusalem to Babylon.

The Destruction of the Temple of Jerusalem, Francesco Hayez, 1867. Gallerie dell'Accademia, Venice. The Second Temple in Jerusalem was destroyed in AD 70 by the Romans. This event led to a long period of exile for the Jews, as they eventually became scattered and settled in many different places.

Returns in the Hebrew Bible

The Book of Joshua describes the Hebrews crossing over the Jordan River and taking possession of Canaan.

In ca. 539 BC, the Jewish people began returning to Jerusalem from Babylon. One of their first tasks at the end of this second exile was to rebuild the walls of Jerusalem.

Modern Jewish Immigration

Jewish survivors of the Holocaust arrive in Israel by ship.
A number of Jews and Christians believe the dispersion that began ca. AD 70, the longest and most far reaching in Jewish history, ended with the establishment of the modern State of Israel, in 1948. They tend to view today's Israel as a fulfillment of biblical prophecies. Others disagree, rejecting any comparison between the modern State of Israel and biblical descriptions of exile and return.

Vocabulary

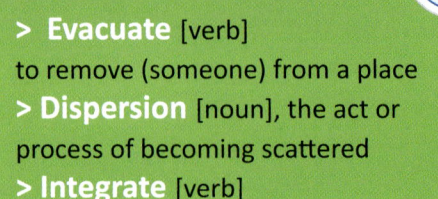

> **Evacuate** [verb]
to remove (someone) from a place
> **Dispersion** [noun], the act or process of becoming scattered
> **Integrate** [verb]
to become a part of the whole

Summary

As the Hebrew Bible's narrative comes to a close, the Jews return from Babylonian captivity to the land they had left earlier. They turn their attention to rebuilding the Temple and the city of Jerusalem but face opposition. The Judeans (who become known as Jews during this period) develop new forms of worship and study; in the absence of the Tabernacle or Temple, the synagogue emerges as a place of learning and prayer. The return from Babylon is but one of many journeys to and from the biblical homeland undertaken by the people of Israel over the centuries. The repeated migrations have strengthened an appreciation for memory and tradition.

Model of the Second Temple (as expanded by King Herod in Roman times), displayed in the Israel Museum, Jerusalem.

Coming Home from Babylon

Rediscovered People

What Do 200 Years of Discoveries Teach Us About the Bible and History?

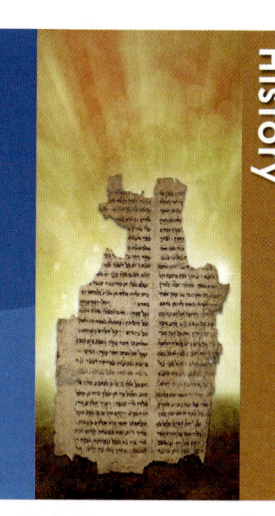

"For they draw from the abundance of the seas and the hidden treasures of the sand."

Deuteronomy 33:19 (ESV)

When a Civilization Disappears

History holds many mysteries. Historians, archaeologists, and others who study earlier times and places follow traces of evidence and look for clues about what may have happened in the past. Sometimes those clues lead to incredible breakthroughs—like the 1922 discovery of King Tutankhamun's tomb by Howard Carter. Other times painstaking research leads only to a dead end.

One of the major mysteries of history is the disappearance of the Maya, a once-flourishing civilization in the region we now call Central America. Around AD 900, this advanced civilization crumbled and largely disappeared. Scholars have offered theories to explain the rapid collapse: perhaps it was a brutal civil war, or a famine, or a natural disaster. Or maybe environmental changes led to mass starvation.

It was a vast empire at its peak. Powerful city-states engaged with the Maya in long-distance trade. Yet somehow the empire collapsed. Though millions of Maya have a link to this past stronghold, their historic landmarks remain in ruins.

Archaeologists at work, looking for clues that may shed light on the past.

The Bible and History

The Maya are just one of many groups of people about whom there are still unanswered questions. In some cases, historians have an abundance of evidence but disagree about what the evidence means. In other cases, there isn't much evidence to begin with. What about the Bible? Is there historical evidence for individuals or groups mentioned in the Old and New Testaments?

In this chapter, we will look for individual characters and whole groups that seem to have disappeared into thin air, for still-unknown reasons—if they did indeed exist as historical entities. The time periods we will examine stand even further in the past than the era of the vanishing Maya.

Why Is This Important

The Bible is a sprawling and complex book. It contains different genres of literature written at different times. Studying it thoroughly requires many different angles and approaches. Manuscript experts pore over ancient writings, studying variations among versions and translations. Art historians examine artifacts that have survived many centuries, sometimes intact. Archaeologists look for clues to the past in the remains hidden below ground. These and other specialists examine the relationship between the Bible we have today and the historical settings in which it was written.

Why Is This Interesting

Scholars sometimes find what could be a match between a name mentioned in the Bible and a similar name found in historical records—which could be pottery, a scrap of papyrus, a coin, a piece of a building, or many other objects. Of the approximately 3,200 individuals mentioned in the Bible, some important and others less so, so far there is historical evidence for about 60 to 80 of those names.

Digging through the accumulated rubble of hundreds, or even thousands, of years is painstaking and tedious. Biblical archaeology as a field of scholarly activity is still a fairly young science; it is only about 200 years old. Archaeologists have only scratched the surface of a vast treasure trove of information waiting to be unearthed. Even when ancient fragments are uncovered, it can still take decades before all the material is properly gathered, cleaned, organized, reassembled, translated, numbered, filed, researched, reviewed, and published. Yet, time and again, the extraordinary patience of scholars has yielded huge rewards.

Missing People of the Bible

Like other scientific pursuits, archaeology proceeds slowly and cautiously. Hypotheses are formed that are then carefully tested against the evidence. The supply of evidence is continually expanding as researchers discover new remains. Sometimes newly discovered evidence supports a hypothesis, while other times the hypothesis is refuted and has to be replaced by a new theory.

Through such meticulous efforts, archaeologists have unearthed long-buried cities and buildings and have shed important light on the past. As explained in an earlier chapter, for instance, the ancient city of Troy (famous for being the setting of the Trojan War in Greek literature) was long thought to be merely mythical until it was perhaps identified with Hisarlik, uncovered in the 19th century in modern-day Turkey. Similarly, the ancient Egyptian city of Amarna was an important political and economic capital in the second millennium BC. Yet its historical existence was only confirmed in modern times through careful archaeological research.

The Mystery of the Horites

Genesis and Deuteronomy refer to a people called the Horites (Genesis 14:6 and 36:20), but there is no independent evidence that such a people ever existed. For a while, scholars debated whether the Horites were the same as a Mesopotamian people called the Hurrians. Today, however, scholars think that the Horites were an early group of people living in what later became Edom, the land associated with Esau in Genesis. The name Horite may refer to a Hebrew word meaning "cave" or "noble, free" used by the Horites to describe themselves as either cave-dwellers or a free people group.

Vocabulary

> **Meticulous** [adjective]
showing extreme care for details

Remains of the Old Citadel in Kirkuk, Iraq, built in about 860 BC. Kirkuk is located about 150 miles north of Baghdad.

A clay tablet and envelope, dating from the late 1400s BC, discovered in Nuzi, Iraq. Courtesy of the Oriental Institute of the University of Chicago.

Rediscovered People

Remains of the large ancient city of Hattusha, once the Hittite capital, located in central Turkey.

The Lion Gate, part of the ruins from the ancient Hittite city of Hattusha.

A depiction of the ancient Hittite storm god, Teshub, located in southeastern Turkey, near the remains of an ancient Hittite fortress called Karatepe.

Vocabulary

> **Prominent** [adjective]
important and well known

Here Come the Hittites

Biblical archaeology is today an active if controversial field, and many dramatic discoveries have been made in recent years. Consider the people described repeatedly in the Old Testament as the Hittites.

The Hittites figure prominently early in the Bible. They are said to be "the sons of Heth" (Noah's great-grandson, Genesis 10). They once owned the burial place of Sarah, Abraham's wife (Genesis 23:19-20). Esau, Jacob's brother, married Hittite women (Genesis 26:34-35). The Hittites are listed among the groups that Joshua conquered when the Israelites crossed the Jordan River and entered Canaan (Joshua 3:10). Probably the most famous reference is "Uriah the Hittite," whose death King David arranged after he fell in love with Uriah's wife Bathsheba (2 Samuel 11:3).

For many centuries, there was no historical evidence that the Hittites mentioned in the Bible ever existed as a real people. Was it possible that all evidence of the Hittites had vanished? Or was it a case of fabrication by the biblical authors, or at least an exaggeration of the size and influence of their civilization?

However, in the late 1800s, as the field of biblical archaeology started to emerge in earnest, several discoveries were made that may help us understand who the Hittites were. Archaeologists uncovered cuneiform tablets (the Amarna letters) that refer to a people from Anatolia (roughly where modern Turkey is today) called the Hatti. A pioneering British linguist and Assyriologist named Archibald Sayce argued that the "people of Hatti" mentioned in the cuneiform tablets are the same as the biblical people we call the Hittites. Then, early in the 20th century, excavations revealed the Hatti Empire centered in Hattusa in modern-day Turkey.

Today scholars line up on both sides of the debate. Some think the Hatti and the biblical Hittites are the same; others argue that they're not connected. It's also possible that both are correct: biblical references to the Hittites may refer to several related groups of people, including the Hatti.

In this case, a missing civilization came to light that scholars today call the Hittites. How precisely these Hittites match up with the biblical Hittites is still disputed, but what is not disputed is that a once-lost civilization has been uncovered that has shaped the way we understand the biblical stories and their context.

Rediscovered Individuals

We have seen how people and places known from antiquity can eventually resurface. What about specific people mentioned in the Bible? Let's look at a few examples.

Sargon II of Assyria

Sargon II is mentioned in Isaiah 20:1. Until the 1800s, historians had not confirmed the existence of this Assyrian king. Scholars of the time failed to find his palace where they expected it, in the great Assyrian capital of Nineveh—the setting for the biblical story of Jonah and the focus of the Book of Nahum. Some scholars found the absence of evidence for this Assyrian king problematic. Circumstances changed in 1843, when Paul-Émile Botta discovered Sargon II's capital city, Khorsabad, 12 miles northeast of Nineveh. Botta also discovered the remains of the king's huge palace.

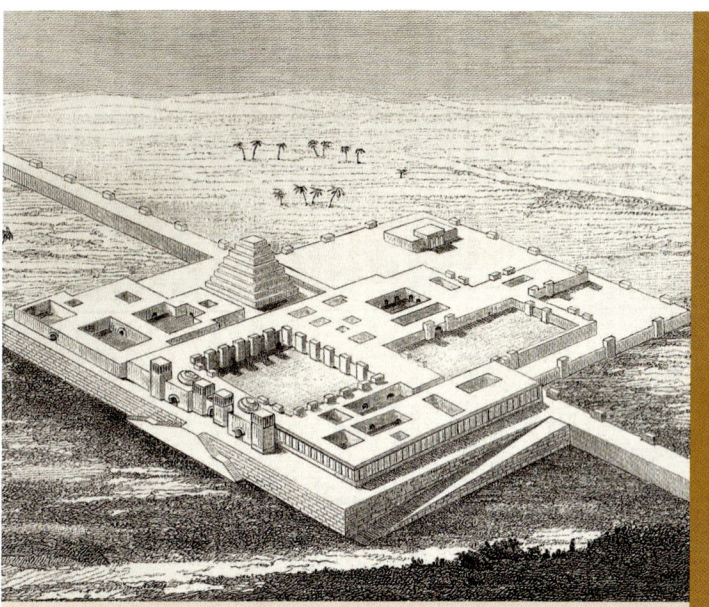

Palace of Sargon II, as recreated in a sketch by Sellier and Meunier, published in Paris, 1882.

Paul-Emile Botta (1802–1870), portrait by Charles de Champmartin, 1840. Louvre Museum, Paris. Botta was the controversial French diplomat and archaeologist who in 1843 discovered the ancient Assyrian city Dur-Sharrukin (modern Khorsabad), about ten miles from Mosul in present-day Iraq.

Vocabulary

> **Problematic** [adjective]
not definite or settled; posing a problem

Sargon II, stone reliefs from the Palace of Sargon II. Louvre Museum, Paris.

Rediscovered People

The Cyrus Cylinder, ca. 539–530 BC. British Museum, London. Discovered in 1879 in the ruins of ancient Babylon, in modern Iraq.

The Nabonidus Chronicle, describing events in ancient Babylon from ca. 556 to 539 BC. British Museum, London. It tells of the fall of King Nabonidus and the events leading up to the final days before Cyrus of Persia takes over. References on other various cylinders are made to Belshazzar, the son of Nabonidus, who is also mentioned in the Bible as King Belshazzar.

Lion hunt, from an ancient Assyrian relief, ca. 645-35 BC. British Museum, London.

King Belshazzar

King Belshazzar is one of the most unforgettable characters in the Book of Daniel. The story of "Belshazzar's Feast" in Daniel 5 is the source of the modern phrase "the writing on the wall."

The Greek historian Herodotus does not mention this ruler. Nor do other ancient texts that might be expected to mention him. Until the early 1900s, in fact, the accepted list of Babylonian kings omitted his name:

- Nabopolassar   626 – 605 BC
- Nebuchadnezzar II   604 – 562 BC
- Amel-Marduk   562 – 560 BC
- Neriglissar   560 – 556 BC
- Labaši-Marduk   556 BC
- Nabonidus   556 – 539 BC

Even the highly important Cyrus Cylinder, excavated in 1879, which provides clear evidence of Cyrus of Persia's seizure of the throne from Nabonidus in 539 BC, contains no mention of Belshazzar.

As it turns out, though, the absence of Belshazzar from the historical lists seems appropriate now, given what we have learned about Babylonian history.

Around 1930, cuneiform texts from the time of King Nabonidus were published after their discovery in modern Iraq. These ancient texts explain that King Nabonidus left Babylon and lived for about ten years in Arabia—and that he left Belshazzar, his eldest son, in Babylon to rule in his place. Though Nabonidus was legally the king, in practice Belshazzar was co-ruler with his father. Both locals and foreigners probably treated Belshazzar as the crown prince.

Vocabulary

> **Relief** [noun], a mode of sculpture in which forms are distinguished from the surrounding surface

Rediscovered People

And the List Goes On

A few other biblical figures are worth mentioning. Each has gained increased historical clarity in recent years.

Information about the Jewish king Jehoiachin (2 Kings 24:8-17) emerged during excavations near the Ishtar Gate in Babylon in the early 1900s. Jehoiachin's name was found on food ration tablets, written in the Akkadian language in the cuneiform script. His five sons are also mentioned in these tablets from King Nebuchadnezzar's archives.

For another example, the Old Testament refers to a man named Sanballat, said to be a contemporary of the prophet Nehemiah (Nehemiah 2:19). That name is mentioned in papyrus documents found in the 1800s on an island in the Nile river in southern Egypt. The dating of the documents suggests that the two men could have lived around the same time.

Uncovered texts from the ancient world also mention Hanani (Nehemiah's brother, Nehemiah 7:2) and Nehemiah's high priest, Johanan (Nehemiah 12:22). And there is historical support for the existence of the biblical kings Menachem, Ahab, and Hezekiah, and for a prophet named Balaam.

Jehoiachin ration cuneiform tablet. Pergamon Museum, Berlin. The tablet was made ca. 595–570 BC and was discovered in the year 1900 in an area that is today part of Iraq.

Elephantine Island, in the Upper Nile near Aswan, in southern Egypt.

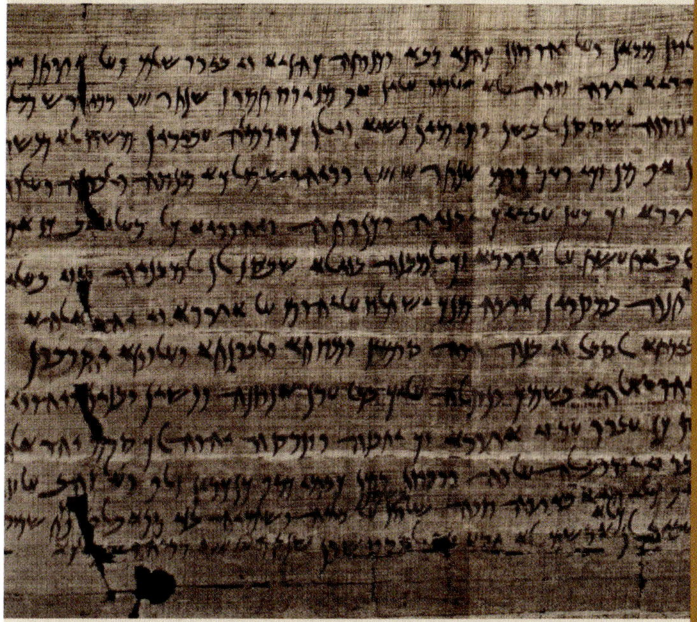

A terracotta statue (1575–1578) of the prophet Balaam by the Italian sculptor Tommaso Porlezza della Porta. Rijksmuseum, Amsterdam.

A letter, written on papyrus, from the Jewish community in Elephantine in Egypt. It is written by Yedoniah and his colleagues, to Bagoas, Persian governor of Judah. The letter requests help for rebuilding a Jewish temple to YHWH at Elephantine, which had been damaged. It is dated to ca. 407 BC. Egyptian Museum, Berlin.

The city of Jericho is located on the western side of the Jordan River Valley. In the background rise the steep foothills of the Judean wilderness.

Vocabulary

> **Diligent** [adjective]
characterized by steady and earnest effort

Still Missing

Despite the diligent efforts of historians, archaeologists, and other scholars who help us better understand the Bible, many questions about the past remain unanswered. In fact, some questions may never be answered.

Many of the stories told in the Bible lack any confirming evidence outside of the biblical narrative. Historians know very little about Joshua's conquest of Canaan, for example. Scholars have proposed locations for the cities mentioned in Joshua 7:2 (such as Ai and Bethel), but there is no consensus. All concede that Beth Aven is completely unknown. Further, we possess no record outside the Bible that Joshua himself ever existed. For that matter, direct reference from outside the Bible is lacking for all of the patriarchs (Abraham, Isaac, Jacob), and the same is true for Joseph, Moses, and many others. Most people from the ancient world, unless they constructed monuments to themselves or commissioned court histories, leave little trace.

Darius the Mede, in the Book of Daniel, is another biblical figure who remains absent from the records of history. Bible scholars have proposed various theories about his identity but none is convincing. There is a wide spectrum of beliefs among scholars regarding the historical accuracy of Daniel (or any other biblical book). Archaeologists have yet to excavate and examine fully a large amount of historically significant sites. Whatever they find will continue to shape and refine our understanding of the people of the past.

Summary

Over the past 200 years, archaeology has made many valuable contributions to the study of the Bible. Some findings seem to lend support to the historical existence of individuals or entire cultures, while other research seems to point in the opposite direction. Scholars disagree about the meaning of the evidence available so far. As more fragments of the past are uncovered, new theories will be proposed, new views will emerge, and the quest to understand the Bible in its historical context will continue.

The Septuagint

Why Was the Hebrew Bible Translated into Greek?

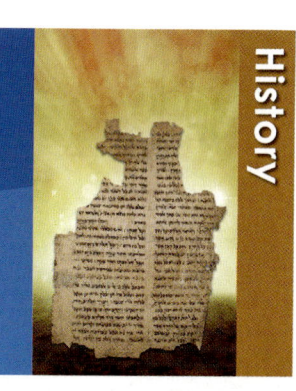

History

"All Scripture is breathed out by God and profitable for teaching."
2 Timothy 3:16 (ESV)

Translation

Translating a book into another language is a laborious process, taking months or even years. Today, even though modern digital tools like Google Translate can convert almost any text from one language to another instantly, it still takes effort and experience to produce an accurate and elegant translation.

In ancient times, traveling merchants carried not only the perfumes and spices of their trade, but also the stories they brought from home and others they picked up along the way. In the taverns each evening, beside crackling fires, eager audiences gathered round and heard their stories. Merchants such as these were traveling storytellers, and arguably the first translators of ancient tales. Those conversant in multiple languages had considerable advantages in many aspects of their routines.

Vocabulary

> **Septuagint** [noun]
an ancient Greek version of the Hebrew Bible, traditionally said to have been translated by 72 Jewish scholars at the request of Ptolemy II

> **Circulate** [verb], moving around from place to place or person to person

The Septuagint 127

Lost in Translation

It's often said that every translation is also an interpretation, because the act of translation is never simply mechanical or automatic. Since the text in the original language can always be rendered in multiple ways, translators who want to find the best translation must always make decisions regarding what they think the author wanted to communicate. Given a particular phrase in Greek or Hebrew, the translator will recognize several different ways in which it can be rendered into English. They will be guided by (among other things) their understanding of the context of the sentence, the historical background, and what they think were the author's intentions.

Two translators may approach the same phrase with different beliefs about the author and the text, and produce different translations as a result.

Consider the following example from the New Testament. The proper understanding of Paul's Letter to the Romans was a point of contention between Catholics and the emerging camp of Protestant Reformers in the 1500s, and remains so today. It discusses the theological concepts of sin, redemption, and the relationship between God and humankind. Notice the similarities as well as the differences in the translations of the following passage (Romans 3:21 and part of 3:22):

- But now the righteousness of God apart from the law is revealed, being witnessed by the Law and the Prophets, even the righteousness of God, through faith in Jesus Christ, to all and on all who believe (NKJV).
- But now apart from the law the righteousness of God has been made known, to which the Law and the Prophets testify. This righteousness is given through faith in Jesus Christ to all who believe (NIV).
- But now apart from the law the righteousness of God (although it is attested by the law and the prophets) has been disclosed—namely, the righteousness of God through the faithfulness of Jesus Christ for all who believe (NET).
- But now the righteousness of God has been manifested apart from the law, though testified to by the law and the prophets, the righteousness of God through faith in Jesus Christ for all who believe (NABRE).

There is generally greater debate about passages that have special theological or moral significance. If a passage reflects on critical beliefs for Jews or Christians, or if it is employed in arguments today about hot-button topics, there will be greater concern to get the translation right. In this case, whether the verse is translated to read either "faith in Jesus Christ" or "the faithfulness of Jesus Christ" —or whether it refers to "the righteousness of God apart from the law" or just to a righteousness that is "manifested apart from the law"—will matter a great deal to some people of faith.

The nuances intrinsic to ancient words in different languages mean that there is not always a single English translation that is clearly correct. This puts tremendous pressure on translators to handle these texts that are sacred to many people and develop the best possible translation. Faith communities tend to gravitate toward Bible versions that reflect their deeply held beliefs on what the Bible is and what it says.

From Hebrew to Greek

After the Babylonian exile, Jewish communities emerged in multiple locations around the ancient world. Most of these communities came to speak the language of their new homes, which was most often Greek. In turn, these communities forgot how to speak Hebrew. But this presented a problem for these communities: they could no longer read their sacred texts. To remedy this, Jews began translating the Hebrew Bible into Greek as early as the third century BC, and soon more Jews were reading the Greek version than the Hebrew texts.

Why Is This Interesting

> The Bible has been translated into more languages (2,932 at last count) than any other book. Many debates and controversies over the Bible concern how it is best translated and understood. The Septuagint is one of the most influential translation projects of all time.

A trained Jewish scribe, known as a *sofer*, copies the biblical text word for word.

During Sabbath (Saturday) and High Holy Days services, Jews take the Bible out of the ark and read it aloud in front of the congregation.

How Did Reading These Scriptures Become So Important to the Jews?

In the ancient world, most cultures were more "oral" than "literary." What does this mean? The cost of writing materials and of learning to write were an expense most people found unnecessary. News, stories, and religious practices and teachings were shared through oral communication, not reading.

The writing of official and religious texts was primarily handled by officials at palaces and temples. Texts considered sacred were copied for future generations to study, while religious teachings and practices also continued to be passed on orally by families, priests, and kings in Israel and Judah—until the Babylonian exile.

With the loss of their government and Temple, the Judean exiles in Babylon and elsewhere began to focus increasingly on the sacred texts they had brought with them. Surrounded by new and foreign cultures, these texts were an important connection to their home and their past, and became fundamental to the identity of the scattered Jewish communities.

Vocabulary

> **Scripture** [noun]
sacred writings or religious texts

The Septuagint

The Hellenized Jews

Long after the Babylonian exile, and after Alexander the Great conquered many kingdoms and spread Greek influence across much of the Ancient Near East, the Jews were scattered across many countries. At one point, more Jews lived in one section of Alexandria than in all of Jerusalem, and more Jews spoke Greek than Hebrew. Today they are called Hellenized (Greek-influenced) Jews. It was important for these Jews to be able to engage the Bible in a language they could understand. It is not surprising, therefore, that Jews began to translate the Hebrew Bible into Greek in the mid-third century BC, or that the New Testament was written in Greek. The Septuagint is an important source for biblical scholars who research how the Bible came together, because it was translated from an ancient Hebrew "source text" that we no longer have. When the Greek New Testament quotes the Old Testament, it's often similar to the Septuagint.

The Bibliotheca Alexandrina, the New Library of Alexandria, Egypt. The original Library of Alexandria near the Mediterranean coast of Egypt was built in the fourth century BC and became one of the great libraries of the ancient world. The library was a bustling center of learning and scholarship. According to ancient sources, the library was burned and its extraordinarily valuable collection was destroyed. This may have happened in stages, though, rather than all at once.

Why Translate into Greek?

The conquests of Alexander the Great in the late fourth century BC transformed the world. This Greek-speaking conqueror subjugated the world from Macedonia (north of Greece) all the way to India. He died at age 33, but during his relatively short life he spread Greek language and culture across a tremendous area. Greek became at the time what the English language is today: the language of international trade and commerce.

Jews were scattered across the world at the time of Alexander. After the Babylonians destroyed Jerusalem in 586 BC, some fled to Egypt, some were exiled to Babylonia (modern Iraq), and others ended up in Persia (modern Iran). They grew up speaking the local languages. By the third century BC, many Jews in places like Egypt probably couldn't understand Hebrew anymore, let alone read it.

Interesting Fact

Although Hebrew was spoken in the time of Israel's monarchy and earlier, most Jews spoke Greek or Aramaic during the time of Jesus. Today, for the first time in Israel in at least 20 centuries, most Jewish people again speak Hebrew, the language of their forefathers.

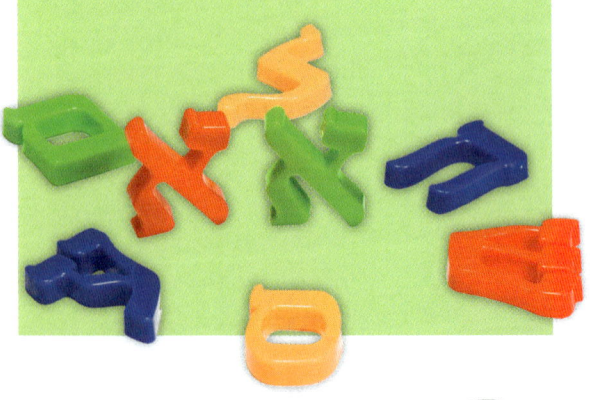

Vocabulary

> **Commerce** [noun]
the buying and selling of goods

Development of the Septuagint

There is a famous legend in the text called *The Letter of Aristeas* that tells how the first five books of the Bible came to be translated into Greek. It says that a librarian wanted a copy of the Pentateuch for the famous royal library of Alexandria in Egypt. So in about 250 BC the king of Egypt, Ptolemy II, who had Greek ancestors, called for expert translators from Jerusalem. These 72 experts translated the Pentateuch into Greek in 72 days. The word *Septuagint* means "seventy," giving the famous translation its name.

It's impossible to know how much of this story is true. It is quite possible that the Hebrew Bible was mostly translated into Greek in Egypt, probably in Alexandria. Alexandria was the most important center for Jewish philosophical learning in the world. The Jewish thinker Philo wrote numerous commentaries on the Greek translation of the Pentateuch, all with a heavy philosophical flavor.

Over time, this legend grew and grew. An early Christian writer known as Justin Martyr extended the claim so that not just the Pentateuch but the entirety of the Hebrew Bible was translated in 72 days. A few centuries later, a Christian theologian named Augustine suggested that each of the 72 translators, under God's inspiration, had independently produced precisely the same word-for-word translation. Scholars often refer to these ancient Greek translations as the *LXX*, the Roman numeral for 70.

The complete translation of the Hebrew Bible into Greek probably took place over a long period, during the third and second centuries BC. For Jews, who no longer knew Hebrew, the Septuagint became their "Bible." Among the Dead Sea Scrolls—which belonged to a very conservative Jewish community—we even find some fragments of the Greek translations of the Hebrew Bible.

Translation of the Septuagint appears to have continued into the late second century BC. Some books, not written in Hebrew but in Greek, such as the Wisdom of Solomon, were gathered together into the Septuagint with the translated texts. Other books in Hebrew outside the Jewish "canon" (see the next chapter) were also translated and included in the Septuagint. Also, some Septuagint versions of the books of the Bible, such as Daniel and Esther, are longer than the Hebrew Bible books today. Others, such as Jeremiah and Job, are shorter.

Given longer and shorter versions of beloved books and stories, it was not always clear which ones were best. Nor was it always clear which books should be "in" and which should be "out." Ancient scribes and translators had to make decisions about which were the most authoritative books and the most reliable sources.

Ptolemy II Philadelphus was the king of Ptolemaic Egypt from 285 to 246 BC. During his time, the ancient Library of Alexandria flourished.

Vocabulary

> **Philosophical** [adjective], pertaining to the rational study of truth and the meaning of existence

The Bodmer Papyri, containing portions of Psalm 108:16-109:4 in Greek, from the third and fourth centuries AD. This group of manuscripts was discovered in 1952 at Pabau, just north of Luxor in Egypt.

Why Is This Important

The Septuagint translation allowed people who did not know the Hebrew language to read Jewish sacred texts for the first time. It restored the Hebrew Bible to Jews spread around the ancient world who could no longer read in Hebrew, and it made the Bible accessible to non-Jewish philosophers and religious writers who could now engage with its ideas.

The authors of the New Testament all wrote in Greek, so it is not surprising that they quote the Hebrew Bible in Greek. Most of the time, they are quoting from the Septuagint. In some instances, they base their arguments on the specific wording of the Greek Old Testament.

The Septuagint was more or less the version of the Hebrew Bible that Christians used for the first few centuries of Christianity. Even today, the Greek Orthodox Church uses the text of the Septuagint as its Old Testament.

Greek Orthodox Church, Santorini, Greece.

Summary

As a result of the conquests by Alexander the Great, the Greek language spread far and wide. By 300 BC, it had become the common language of the Western world. The Jewish scriptures were translated from Hebrew into Greek. The result came to be called the Septuagint. The Septuagint allowed the Bible to be read by Jews scattered around the ancient world, who no longer spoke or read Hebrew. It also made the Bible accessible to non-Jews for the first time.

Alexander the Great, Thessaloniki, Greece.

The Hebrew Bible
How Were the Contents Selected and Distributed?

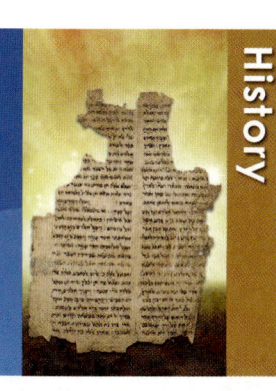

History

"Bind up the testimony; seal the teaching among my disciples."
Isaiah 8:16 (ESV)

Introduction

How do you get an entire people to agree on a single "standard" collection of sacred writings containing their most cherished stories and teachings? Or do you even try? Before Christianity ever developed, the Jewish people started to struggle with this vital issue. Over a period of roughly 600 years, Jewish leaders and rabbis gradually consolidated what they deemed to be their most inspired, reliable, and cherished manuscripts into one large collection. It became known as the Tanakh, or Jewish Bible. According to both the biblical narrative and Jewish tradition, many of the writers of these scrolls were the well-known prophets and poets, such as Moses, David, Solomon, and Isaiah. Other scrolls are attributed to court scribes and historians who will forever remain anonymous. The collection that gradually became accepted over time as the "best document" is the same one that most Christians later accepted (with some variations) as the Old Testament.

Vocabulary

> **Consolidate** [verb], to join several items or units into one whole

The Hebrew Bible

Torah Scroll, ink on gevil, North Africa, 17th century. Gevil is a specially treated animal hide that Jewish scribes and rabbis have always recommended for copying the Torah.

The Hebrew Canon

For Jewish people, the word *Bible* refers to the Hebrew canon. To review, the Jewish Bible, also called the Hebrew Bible, is basically the same collection of books that many Christians generally accept as the Old Testament, but arranged in different order. A canon is a list of books or rulings officially approved by an organized community—in this case by leaders of the Jewish religious community. The word derives from the Greek word *kanon*, implying the standard norm.

Today, and for the past few centuries, printed Bibles have had all the Bible's books bound together in one volume. However, 2,000 years ago, these writings existed only as individual scrolls, carefully copied by hand, one by one. These scrolls formed a collection that gradually became known and accepted as the Bible. Among Christians, these scroll collections were later copied in the form of a single codex—the first real book of hand-written content, starting around AD 100.

The Jewish Bible contains three sections: the Torah, the Prophets, and the Writings. Scholars believe that the Torah (the first five books) and the Prophets gained acceptance before the Writings. Canonization was a gradual process that apparently came to a conclusion by about AD 200. The noncanonical Jewish book 2 Esdras, likely written in the late first century AD, is the first to mention the existence of 24 scrolls. These scrolls would have contained all the canonical books of the Hebrew scriptures, equivalent to the 39 books of the Christian Old Testament.

Vocabulary

> **Canonization** [noun], the process of considering or treating as sacrosanct or holy, especially scriptural works

> **Noncanonical** [adjective], describing those books that do not meet the standards set by the religious community to be included in the canon of authoritative writings

The Leningrad Codex

The Leningrad Codex, copied in Cairo, is considered the oldest surviving complete codex of the Jewish Bible (Tanakh) in Hebrew, dating from about AD 1000.

In Traditional Judaism the Tanakh Comprises 24 Scrolls (39 Books)

The Hebrew canon consists of 24 scrolls in three divisions: Torah (Instructions), Nevi'im (Prophets), and Ketuvim (Writings).

- The Torah (five scrolls, five books): Genesis, Exodus, Leviticus, Numbers, and Deuteronomy.
- The Writings (11 scrolls, 13 books): Psalms, Proverbs, Job, Song of Songs, Ruth, Lamentations, Ecclesiastes, Esther, Daniel, Ezra-Nehemiah (originally, for many centuries, counted by Jews as one book), and Chronicles (two books).
- The Prophets (eight scrolls, 21 books), which divide into two subgroups: the Early Prophetic literature (four scrolls, six books), from Joshua to Kings, which cover the history of the ancient Israelites; and the Latter Prophets (mostly poetic verse and prophecies), comprising Isaiah, Jeremiah, and Ezekiel (three scrolls, three books), plus the smaller group of 12 prophets (one scroll, one set of 12 books), from Hosea to Malachi.

The Bible in Modern Israel

Some 1,800 years after the Jewish Bible was canonized, it is still a popular book among Jews in Israel and influences many aspects of their lives. The study of the Bible, or subjects directly related to the Bible, starts in second grade. At that time, in a classroom ceremony, each child is given his or her own Jewish Bible to take home. They study the Bible for 11 more years, and by the time they finish 12th grade they have gone through the Hebrew canon three times. High scores in four subjects are required for admittance to any of Israel's top universities: Math, English, Hebrew Literature, and the Jewish Bible.

Torah Scroll, ink on gevil, from 15th-century Spain.

Ancient Remarks
about the Sections of the Jewish Bible

Some early writers commented on the way in which the Hebrew canon was divided:

Philo of Alexandria, in the first century AD, mentions "studying . . . the laws and the sacred oracles of God enunciated by the holy prophets, and hymns, and psalms . . ."

Similarly, the author of the Gospel of Luke in the New Testament seems to make reference to three sections: "Then he [Jesus] said to them, 'These are my words that I spoke to you while I was still with you, that everything written about me in the Law of Moses and the Prophets and the Psalms must be fulfilled'" Luke 24:44 (ESV).

Josephus, the first-century Jewish historian, mentions that the Jewish sacred scriptures were divided into three parts: the books of the Torah, the books of the Nevi'im (Prophets), and other books of hymns and wisdom.

The Torah Scribe, by M. Gottlieb, 1876. National Museum, Wroclaw, Poland. A Jewish scribe (*sofer*) must go through special training before he is qualified to copy Bible scrolls in Hebrew.

Finalizing the Hebrew Canon

We don't know precisely when the Jewish canon was fully and finally established. The standardization of the Hebrew Bible's content seems to have occurred sometime in the second century AD. Collecting and arranging the books in the Hebrew canon undoubtedly was a long process, for which we have only indirect evidence.

References to the canonical divisions of Law (Torah) and Prophets seem clear from the second century BC onward. The content of the third division, Writings, however, is not clear until the end of the second century AD, when the full Hebrew canon had formed. All 39 books found within the 24 scrolls were accepted as part of the Hebrew canon. Scholarly debate continues regarding when the last book was written. Jewish tradition suggests that the last of the scrolls was completed by the time of Ezra, in about 450 BC, or before, though many scholars think the last four books of the Hebrew Bible were written around 200 BC.

Vocabulary

> **Oracles** [noun], in the Bible, any messages from God; in other cultures, utterances by priests or priestesses at a shrine as the response of a god to an inquiry

The Dead Sea Scrolls

When the Dead Sea Scrolls were discovered in caves between 1947 and 1956, researchers suddenly had copies of biblical manuscripts and fragments that were nearly 1,000 years older than any existing Hebrew biblical texts. Most of the Dead Sea Scrolls were copied in the last two centuries BC and the first century AD. The Torah makes up a large part of the Dead Sea Scrolls, in terms of both the large number of Torah manuscripts uncovered and the numerous quotations from the Torah in the many extra-biblical manuscripts.

In the Dead Sea Scrolls, books from the Prophets are also represented extensively (particularly Isaiah and the Minor Prophets), and a number of "commentaries" on them were found. However, evidence of the third division, the Writings, is more complicated. For example, while the Dead Sea collection has many manuscripts of most Psalms, there is sometimes a different ordering of the psalms, and one "extra" psalm appears (Psalm 151), which scholars have long known existed but was not included in the Hebrew canon.

Above: A copy of one of the many Dead Sea Scrolls on display at the Shrine of the Book, Jerusalem, Israel. Below: In the desert cliffs near the Dead Sea, at about 1,000 feet below sea level, the first of 11 caves scattered all around the area was explored. Eventually the 11 caves produced more than 900 ancient Hebrew texts between 1947 and 1956.

The Hebrew Bible 137

Why Is This Important

In the history of world literature, there may be no text with a more remarkable story than the Hebrew Bible. It began as a set of stories passed down by obscure people in the Ancient Near East. Scribes and teachers chose these stories, and excluded others, to be included in the collection of writings that were judged sacred and authoritative. This collection—what we now know as the Hebrew Bible—formed the center of Jewish identity, faith, and culture. It became the indispensable first half of the Christian scriptures. Its stories were even taken up in the Qur'an, where they were given a distinctively Muslim expression.

Scholars and philosophers will debate the value and the legacy of the Hebrew Bible. But it's no exaggeration to say that this humble set of stories and scrolls has changed the world. For hundreds of millions of people the stories of the Hebrew Bible have become a familiar story book informing their lives. They know the story of Noah and his ark, of Jonah and his fish, of Esther and her courage. They know the narratives of the creation, the patriarchs, the Exodus, the monarchs, and the prophets. And why do they know these things? Because scribes and teachers wrote these stories down and gathered them together—and a community of people felt that these stories conveyed something sacred and true, so they passed it on to their children and their children's children, and taught them to do the same.

Why Is This Interesting

It seems as though few things in our modern world last for long. Computers are outdated and thrown on the trash heap within a few years. Yet the Hebrew Bible has endured. The canon was closed, and this has given the Hebrew Bible stability over the years. But this does not mean that nothing has changed. Alongside the Hebrew Bible, as with the New Testament, there has been a lively tradition of interpretation and debate. Without the stability of the canon, the Hebrew Bible as we know it might have been lost. Without the tradition of continual reinterpretation, it might have been forgotten.

Simchat Torah

Simchat Torah is a rabbinical holiday celebrated each year at the end of the biblical Feast of Tabernacles (Leviticus 23). It marks the end of the annual reading cycle in synagogues across the globe. During this cycle the Jewish people read every verse from the Torah at least once during the year, and large parts of the rest of the Hebrew canon. On Simchat Torah, in Orthodox synagogues and many Conservative ones as well, people are allowed to dance around the synagogue with Torah scrolls in their arms and even take the sacred scrolls outside, in good weather, for special lively rounds of public dancing in the streets (called *hakafot*).

Summary

Among the ancient Israelites lived prophets, sages, and scribes who passed on writings held sacred by the community. Much of it makes for compelling reading, even today. It contains sections that are not as engaging for modern people (e.g., genealogies or detailed instructions). But the sages and rabbis responsible for Judaism's religious instruction believed that every word in these traditional writings was significant. They were not looking merely for good literature, but rather seeking to organize and hand down sacred texts. Over a roughly 600-year span, they carefully chose and finally assembled their sacred scriptures into one book. They believed these writings were their very best and most inspiring texts. These 39 books, from 24 different scrolls, became their Bible (Tanakh), which many Christians generally refer to and accept as the Old Testament.

The "Obscure" Books of the Bible
What Insights Do These Books Provide?

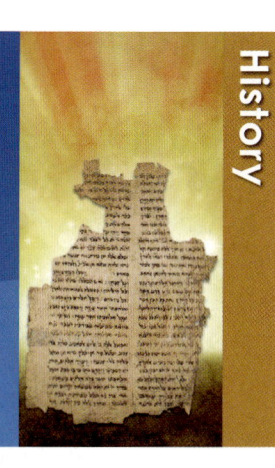

"He [Eleazar] crept under the elephant, and thrust him under, and slew him: whereupon the elephant fell down upon him, and there he died."

1 Maccabees 6:46 (KJV)

Included or Excluded

For many centuries, writing was a laborious and time-consuming activity. Much writing in Mesopotamia and Egypt was administrative and religious, and was closed to most people, though more basic writing and accounting systems were used by merchants and administrators. As the idea of the alphabet spread, a local alphabet developed in Phoenicia—consisting of 22 symbols—and elsewhere, making writing less elite and more common. The ancient Israelites adapted the Phoenician writing system to represent the Hebrew language, creating the Hebrew alphabet. Along with other alphabetic cultures, writing became much more common among the Jews.

Some Jewish books and stories found their way into the collection of sacred writings that became the Bible, and so they were preserved for later generations. Jewish leaders agreed that these books were worthy of inclusion. Yet there were other stories and books that were matters of dispute. Some were rejected and lost to history. Other Jewish literature, including some very inspiring and popular stories, was not included in the Hebrew Bible, but still was preserved by Jews and Christians so that we can read these texts today. Some of these books were included in the Septuagint (the Greek translation and collection of Jewish sacred texts) and most scholars today call them the Apocrypha or deuterocanonical works. They further enrich the Hebrew storybook and give us more insights into the lives and history of the ancient Jewish people.

What Should We Call These Books?

What do we call these books that we find in some Bibles but not others? It depends on whom you ask.

Some key early church writers called them the Apocrypha (Greek for "things that are hidden" or "obscure"). One of the most important teachers of the early Christian church, Jerome, used this term when he produced his important Latin version of the Bible (later called the Vulgate) from about AD 382 to 405. Although he included these books, he argued that they are not accepted in the Hebrew canon. They could be useful for teaching, he suggested, but should not be considered as authoritative as the 39 books of the Tanakh (the Hebrew Bible) or the books of the New Testament. The term *apocrypha* entered modern usage when early Protestant Bible versions like the Luther Bible and the King James Version placed them in a separate section titled Apocrypha. Early leaders of the Reformation, citing Jerome, argued that these books were not as authoritative as the books they included in the Bible, but were nonetheless helpful for historical and spiritual instruction. The King James Version included the Apocrypha until 1885. Most Protestant versions printed today do not include the Apocry

The Catholic Church disagreed with Jerome and rejected his viewpoint on this matter. Catholic versions of the Bible generally include these works in their Old Testament section. Catholics today call them deuterocanonical works (the Greek word refers to their status as part of a "second" or later collection of biblical writings). They are considered canonical (which means that they belong to the collection of authoritative sacred writings) and authoritative, but distinguished from the "protocanonical" works (the works included in the Hebrew Bible) because they were embraced later.

But wait, it gets more complicated! Eastern Orthodox churches use the term *anagignoskmena*, meaning "to be read" or "profitable for reading," to refer to the books that were included in the Septuagint but not in the Hebrew Bible. The Orthodox also use the term *deuterocanonical*, but with this term (unlike Catholics) they mean books that have less authority than the books of the Hebrew Bible. Finally, the lists of books counted among the Apocrypha or the deuterocanonical works can vary slightly from one group to another.

Although all the apocryphal books are Jewish writings, we do not know how the Jewish religious authorities referred to them. Some scholars suggest they were called *sefarim genuzim*, or "stored away books." This may have applied to a larger number of Jewish books that were known to Jewish teachers but excluded from the Hebrew canon.

Even graduate students in biblical studies have a hard time keeping track of all these words and how they are used differently across Christian and Jewish traditions. What's important to understand, for our purposes, is that there is a collection of Jewish texts that ancient Jews and Christians preserved for posterity but did not agree on including in the Bible. Today, neither Jews nor Protestants include them in their Bible, while Catholics and Orthodox Christians do. Regardless, these books offer rich details and insights into the lives and thoughts of the Jewish people, especially during the centuries of the closing of the Old Testament and the writing of the New.

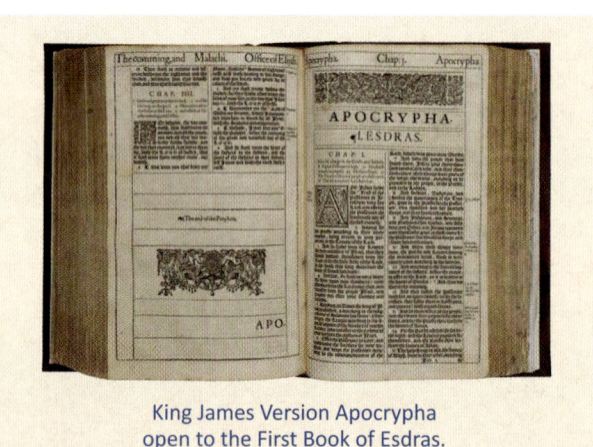

King James Version Apocrypha open to the First Book of Esdras.

What's in the Apocrypha

The Apocrypha includes about 15 texts that were written between around 200 BC and AD 100. Despite the fact that the Tanakh (Jewish Bible) does not include these books as sacred scripture, most of these texts appear in the Septuagint, the Greek version of the Hebrew Bible produced by the Jews of Alexandria in Egypt. As a result, they were included in the "Bible" known to the authors of the New Testament and had an influence on the development of the early Christian church.

Contents of the Apocrypha

The 15 documents that make up the Apocrypha, as printed in the 1611 King James Bible (and thus in most early English Bibles), can be divided into four groups:

Narrative	Wisdom	Apocalypse	Additions
1 Esdras	Wisdom of Solomon	2 Esdras	Additions to Esther
Tobit	Wisdom of Sirach	Baruch	The Prayer of Manasseh (at 2 Chronicles 33:18)
Judith		The Epistle of Jeremiah	3 Additions to Daniel
1 and 2 Maccabees			The Song of the Three Children (includes the Prayer of Azariah)
			Susanna
			Bel and the Dragon

Vocabulary

> **Canonical** [adjective], writings approved by a religious community as meeting the standard for inclusion in a holy book

The Obscure Books of the Bible

A Brief Synopsis of Selected Deuterocanonical Literature

1 Maccabees

This book describes, in part, the situation of the Jews under the rule of Antiochus Epiphanes during the mid-second century BC. Antiochus, a Greek monarch, sought to unify his kingdom under Hellenistic ideals and culture, a program that was resisted by many Jews. In response, he slaughtered many thousands of Jews and banned Torah reading, Sabbath observance, and circumcision. Antiochus vandalized the Temple in Jerusalem and defiled it with the blood of pigs, which were considered ritually unclean. The Jews revolted against Antiochus in 167 BC under the leadership of Mattathias, from the Maccabee family, and his five sons. Through this rebellion, the small army of the Maccabees was able to drive the Greeks out and restore Jewish religious practice in Jerusalem. The Jewish holiday of Hanukkah (the Feast of Dedication), also known as the Festival of Lights, commemorates this victory.

2 Maccabees

This book rehearses a part of the story from 1 Maccabees but largely focuses on the story of Judas Maccabee, one of the sons of Mattathias. It portrays martyrs as models of religious devotion. Significantly for both Christianity and Judaism, 2 Maccabees describes resurrection after death in a restored physical state (chapters 7 and 12) and the dead in heaven praying for people on earth (15:14).

Angel of Maccabees, Gustave Doré. This drawing and the ones on the next page are by the French artist Gustave Doré, from his Illustrated English Bible, published in 1885.

Vocabulary

> **Circumcision** [noun], the surgical removal of the foreskin of the penis

Wisdom of Sirach

This poetic book, also known as Ecclesiasticus, is about Sirach, a Jewish sage in Jerusalem in about 250 BC. The longest of the apocryphal books, Sirach was often quoted by the Jewish rabbis. The book was highly regarded in the early Christian church, and regularly read as part of Christian worship. Thus it came to be called by the Latin name Ecclesiasticus, meaning "(book) of the church."

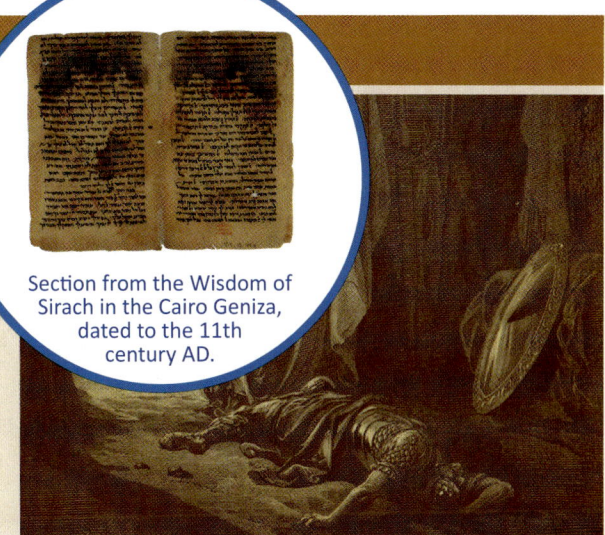

Section from the Wisdom of Sirach in the Cairo Geniza, dated to the 11th century AD.

Wisdom of Solomon

The style of this beautiful and poetic book—attributed to the biblical King Solomon—is similar to that of the biblical books of Proverbs and Ecclesiastes, though it is clearly influenced by Greek and Egyptian thought.

Tobit

Set in Nineveh (Assyria) after the fall of the northern kingdom of Israel, this book tells the story of Tobit, a pious Jew who maintains his loyalty to God, even while captive in a foreign land. The book sheds light on second-century BC views of angels and demons.

Judith

Describing the period shortly after the Jewish captives were exiled to Babylon (ca. 538 BC), the book tells the story of Judith, a devout and daring widow who lives in Israel prior to the captivity. Judith encourages her fellow Jews to maintain their faith. She also endears herself to a foreign commander in Judah, named Holofernes. She promises to help him conquer her people, but through flattery and deception eventually beheads a drunken Holofernes. Judith's courage and determination inspire her oppressed countrymen.

Vocabulary

> **Martyr** [noun], a person who willingly dies for a principle, usually his or her faith

The Obscure Books of the Bible

Some Obscure Facts about the "Obscure" Books

- The New Testament text contains hundreds of references to the Hebrew canon, but barely any references to deuterocanonical texts. The Book of Jude (1:14) refers to the Book of Enoch, and the Gospel of John (10:22-42) depicts an event that takes place during Hanukkah, an indirect reference to the events described in the time of the Maccabees.
- Two of the archangels (the seven most important angels) in Judaism are mentioned in the Bible: Michael, God's warrior, the protector of Israel (Daniel 12 and Jude); and Gabriel, God's messenger (Daniel 8 and 9, Luke 1). Another archangel, Raphael, God's healing messenger, is mentioned only in the Apocrypha, in the Book of Tobit.
- Tobit had a pet dog.
- The Christian tradition that Jesus was born at midnight may come from the Wisdom of Solomon (18:14-15).

Why Is This Important

Scholars see these texts as a treasured literary resource that helps us understand a very important period in the history of Jewish religion, philosophy, and thought. They shed light on a time of political turmoil for the Jews, mostly (with the possible exception of 2 Esdras, which may have come after AD 70) before the Second Temple was destroyed. They also show us a time rich with new ideas. Some of those new ideas led to rabbinic Judaism after the destruction of the Temple. Other ideas became a part of Christian thought. The stories and ideas of the deuterocanonical books were very much a part of the culture inhabited by the earliest Jewish followers of Jesus of Nazareth.

Why Is This Interesting

These documents provide a window into the development of some concepts that would become extremely important in Christianity, such as spiritual warfare, the afterlife, resurrection from the dead, and apocalyptic visions of the future. They also illuminate the variety of Jewish books and stories that were available when Jews and Christians began to decide what to include in the canon of their most sacred texts.

Summary

Although the deuterocanonical writings were not accepted into the Tanakh, they were preserved first by Jews and then by Christians and in many cases honored and celebrated. While theologians argue about whether the books are sacred scripture, these books provide helpful insight and information about the Jews and their religion during this time. The Apocrypha or deuterocanonical works, for them, open a valuable window into the thoughts, attitudes, and views circulating in Israel among the Jewish people at a critical juncture in their history.

Daily Life in Bible Times

What Do Ancient Customs Teach Us?

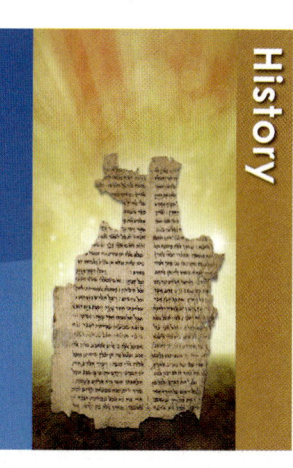

History

> "I have observed the business that God gave man to be concerned with."
> Ecclesiastes 3:10 (NJPS)

The Basic Human Drama

The Bible is full of big stories—from poetic portrayals of the creation of the world to prophetic visions about the end of days. Wars, floods, earthquakes, and other upheavals—the biblical narratives are packed with major dramas. But the Bible speaks about far more than these grand accounts. The stories also describe the challenge of everyday life, and so connect with us on a simpler level. How did people in biblical times take care of themselves and their families? What did they eat, wear, and worry about day to day? What might their everyday schedule have looked like? We can gain insights from archaeological discoveries and ancient records, but we can also piece together clues from the Bible itself.

Daily Life in Bible Times 145

Why Is This Interesting

When the Bible was being written, many people lived their whole lives without traveling far from where they were born. Today news travels fast, and many people move across regions, countries, or even across the globe. Until fairly recently, news, like life itself, traveled much more slowly. While the many contrasts between life then and life now are striking, you might be surprised by how little people's basic needs and aspirations have changed.

Why Is This Important

Life today—with its social media, modern conveniences, and swiftly changing cultures—can seem so disconnected from the past. Despite the outward differences, people remain much the same in their basic needs, hopes, and fears. The more we learn about both the differences and similarities between modern societies and ancient times, the better we can understand the stories and characters of the Bible.

Daily Life in Bible Times

Jacob Urging Leah and Rachel to Flee from Laban, Pieter Symonsz Potter, 1638. Saint Catherine's Convent Museum, Utrecht, Netherlands. The artist attempts to show Jacob and his family before they begin their long journey to the land of Canaan, where Jacob grew up.

Family Structure Then and Now

How long does it take you to get to your grandparents' home? For some people, this question would probably not even be asked. If it had been, the answer might have been "My grandparents live in the next room! My grandmother bakes bread every morning in the courtyard, and my grandfather helps in the field as much as he can." In the ancient world, extended families oftentimes lived and worked together, a pattern that is still common today in rural communities in some parts of the world. Even the kids contributed to the "household," which, together with servants and other workers, might have included dozens of people.

Most young women only left home when they married to join their husbands' households. Today many young people leave home regardless of marriage, to live on their own. Jesus' story of the "prodigal son" who took his portion of his inheritance early and went to live on his own in a distant country may have been seen as odd (Luke 15:11-32).

Think of the stories about the biblical patriarchs and matriarchs. In the Genesis narrative, sisters Rachel and Leah (who both married Jacob, Abraham's grandson) live together their whole lives. Rachel and Leah are also Jacob's cousins, just as Jacob's father, Isaac, himself married his cousin Rebekah (Genesis 24). Such marriages between blood relatives were not unusual. They often ensured that property stayed in the family.

As the story of Jacob shows, wealthy men sometimes had more than one wife. Such extended families, with multiple children, helped support the larger household. Children's responsibilities went far beyond today's household duties, such as taking out the garbage or walking the dog. A young person's job might be tending sheep, as the Bible describes Rachel, Joseph, and David (Genesis 29:9; 37:2; 1 Samuel 16:11). This could be a huge responsibility. Imagine being entrusted to care, by yourself, for the welfare of 50 to 100 valuable sheep on a remote hillside. A benefit of extended families is that there are more family members to provide care during hard times.

Daily Life in Bible Times

Abraham's Servant Meets Rebecca, James Tissot, 1902. The Jewish Museum, New York, New York.

Matchmaking

How did couples in biblical times meet and marry? Not by first dating each other, which is popular in modern culture. Marriages were almost always arranged ahead of time between families. The story of Jacob and Rachel describes an exception. While most marriages in ancient times were more about economic concerns and community relations than romance, the text says that Jacob pursued Rachel because of his love for her (Genesis 29:18).

Arranged marriages, which are still commonplace in some places today, allowed the parents of the couple to make a deal based on the interests of both families. Many modern Western critics raise concerns about the freedoms of women, who are sometimes very young when they are sent away from their homes to live with older husbands. Cultures around the world practice, and view, arranged marriage differently.

One example of an arranged marriage in the Bible occurs in the story of Isaac. Abraham sends his servant Eliezer to find Isaac a bride from his extended family. Eliezer travels to Abraham's homeland, Nahor, in Mesopotamia. Eliezer is impressed with the hospitality of a woman (Rebekah) who provides water for both him and the camels (Genesis 24:16-24).

In the Genesis story, Rebekah does not even get to meet Isaac before their wedding. Abraham's servant takes her on a long journey back to Isaac to consummate the marriage.

Doctors did not have the technology or medicines that we have today. There were no microscopes to discover viruses. While doctors used many kinds of plants and foods to treat diseases, including herbal remedies that are still used today, they had little understanding of how simple things such as washing hands could prevent disease. In ancient times, and even fairly recently, people often died from infections that are easily treated today. Infant mortality and maternal mortality rates were also much higher than today, since people did not have the benefit of modern birthing techniques, the science of nutrition, or all the technologies we use to monitor the health of pregnant women and babies.

Women provided most of the child care. Grandmothers, mothers, and sisters shared a long list of tasks. Although wealthier women might have had servants, households of ordinary means produced many things used by the family, in addition to sharing responsibilities in raising the children. Most men and women worked long hours. The women wove (Proverbs 31:13), ground the grain, baked the bread (Genesis 18:6; Leviticus 26:26; Job 31:10), and cooked the other food (Genesis 27:9, 14). Some young women were shepherds, like Rachel (Genesis 29:9). Women also worked in the fields (Ruth 2:5-9). With so many responsibilities, most women stayed close to home. The famously industrious "woman of valor" described in Proverbs 31 not only manages the household but also engages in major business transactions.

Vocabulary

> **Woman of valor** [noun]
a Jewish prayer (based on Proverbs 31) said by husbands before the Friday meal, extolling a woman's virtues

> **Consummate** [verb]
to make (something) complete

Daily Life in Bible Times

Lodgings

Most modern American houses today look nothing like houses back in biblical times. The stories in the Pentateuch often describe people living in tents, because the households and tribes often lived in nomadic groups. Depending on the season and local weather patterns, people moved their flocks of sheep and goats to new pastures and water sources. Today the Bedouin people still live in tents in Israel and in neighboring countries—typically in desert areas. Although most Bedouin have settled down in cities and towns, the rest experience a lifestyle very similar to the lifestyle described in some biblical stories, such as that of Abraham.

Archaeologists have found many stone foundations of houses first built sometime before 1000 BC. These dwellings could be arranged around a central courtyard. Ancient sources tell us that the family often slept in just one of the rooms, and only rich people had beds. Most people slept on homemade, woven mats that could be rolled up and stored during the day. Many dwellings had straw roofs and hard-packed dirt floors, often painted or plastered. Houses varied between one and two stories.

Women from wealthy homes might watch community activities from their windows. We can see a possible reference to this practice in a passage about Michal, David's wife (2 Samuel 6:16), and also in the song (poem) of Deborah and Barak, which depicts the mother of the slain Canaanite general Sisera (Judges 5:28) waiting in suspense for word about her son.

Because rooms were small and because regional weather was typically sunny and dry for about seven months of the year, much of the daily routine took place outdoors. On warm nights, it would be cooler to sleep on the roof, which was also used for storage (Joshua 2:6). The courtyard had ovens for baking and cisterns for water storage. You might even see some chickens or other small farm animals in the courtyard.

Even today some Bedouin families in the Middle East still camp out close to their flocks.

Bedouin tent, early 1900s. Library of Congress, Washington, D.C.

Bedouin girls, early 1900s. Library of Congress, Washington, D.C.

Daily Life in Bible Times

Pedagogue and Boy, terracotta statue, third century BC (Hellenistic period), Greece. The Walters Art Gallery, Baltimore, Maryland.

Education

Education in many ancient cultures was organized in learning centers or around individuals. These "masters" taught on religious and civil matters, as well as writing and reading. Scholars believe that by about 800 BC there were some school teachers, but the vast majority of youth were taught at home by their parents (Deuteronomy 6:20). And in those days, everything devout Hebrew parents needed to teach their kids dealt basically with how to operate in society and whatever religious and cultural rules are deemed necessary. For girls, this might include weaving, cooking, sewing, and selling produce. For boys, it might include helping their father in his work, finding a labor job, or becoming a priest or a scribe.

For the children of very rich parents, like the 70 sons of King Ahab (2 Kings 10:1, 6), so-called "guardians" may have provided limited instruction. Schools and school teachers existed in the New Testament era. At that time, some of the wealthier families in Greece and Rome might have deployed a trusted servant in the role of "pedagogue" or guardian for the family's male children. The use of pedagogues (who were custodians more like a "big brother" than an actual teacher) is mentioned in 1 Corinthians 4:15 and Galatians 3:24-25. The Jewish historian Josephus writes about his own son (educational opportunities were much more limited for girls) having a pedagogue.

A Bedouin girl weaving, early 1900s. Library of Congress, Washington, D.C.

Re-enactment of a family meal during the late Second Temple period. Nazareth Village, Nazareth, Israel.

A dish of salt recovered from Roman ruins at Masada, Israel.

Roman-period olive seeds recovered from Masada, Israel.

What's for Dinner?

Growing vegetables, fruits, and grains; herding sheep or goats; preparing bread, wine, and oil; or fishing or hunting occupied most people during their waking hours. The land of Canaan was described as "a land flowing with milk and honey" (Exodus 3:8; Deuteronomy 26:15). Cheese making was an ancient art (Genesis 18:8; 2 Samuel 17:29). *Afiq* is a dried and salted curd cheese that kept best in the heat and was later reconstituted with water before eating. The Bedouin still make this kind of cheese, which is available in open-air markets in many Middle Eastern cities, including Jerusalem and Nazareth. Carvings from ancient Mesopotamia show men tending the flocks and milking the animals, with women churning the butter. People enjoyed fresh fruit (in season) and dried fruit (year round). Wine was a staple. Lentils were turned into savory stews and soups, reminding us of the story about Esau, who was willing to surrender his birthright to Jacob for a bowl of stew (Genesis 25:27-34).

People in biblical times probably ate less meat than we do. They depended on their animals in several ways. As Proverbs 27:26-27 says,

> The lambs will provide you with clothing,
> The he-goats, the price of a field.
> The goats' milk will suffice for your food,
> The food of your household,
> And the maintenance of your maids. (NJPS)

Beef was an especially precious food item, probably served mainly on special occasions (see Luke 15:22-32).

People in the Ancient Near East used a variety of spices to flavor their food, including cinnamon and saffron (Song of Songs 4:14) and black cumin (Isaiah 28:27)—which some people in Israel still sprinkle on their bread, yogurt, and soft cheese. But the most basic flavor of ancient times—salt—is still the most common one. In ancient Rome, salt was so important that Romans once connected the payment of soldiers with salt, which in Latin is *sal*—and this is the origin for the English word *salary*. The other basic food of the region—bread—finds its way into dozens of Bible stories, sayings, and miracles, both symbolically (John 6:35) and as essential food (1 Kings 17:12-15; Luke 11:3). The psalmist gave thanks to God for the basic elements of sustenance enjoyed by the people of his day: wine to drink and bread to eat, along with multipurpose olive oil (Psalm 104:15). The oil was consumed and also used as an ointment for the skin.

Daily Life in Bible Times

Re-enactment of a carpenter at work during the late Second Temple period. Nazareth Village, Nazareth, Israel.

Nazareth Village

What was life like in Galilee at the time in which the Jesus stories are set? Some local Arab Christians in Israel, with international support, created a nonprofit venture called Nazareth Village to showcase their findings. This "open-air" museum opened in 2000 and attracts thousands of visitors every year. Nazareth Village is on a hillside close to the town named in the New Testament as Jesus' childhood home. Excavations on this hillside have uncovered ruins of a first-century vineyard with a watch tower, terraces, and a spring-fed irrigation system. These discoveries have been restored. Several stone buildings have been constructed nearby using ancient building techniques to give the feel of a small farming community from that period. Guides dressed in period costumes lead visitors through the site, while other staff members reenact some of the daily activities from 20 centuries ago, including bread and wine making, weaving, carpentry, and pottery creation. Many TV and movie companies use the site for historically accurate productions.

Some New Testament Advances

By the time we reach the New Testament period, the lifestyles of ordinary people had changed a great deal. More were living in permanent homes in villages and cities. The religious life of the people was different, too. The biblical narrative shows a progression of the Israelite holy place from an elaborate tent in the desert—the Tabernacle—to the Temple in Jerusalem. By the time of Jesus, however, the people also had local places for prayer and worship, the synagogues.

There were changes in technology, too. For example, the olive press, which for thousands of years was a simple tree trunk weighted down with heavy stones, gave way to a new invention, where the necessary pressure was exerted by a large hand-crank or wheel press. Basic schools also came into existence. They were a regular feature of villages and cities. The Book of Romans refers to someone who teaches young children (Romans 2:20). By the time of the Jesus narratives, the Roman Empire had established roads across the Mediterranean.

Vocabulary

> **Tabernacle, the** [noun]
the portable tent of the Israelites noted in the Bible that housed the Ark of the Covenant and other sacred objects, from the exodus from Egypt to the Temple period

Summary

The details of daily life in biblical times were far different from our own experiences in the 21st century. Yet when we look at how ordinary people performed their everyday activities, we can recognize that many of their essential acts were much the same as ours: establishing a home and family, working, sleeping, eating, drinking, learning, and celebrating.

The Dead Sea Scrolls

Why Do We Care So Much about Dusty Sealed Jars Hidden for 2,000 Years?

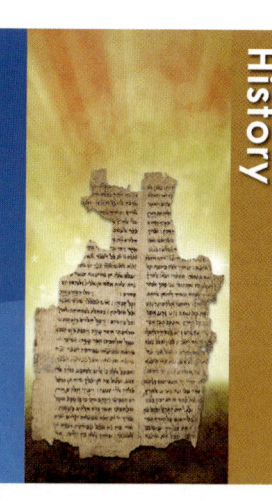

"They shall go into the holes of the rocks, and into the caves of the earth."

Isaiah 2:19 (NKJV)

An Amazing Discovery

Many archaeologists work for decades, or even their entire careers, without making a major discovery. Then there are non-archaeologists, with no training and no years of back-breaking labor, who stumble by chance on historical treasures that change the world. That's what happened with the Dead Sea Scrolls.

Three Bedouin shepherds, sometime between November 1946 and February 1947, accidentally discovered what is arguably the greatest archaeological find of the 20th century. In a dry riverbed near the Dead Sea, a young goatherd named Jum'a playfully threw some rocks up toward a cave opening. One of them shattered something inside. Two days later, his cousin Muhammad squeezed into the cave, found ten large jars, and retrieved three scrolls. While no one can verify every detail of the story, the two young men had made a major archaeological discovery. The problem

Time Travel

The Dead Sea

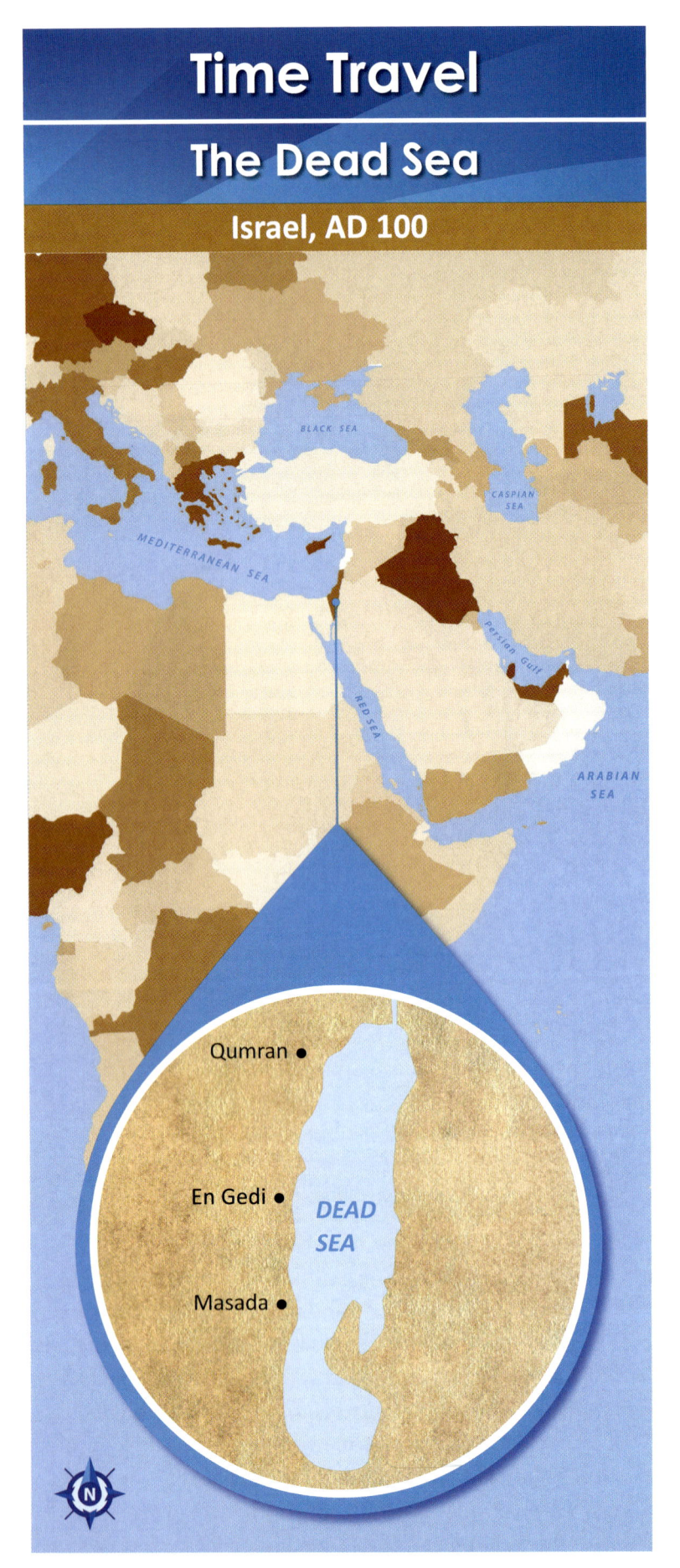

Israel, AD 100

was, they didn't know it yet. Months later, these boys sold some of their scrolls (they found seven in all) to a part-time antiquities dealer for just seven British pounds. That's the equivalent of about $40 today. The actual worth of the scrolls? Priceless. For what they had found were some pieces of the Hebrew Bible and other ancient texts that had been hidden from human eyes for about 20 centuries.

Today the site of these finds is known as Qumran. It's located about 12 miles southeast of Jerusalem and is now one mile inland from the steadily receding northwestern shore of the Dead Sea. Between 1947 and 1956, the Bedouin and a dedicated group of searchers and archaeologists would find 11 caves, with a few hundred scrolls and documents and thousands of smaller fragments.

The Telephone Game

Imagine that someone has handed you an ancient text written 20 centuries ago. The text may have been copied multiple times, passing through many hands. It's been translated and sometimes edited and commented upon. How can you be sure that what's in your hands matches well with what the original author wrote down 2,000 years ago?

If you've ever played Whisper Down the Lane (also called the Telephone Game), you can easily understand the potential problem. In this game, a group of people stand in a line. The first person in line is given a message. Let's say the message is "The fox invaded the hen house." The first person whispers the message to the

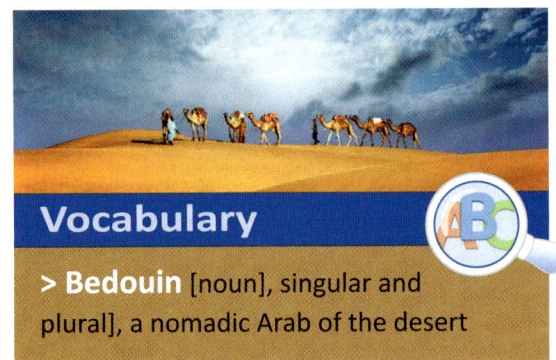

Vocabulary

> **Bedouin** [noun], singular and plural], a nomadic Arab of the desert

154 The Dead Sea Scrolls

second person. Whispers are easily misunderstood. The message might change a tiny bit (perhaps "the fox" changes into "the foxes") or it might not change at all. But as the second person whispers the message to the third, and the third to the fourth, and so on, changes usually build up. When it reaches the end of the line, the final person repeats what she thinks she heard. She might declare, "A boxer weighed in and went pow."

In other words, messages can change dramatically when they're copied and passed down many times. We would expect many fewer changes with a written text, but the question still stands. How can we be sure an ancient text hasn't been dramatically changed when it's been handed down for centuries? What if our version of "Genesis" is nothing like the original version that was first written down?

Imagine, in the telephone game, that you were the last person in the line. You want to make sure that your version of the "text" is as close as possible to the original. One of the best approaches would be to compare your version with earlier people in the line. Since changes tend to accumulate, if you could check your version against the third person in the line, or even the second, you can expect that you will get closer to the original message.

This is one reason why the Dead Sea Scrolls are so important. They get scholars back much closer to the original biblical texts. Prior to their discovery, the oldest existing copies of the Old Testament in Hebrew were two manuscripts from about AD 1000. They were known as the Aleppo Codex (portions missing) and the Leningrad Codex. With the discovery of the Dead Sea Scrolls, however, scholars can study biblical texts that are about 1,000 years older. These scrolls allow researchers, for the first time, to compare biblical texts from about AD 1000 with earlier versions from about 200 BC to about AD 100. This side-by-side comparison enables us to see how much the wording of the Bible may have changed over time.

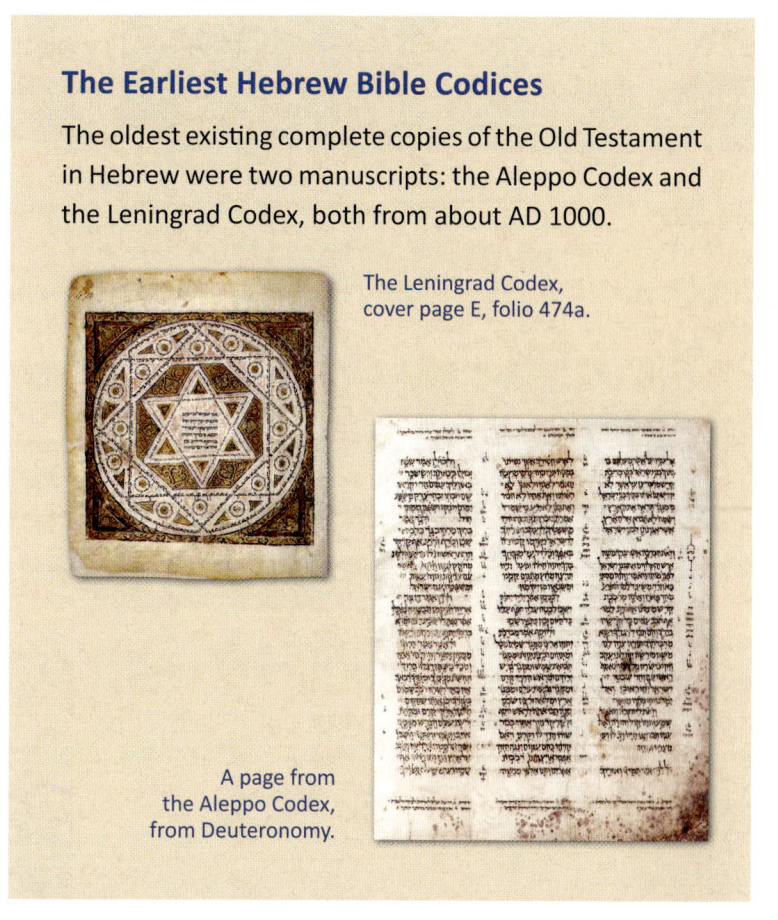

The Earliest Hebrew Bible Codices

The oldest existing complete copies of the Old Testament in Hebrew were two manuscripts: the Aleppo Codex and the Leningrad Codex, both from about AD 1000.

The Leningrad Codex, cover page E, folio 474a.

A page from the Aleppo Codex, from Deuteronomy.

How Much Did the Texts Change over 1,000 Years?

What Did the Scholars Find?

Let's take one example. The only complete book of the Bible found at Qumran, with no chapters or verses missing, is the Isaiah Scroll. It was one of the first scrolls found and also one of the most important. It turns out that the copy of Isaiah in the Leningrad Codex (from ca. AD 1000) is virtually identical with what the Bedouin discovered in the Qumran caves. After 11 centuries, only 5 percent of the text showed any differences. These consisted mainly of stylistic changes, slips of the pen, and some grammatical developments over time in the written Hebrew language.

Most of the other scrolls were fragmentary, not complete books like the Isaiah Scroll. Yet content analysis and comparisons with existing, later manuscripts suggest that the biblical texts were preserved and copied over time with remarkable accuracy. The Dead Sea Scrolls, therefore, strongly confirm just how carefully the Jewish scribes copied and preserved the texts from generation to generation. Later, Christian monks would continue this work as well.

What Can We Learn from the Dead Sea Scrolls

The Dead Sea Scrolls also tell us something about how the Hebrew Bible came together. About a quarter of the texts found at Qumran are "biblical," from the traditional Hebrew canon. Among this portion are pieces of every Old Testament book except for Esther. Most of the biblical texts are, however, highly fragmentary. Of the approximately 200 biblical fragments found, 87 are from the first five books of the Bible, the Torah. These books, which include the stories of the Exodus and the Mosaic Law code, had special value to the Jewish people in general and to the religious community at Qumran in particular. Psalms is also well represented, with more than 35 partial scrolls. Some of the Psalms scrolls contain a handful of "extra" psalms that were not included in the Hebrew canon while Psalms 110 and 111 are missing. Other books not included in the Jewish Bible, like the Book of Enoch, were also part of the Qumran collection.

Names of Dead Sea Scrolls
- The Community Rule Scroll
- The War Scroll
- The Isaiah Scroll
- The Temple Scroll
- Habakkuk Commentary

Every piece of parchment discovered has been carefully cataloged and labeled according to its cave of origin. For example, an extra-biblical text was found full of ancient titles for the messiah that seem similar to names applied to Jesus in the New Testament, such as "Son of the Highest" (Luke 1:32). That specific text has been labeled 4Q246. The "4" is the number of the cave where it was found; "Q" means it was discovered at Qumran; and "246" means it was the 246th text to be recorded from that cave. The Community Rule Scroll was named and cataloged as 1QS, meaning Cave 1, Qumran, *Serekh ha-Yahad* (its Hebrew name). It was one of the first scrolls found.

Which Books Were Held in High Esteem

Two characteristics indicate that the people of Qumran considered a book to be important: that they quoted from it as coming "from God" and that it was accompanied by a commentary. Either of these two indicators is like seeing the word *important* stamped on the text. Accordingly, all the books of the Law and the Prophets in the Hebrew canon, plus a few historical books, such as Samuel, Enoch, and Jubilees, appear to have been viewed as important by the people of Qumran by the first century AD.

Photograph of some of the first caves in which the Dead Sea Scrolls were found, near Qumran, Israel. Circled: remains of some living quarters at Qumran.

View of the archaeological site at Qumran, looking from the west. It is located about a mile from the Dead Sea, and in the summer temperature can reach 120°F.

Who Were the People of Qumran

The scrolls provide a remarkable window into the Qumran community. But who were the people who collected and preserved these texts? Scholars label a fourth of all the scrolls as "sectarian" because they promote the philosophy of the Jewish sect that lived there. This remote community at Qumran had separated itself from the larger Jewish community, to remain holy according to its own strict beliefs. Members waited for God to deliver them. The Community Rule states that the goal of their lives and studies is to "seek God with a whole heart and soul, and do what is good and right before Him as He commanded by the hand of Moses and all His servants the Prophets."

The sectarian community at Qumran is identified most commonly with the Essenes. Jewish historians Josephus and Philo describe the Essenes as being fervently devoted to the study of the holy books, to the practice of all sorts of purification rites, and to ethical standards rooted in the Law of Moses. They lived in isolated communities that focused on interpreting the Prophets for the present day. Others, however, identify the Qumran community with the Sadducees in light of the legal content and Temple traditions in the scrolls.

Many of the sectarian texts describe the rules for living in the community (such as ritual baths for purification and a ban on spitting in public). Other texts describe how God will destroy their enemies and deliver them in fulfillment of his prophetic promises. According to the War Scroll, members of the community at Qumran called themselves the "sons of light" who would one day defeat the "sons of darkness."

Vocabulary

> **Sectarian** [adjective]
adhering or limited to a particular group

The Shrine of the Book

The Shrine of the Book is located at the Israel Museum in Jerusalem and houses the first seven scrolls discovered at Qumran, plus the finds from Cave 11. It has a large white dome representing the "sons of light." An adjacent, contrasting black wall symbolizes the "sons of darkness."

The Shrine of the Book at the Israel Museum in Jerusalem. The shape of the roof at this famous exhibit was designed to imitate the lids that covered the clay jars in which many of the ancient scrolls were stored.

Discovering the Dead Sea Scrolls—The Story in Pictures

(All photos courtesy of l'École biblique et archéologique française de Jérusalem.)

Roland de Vaux, director of the French Biblical and Archaeological School, and co-director of excavations at Qumran in the 1940s and 1950s, seen here on the left examining small fragments of broken earthenware known as shards.

Roland De Vaux, handling small finds from the field.

A fragment from the Dead Sea Scrolls consisting of portions of Genesis 32:3-7. This is among the earliest surviving biblical texts. It was apparently preserved by a member of the Qumran community, a Jewish sectarian group, ca. AD 50.

De Vaux and his excavation team in discussion with local Bedouin men.

Excavation worker holding a large storage jar with Hebrew inscription.

158 The Dead Sea Scrolls

Large storage jar exposed in its original setting at Khirbet Qumran.

Scroll jar, with small ceramic lamp and other pottery, following reconstruction.

Scene of Khirbet Qumran being excavated, looking east toward the Dead Sea.

The Dead Sea Scrolls and Jesus

The Dead Sea Scrolls also reveal how some Jewish religious communities interpreted the Law and the Prophets at around the same time as the life of Jesus. For example, in the War Scroll, we discover that the community at Qumran believed God was about to judge the "sons of darkness"—a group of Gentiles and Jews they thought had broken the covenant with God. The Qumran community believed that Jewish leaders in charge of the Temple in Jerusalem were corrupt and faced impending judgment. The New Testament depicts Jesus holding a similar view of the corrupt religious leadership in Jerusalem. Jesus told parables that condemned corruption and predicted the imminent destruction of Jerusalem's leaders (Luke 20:1-19; Matthew 23:13-39).

The Temple Scroll found at Qumran describes how the Temple in Jerusalem will be replaced and how the Law of Moses will be altered, in the spirit of the new era. In the New Testament stories, Jesus expands on laws from Deuteronomy in the Sermon on the Mount (Matthew 5:21-48) and predicts the destruction of the Temple in Jerusalem (Matthew 24:2; Mark 13:2; Luke 21:6). No direct link between the Qumran community and the early Christians has ever been established, but these and other examples suggest some parallels between the Dead Sea Scrolls and what Jesus is said to have taught.

On the other hand, the many purity laws from Qumran contrast sharply with what the New Testament says Jesus taught (Mark 7:1-9). One scroll recounts how the laws of purity followed by the Qumran community were much stricter than even those followed by the Jerusalem priests. While Jesus taught that the religious authorities had gone too far in such matters, focusing too much on outward ceremonies and rituals, the Essenes believed they had not gone far enough.

Why Is This Important?

The Dead Sea Scrolls have had an extraordinary impact on our understanding of the Bible and the way it came together. When we compare later manuscripts (such as the Leningrad Codex and the Aleppo Codex) with the scrolls, which were written roughly a millennium earlier, we see how carefully some of the texts that will become the Hebrew Bible have been preserved. We also find a window into the life of a devout Jewish community: how they lived, what they valued, what texts they considered sacred and authoritative. The Dead Sea Scrolls shed light on a moment when Judaism was changing, and they give context for some views and beliefs found in the New Testament.

Why Is This Interesting?

While it's important to see that most things in what will become the Old Testament texts have not changed from the time of the Dead Sea Scrolls until today, it's also important to grapple with the changes. Does the absence of Esther from the Dead Sea Scrolls tell us something? Or might an "Esther Scroll" (if there ever was one) have simply been lost or destroyed? One change seems clear: the people of Qumran appear to have regarded some texts as sacred that do not appear in our Hebrew Bible or Old Testament. The "canon" was still in formation at the time, as devout Jews sorted through the ancient stories and determined which were most important and which should have authority over their lives together.

Summary

The Dead Sea Scrolls are considered by more than a few scholars to be the greatest historical find of the 20th century. The scrolls show how one sect lived according to its beliefs while preserving Jewish holy books and other texts. They seem to confirm that today's Hebrew Bible, or what Christians call the Old Testament, is very close to the texts people were reading 2,000 years ago.

Digging Up Jerusalem

What Can the Stones of Jerusalem Tell Us about the Bible?

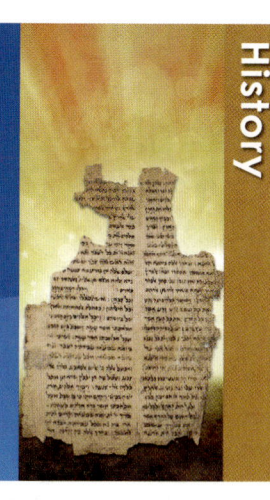

History

"For out of Zion shall go forth instruction, and the word of the LORD from Jerusalem."

Isaiah 2:3 (NRSV)

Why Is This Interesting

When reading Bible stories, we meet interesting characters from long ago and visit cities that have since crumbled into dust. It taxes our brains to think what these people and places might have looked like. But the ancient biblical accounts seem to come alive in vivid color when we visit Jerusalem. There visitors can literally touch the stones of the streets and buildings described in the stories of King David, Jeremiah, and Jesus.

Why Is This Important

The history of Jerusalem goes back many thousands of years. While the first signs of habitation in the extended region date to the Neolithic era, the first documented settlement at the site of Jerusalem is Chalcolithic. The first signs of a fortified city reach back as far as 1800 BC. Jerusalem has been besieged over twenty times, completely destroyed at least twice, and survives as a living testimony to the past. A mass of rich archaeological evidence is buried under the streets and buildings of the modern city. Piece by piece, archaeological excavations are shedding light on the historical accounts and biblical stories.

Vocabulary

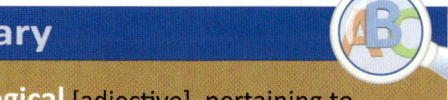

> **Archaeological** [adjective], pertaining to the study of past cultures through artifacts and relics

> **Excavation** [noun], a site where archaeologists unearth artifacts and relics

Tracing the Story of Jerusalem as Told in the Bible

The Hebrew Bible (the Old Testament) refers to Jerusalem more than 600 times. The New Testament mentions Jerusalem about 140 more times. Some verses refer to the city as a sacred place; in many verses Jerusalem is the site of warfare and bloodshed. In the verses listed below, we see a glimpse of the story of Jerusalem as told in the Bible:

Joshua 10:1

The first mention of Jerusalem is when Adoni-Zedek, king of Jerusalem, hears that Joshua has captured and completely destroyed Ai and killed its king, just as he had destroyed the town of Jericho and killed its king.

Joshua 15:63

The tribe of Judah cannot drive out the Jebusites, who live in the city of Jerusalem.

Judges 1:8, 21

The men of Judah attack and capture Jerusalem, setting the city on fire. The tribe of Benjamin, however, fails to drive out the Jebusites, and so the Jebusites live in Jerusalem alongside the people of Benjamin.

2 Samuel 5:6-7

King David, looking for a place to serve as his capital, leads his men to Jerusalem to fight against the Jebusites. The Jebusites taunt David, saying, "You will not come in here, even the blind and the lame will turn you back" 2 Samuel 5:6 (NRSV). According to this verse, the Jebusites believe there is no way for David to get into Jerusalem. But David captures the fortress of Zion (Jerusalem of that time, south of the current Temple Mount area), which also received the name City of David.

1 Kings 6:1

King Solomon begins to build the First Jewish Temple in Jerusalem during the fourth year of his reign.

1 Kings 8:1

King Solomon summons to Jerusalem the elders of Israel and all the heads of the tribes—the leaders of the ancestral families of the Israelites. They are to bring the Ark of the Covenant to the Temple from its location in the City of David.

1 Kings 14:25-26

In the fifth year of King Rehoboam's reign, King Shishak of Egypt attacks Jerusalem. He ransacks the Temple treasury and the royal palace; he steals everything, including the gold shields Solomon had made.

View of the hills surrounding Jerusalem. In the distance to the left is the suburb of Mevaseret Zion, about five miles west of Jerusalem, which gets its name from Isaiah 40:9, meaning "bringing good tidings to Zion."

2 Kings 18:14–19:36

The Assyrian Empire rules the area, including the cities of Judah. Sennacherib, the king of Assyria, confronts King Hezekiah in Jerusalem, while his army is nearby at Lachish. According to another biblical mention of the story, an angel enters the Assyrian camp and kills 185,000 Assyrian soldiers. When the surviving Assyrians awake the next morning and find the corpses, they break camp and return to their homeland.

2 Kings 21:7

King Manasseh makes a carved image of Asherah, a goddess. He sets it up in the Temple, the very place that, according to the Bible, YHWH had chosen for his own name.

2 Kings 23:29-30

King Josiah and his army march out to fight Pharaoh Necho, king of Egypt, but Necho kills Josiah when they meet at Megiddo. Josiah's officers take his body back in a chariot to Jerusalem and bury him in his own tomb.

2 Kings 24:10-17

During King Jehoiachin's reign, King Nebuchadnezzar of Babylon lays siege to Jerusalem. Then Jehoiachin surrenders to the Babylonians. Nebuchadnezzar strips away all the treasures from the Temple and the royal palace. He also leads Jehoiachin away as a captive to Babylon, along with all of Jerusalem's elite.

2 Kings 25:1-2, 8-11

During the ninth year of King Zedekiah's reign, King Nebuchadnezzar of Babylon leads his army in an attack against Jerusalem. They surround the city and lay siege to it. Jerusalem is kept under siege for two years. On about August 14 of that year, the Babylonian army burns down the Temple, the royal palace, and all the houses. Then they tear down the walls of Jerusalem on every side.

Most of Jerusalem's Old City walls were built in the 16th century by the Turkish sultan Suleiman the Magnificent. However, Suleiman himself built them on even more ancient walls. On the southeastern side, the walls are older, parts of them dating to the Second Temple period and even earlier. Of the gates, one of them, the Golden Gate, is sealed.

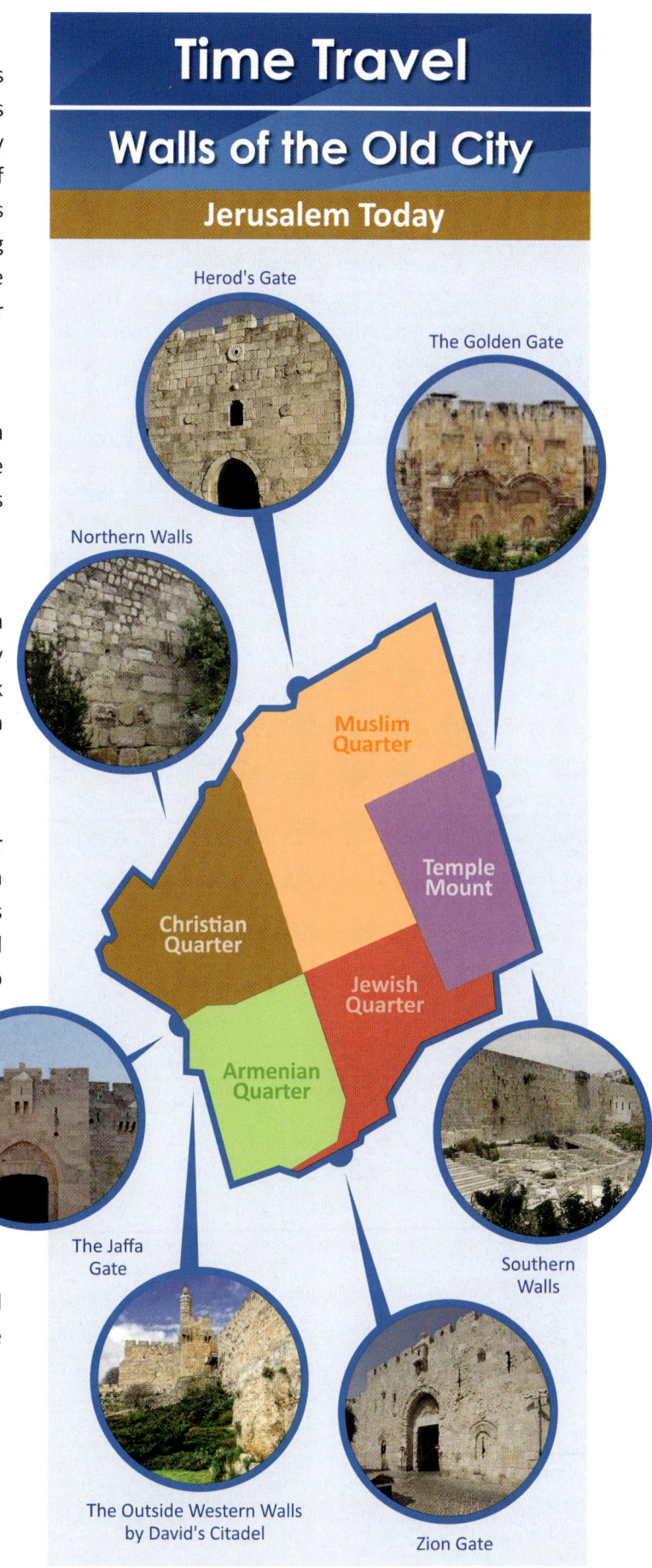

Time Travel
Walls of the Old City
Jerusalem Today

- Herod's Gate
- The Golden Gate
- Northern Walls
- Muslim Quarter
- Temple Mount
- Christian Quarter
- Jewish Quarter
- Armenian Quarter
- The Jaffa Gate
- Southern Walls
- The Outside Western Walls by David's Citadel
- Zion Gate

Digging Up Jerusalem 163

King Solomon Building the First Temple

In the biblical account, King Solomon builds the First Temple close to the royal palace. Archaeological excavations revealed relics at the foot of the Temple Mount, in the area called Ophel located between the Temple and the royal palace. Amongst the findings were a portion of city wall and gatehouse, which some suggest are remains from Solomon's First Temple (1 Kings 5 and 7). While no direct remains of the First Temple have been found to date, based on the findings around the wall, it can be dated to the beginning of the ninth century BC. This is a possible date for the reign of King Solomon. No direct evidence links it to the wall mentioned in 1 Kings 3:1, though the remains of the Second Temple at that location often biased observers in that direction.

Several inscriptions have also been discovered that may be associated in some way with Solomon's Temple, or they may be examples of the modern forgery trade. One of the most famous is a stone tablet known as the Jehoash Inscription. The tablet may be an account of King Jehoash's repairs to the Temple (2 Kings 12:6-7). However, the authenticity of this inscription is debated. One major investigation concluded the tablet is a forgery.

Another article is an ivory-colored piece of hippopotamus bone shaped like a pomegranate that may have been attached to the staff of a priest who served in the Temple. While many scholars consider the item historical, and the most recent scholarship leans towards the authenticity of the writing, the debate continues.

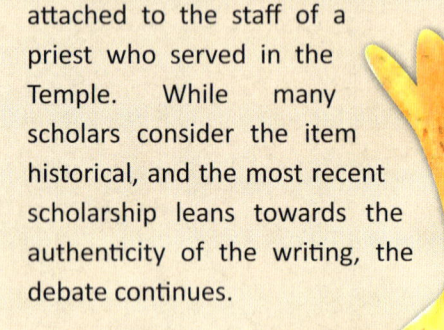

Ivory-colored piece of hippopotamus bone shaped like a pomegranate. Israel Museum, Jerusalem.

The City of David

Excavations on the southwestern slope of the Kidron Valley have uncovered structures that date to the earliest period of Israelite habitation. It was King David, according to the Bible, who captured the area, then called Jebus, from the Jebusites (a Canaanite people) and used their fortifications and water systems. A stepped-stone structure, possibly Jebusite, perhaps served as a retaining wall for a large building, perhaps related to David or Solomon's building activities. Israeli archaeologist Eilat Mazar reported in 2005 that she may have found parts of his palace, buried beneath later constructions. What came to be called the City of David is a fortified city, dating back to about 1800 BC. Its Canaanite fortress would have projected power over the region.

Archaeological digging in the City of David. According to the Bible, King David conquered this original Jebusite stronghold (ca. 1000 BC) and turned it into his capital city, Jerusalem.

Vocabulary

> **Fortifications** [noun]
barricades constructed for defense

Does an Ancient Clay Seal Refer to an Official in the Book of Jeremiah?

Archaeologists working at the City of David in 1982 excavated the "House of the Bullae," a home that was burned when the Babylonian army destroyed Jerusalem around 586 BC. The fire baked and preserved more than 50 bullae (clay lumps that are stamped and used to seal important documents or parcels).

The seals refer to names mentioned in the Bible, especially the Book of Jeremiah. One bulla now displayed at the Israel Museum, thought to have come from the House of the Bullae, features the stamp of Gemaryahu, son of Shaphan. In the Book of Jeremiah, Baruch, Jeremiah's scribe, is said to read from Jeremiah's scroll "in the house of the LORD, in the chamber of Gemariah son of Shaphan the secretary" (Jeremiah 36:10, NRSV). Other seals excavated from the "House of the Bullae" refer to other biblical people, such as Hilkiah, a high priest (2 Kings 22:4).

Bulla bearing the Hebrew inscription "belonging to Gemaryahu ben Shaphan," City of David ('House of the Bullae') Iron Age II from the IAA.

Why Is This Interesting

Inscriptions and other discovered artifacts shed light on the biblical narrative and help bring the ancient world to life.

Sources of Information about the First Temple

We are just scratching the surface of biblical artifacts from Jerusalem, but already we have multiple streams of information providing a richer picture, for instance, of the biblical prophet Jeremiah. He lived in the area of Jerusalem at about the same time where there is also extrabiblical evidence for a priesthood there. From the "stories" as well as the "stones," pictures of the Temple and its priesthood emerge.

Sources from the First Temple Period (ca. 1025 BC–586 BC)

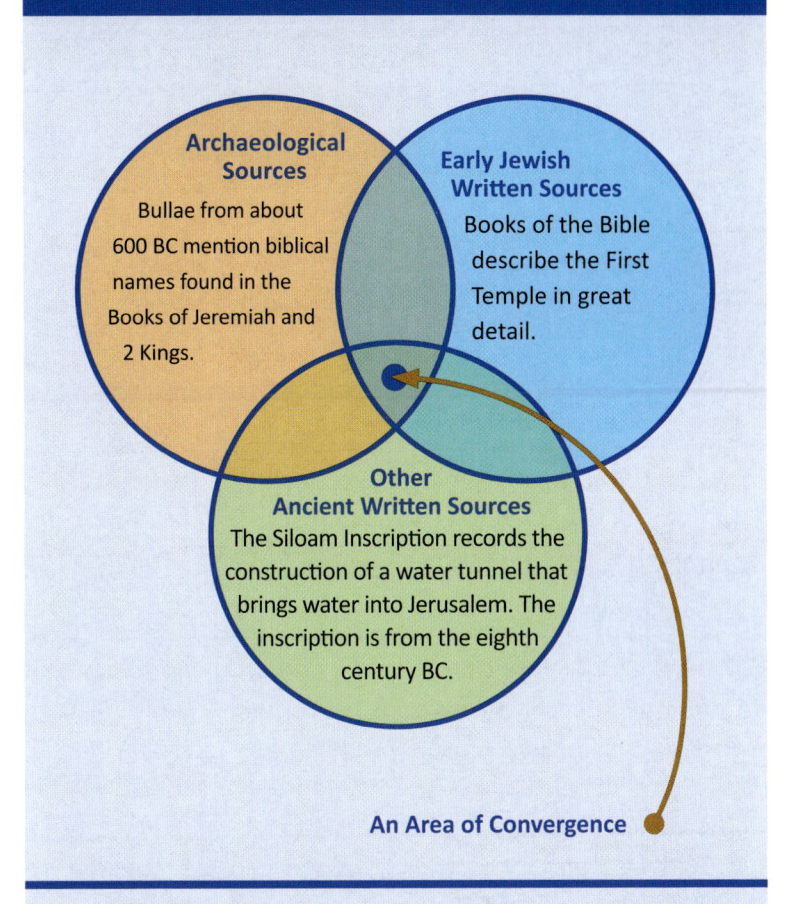

Archaeological Sources: Bullae from about 600 BC mention biblical names found in the Books of Jeremiah and 2 Kings.

Early Jewish Written Sources: Books of the Bible describe the First Temple in great detail.

Other Ancient Written Sources: The Siloam Inscription records the construction of a water tunnel that brings water into Jerusalem. The inscription is from the eighth century BC.

An Area of Convergence

Scholars examine, evaluate, and compare different sources of evidence when researching any historical period. The Venn diagram above helps us visualize how different sources of evidence for the First Temple overlap. Biblical books provide one source of evidence. As Israel's narratives and histories, these books provide us with their own understanding of their past. A second source of evidence is extrabiblical texts. These texts include those from Israel's neighbors and Hebrew texts and inscriptions that were not included in the Bible. The third source of evidence in our Venn diagram is archaeology. Artifacts found in excavations give scholars an idea of the physical, or material, culture, including names and offices. Taking these three sources of evidence together, scholars can identify what information is found in only one source and what information is found in multiple sources. An enormous amount of evidence from the First Temple period keeps scholars busily engaged in reconstructing its history.

Digging Up Jerusalem | 165

Do the Stones Tell a Story?

Some of the stones in the eastern retaining wall of the present-day Temple Mount are from the time of Maccabean rule (about 140 BC). Additionally, excavations have found several buildings from this time under a nearby parking lot. After the Roman conquest of Jerusalem in 63 BC, Herod the Great significantly improved and enlarged the Second Temple starting in about 20 BC. This long project of rebuilding was still going on, according to the New Testament, at the time of Jesus and his disciples (John 2:20). The Romans destroyed it in AD 70 while putting down a Jewish revolt during the First Jewish-Roman War.

Discovering the Tomb of Shebna

Adjacent to the modern area of the Western Wall, excavations have uncovered the remains of an administrative building containing a number of bullae and similar inscribed stone seals from the eighth century BC. This was apparently part of the royal court that was in that area during the time of the First Temple.

Modern houses on the eastern ridge of the Kidron Valley, known today as the Jerusalem neighborhood of Silwan, were built above tombs from the First Temple period. Scholars have argued that one inscription on a tomb there refers to Shebna, a royal steward. This otherwise obscure figure was condemned by name by the prophet Isaiah for building a magnificent burial plot for himself (Isaiah 22:15-17). Ironically, he may have achieved his coveted prestige in a most unlikely way, by leaving behind an inscription that illuminates the biblical text. Jerusalem was resettled, and a Second Temple was built around 516 BC, after the Jews' return from the Babylonian exile.

Eyewitnesses from 2,000 Years Ago

Many archaeologists hope to find evidence from the First Temple. However, they have never been able to dig directly for remains of this Temple. This is due to the sensitive nature of excavating in and around Jerusalem, where the sacred claims of many cultures and religions overlap in both time and space. In the 1960s, excavations began at the foot of the Temple Mount along the western and southern retaining walls. The findings of these excavations have confirmed some of the statements from first-century eyewitnesses to the Second Temple, such as Flavius Josephus and rabbinical authors. Several ancient quarries have also been discovered, containing still-unfinished blocks of stone that may have been intended for use in the Second Temple.

A paved street that ran along the Temple area was uncovered and has been left as it was found. The pavement was likely damaged by giant blocks of stones falling from the Temple walls during its destruction by the Romans in AD 70.

166 Digging Up Jerusalem

Josephus Describes the Sacking of Jerusalem

Titus Flavius Josephus was a first-century Roman-Jewish writer and historian. His most important surviving works are *The Jewish War* and *Antiquities of the Jews*.

"So the Romans being now become masters of the walls, they both placed their ensigns upon the towers, and made joyful acclamations for the victory they had gained, as having found the end of this war much lighter than its beginning; for when they had gotten upon the last wall, without any bloodshed, they could hardly believe what they found to be true; but seeing nobody to oppose them, they stood in doubt what such an unusual solitude could mean. But when they went in numbers into the lanes of the city, with their swords drawn, they slew those whom they overtook, without mercy, and set fire to the houses whither the Jews were fled, and burnt every soul in them, and laid waste a great many of the rest."

The Wars of the Jews, Book 6, Chapter 8.

All that exists of an ancient staircase and bridge today is Robinson's Arch, a stone abutment seen here that protrudes from the western retaining wall of the Temple Mount. At the time of Jesus this area would have served as one of the main passageways for people going in and out of the Temple precincts.

Great Staircases

One of the architectural features of the Second Temple was a great staircase which brought worshipers from Jerusalem's lower market area up to the Temple precincts. (A small remaining portion of the staircase is known today as Robinson's Arch, named after the 19th-century scholar Edward Robinson.) In soil sifted from the bottom of this staircase, a small clay seal was found with an Aramaic inscription. Scholars disagree on its reading. Some believe it said "Pure to God" in Aramaic. The Temple priests would likely have carried such a seal to identify items qualified as "pure" for use in worship.

Other Aspects of the Second Temple

At the southern wall, another monumental staircase was discovered. Apparently it began near the Pool of Siloam in the Kidron Valley and carried crowds of worshipers and priests up through the Huldah Gates and onto the Temple Mount. In addition, numerous *mikvot* (ritual immersion baths) were unearthed. Such baths were likely used for ritual purification prior to entering the holy Temple precincts. (Many religiously observant Jews still use *mikvot* today for purposes of ritual purification.) These uncovered baths feature distinct staircases with a dividing wall in the center to keep those entering (considered "unclean" and therefore not ready for Temple rituals) from having contact with those leaving (considered "clean" and ready to enter the Temple).

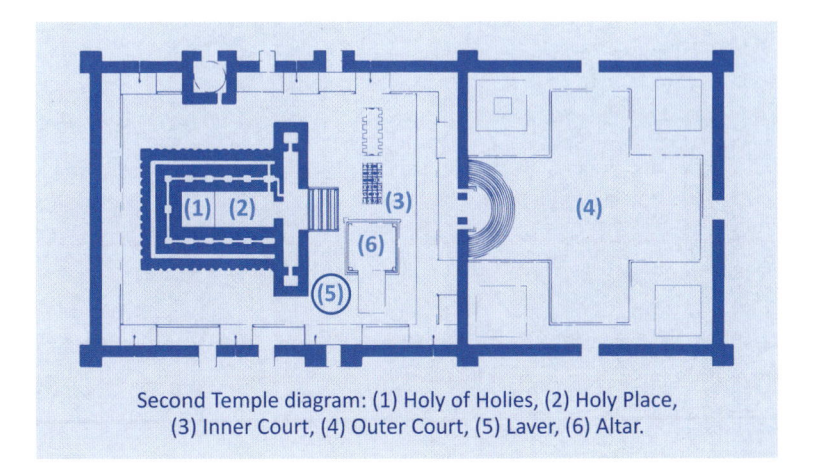

Second Temple diagram: (1) Holy of Holies, (2) Holy Place, (3) Inner Court, (4) Outer Court, (5) Laver, (6) Altar.

About 200 yards to the northeast of the Huldah Gates was another entrance to the Temple Mount from the eastern side, called the Beautiful Gate (and later the Golden Gate). The gate visible today is from the 16th century, and stands atop an earlier gate from the New Testament era, discovered by James Fleming in 1969. Considerable debate remains whether the Beautiful Gate, noted in Acts 3 in the healing of the lame man, was in the outer wall or closer to the Temple.

Digging Up Jerusalem

Why Is This Interesting

The inscription on one of the stones discovered in the Jerusalem area appears to direct the priests where to stand when blowing the trumpets, signaling the beginning of the Sabbath. Another find was the lid of a stone sarcophagus, engraved with the words "son of the high priest," the chief religious leader who presided over worship in the Temple.

The Hebrew inscription reads, "For the place of trumpeting to ..." This is thought to have been the corner railing located at the top of the southwest corner of the Temple Mount.
The image below shows another angle on the same artifact. The full inscription (before a piece was broken off) might have read, "For the place of trumpeting toward the Temple."

Because of the sensitive nature of the area, excavations around the Temple Mount have been limited. While to date no direct physical evidence of the First Temple has been found, some discovered artifacts point to the existence of the Second Temple and its priesthood. For example, the inscription above reads in Hebrew "... son of the high priest."

Vocabulary

> **Sarcophagus** [noun], a stone coffin

Jesus Drives Out Merchants

Archaeologists have uncovered a stretch of an ancient street that ran along the retaining wall of the Temple, now called the Western Wall or Kotel. In antiquity this street was lined with shops. Remains of these shops have been found with coins and other items used by merchants. In these shops, Jews likely bought sacrificial animals for the Temple. The four New Testament books known as the Gospels indicate that the spread of these shops angered Jesus; he overturned their tables and drove merchants out on two separate occasions. Not only were the merchants not maintaining a level of reverence appropriate for the Temple environs, but they had also taken over an area reserved for non-Jews to gather near the Temple. What should have been a "house of prayer," the gospel writers quote Jesus as saying, was instead being used as "a den of robbers" Mark 11:17 (NRSV).

Model of the Second Temple and its surroundings looking from the east. The stone towers on the upper right were part of a large structure known as Antonia's Fortress. This is also a likely area of Pontius Pilate's palace in Jerusalem and of the Praetorium, or Judgment Hall, where Jesus is said to have stood for final sentencing before Pilate, the military governor, who was appointed by Rome (Matthew 27:27-31).

Why Is This Important

Near these same shops was found a large inscribed stone that had been pushed down from the top of the wall. Lying on this ancient street were many tons of the building stones of the western side of the Temple complex. These stones were likely pushed here by Roman soldiers during their assault on the Temple in AD 70. In some places, archaeologists left this stone-littered street just as they had found it, to show modern visitors the magnitude of the devastation.

Digging Up Jerusalem

Treasures in the Soil

Coins minted during the First Jewish Revolt (AD 66–70) offer additional evidence of these final days of Jerusalem before its devastation by Rome. The coins contain inscriptions such as "Holy Jerusalem" and "Freedom of Zion." Scores of iron arrowheads used in the Jewish war against the Romans have been found in the ground near the Temple Mount. Other discovered objects include a bulla which scholars believe would have read "Belonging to Gaalyahu son of Imer," of the Imer family of priests.

Other artifacts of Jerusalem's history that relate to the New Testament are the burial box (ossuary) of "Joseph son of Caiaphas," and an inscription from Pontius Pilate, the Roman prefect who governed Judea from AD 26 to 36. In the New Testament account, a high priest named Caiaphas presides over the Jewish religious trial of Jesus, and Pilate presides over the Roman civil trial with the power to deliver and execute his death sentence.

In 1961 a stone tablet was unearthed bearing a famous name: "Pontius Pilate, the Prefect [governor] of Judea." The stone comes from the steps of the Roman theater in Caesarea and provides rare archaeological support for a ruler named both in the New Testament and in the writings of historians Josephus and Tacitus. Israel Museum, Jerusalem.

The fire that burned this fragmentary bulla black also baked and preserved it. The clay seal impression would have been used to seal a document or parcel. Only a part of the bulla remains, but scholars have reconstructed the partial paleo-Hebrew text to read "(Belonging) to Gaalyahu son of Imer." The house of Imer was a well-known priestly family from the seventh and sixth centuries BC. If the scholars are correct in their reconstruction, this artifact could be the earliest written item from the First Temple period to come from the Temple area itself. Temple Mount Sifting Project, Jerusalem.

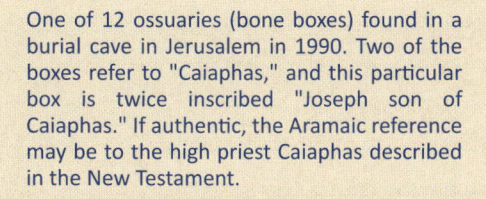

One of 12 ossuaries (bone boxes) found in a burial cave in Jerusalem in 1990. Two of the boxes refer to "Caiaphas," and this particular box is twice inscribed "Joseph son of Caiaphas." If authentic, the Aramaic reference may be to the high priest Caiaphas described in the New Testament.

Interesting Archaeological Trivia

● At the end of the 1967 Arab-Israeli War, the Temple Scroll, one of the Dead Sea Scrolls, was found at an antiquities dealer's home in nearby Bethlehem. More than 2,000 years old, the scroll describes areas of increasing holiness as one approaches the Holy of Holies, where the presence of God was to be found.

● There are known cases in modern Jerusalem where homes were likely built in part with stones that once formed part of the Second Temple. Also, pillars from the Royal Stoa that surrounded Herod's Temple complex were reused to build the Néa Church (AD 543), one of early Christendom's famous churches in Jerusalem. Based on its huge dimensions (approx. 70,000 square feet), the Néa Church was able to hold more than 8,000 worshipers.

● Archaeologists excavating the home of a prosperous family found an iron spear and human remains on the floor. Other artifacts, such as coins scattered on the ground from AD 67 to 69, strongly suggest that the young woman was a victim of the Roman destruction of Jerusalem in AD 70.

● A bone box (ossuary) that may have held the bones of James, the brother of Jesus and leader of the early church in Jerusalem, was once used as a flower box by an unwitting Jewish mother. Many scholars believe that the inscription was added later, but almost no one disputes the authenticity of the ossuary being from the first century.

This 2,700-year-old personal seal was set in a ring and used for signing letters. Clara Amit, courtesy of the Israel Antiquities Authority.

● The Jerusalem city and streets of the time Jesus is thought to have lived are now more than 30 feet below the ground of the present-day city of Jerusalem, mostly buried under the rubble of the ages.

● The ancient Pool of Siloam, where the New Testament recounts Jesus performing a miracle (John 9:7), was lost for almost 2,000 years. Only recently was it discovered by accident during a construction project. Only half of the site has been uncovered. The other half belongs to the Greek Orthodox Church.

Vocabulary

> **Royal Stoa** [noun], a grand covered portico that existed later in the Second Temple period

Summary

The artifacts and other archaeological findings profiled in this chapter shed light on the biblical narrative. However, they represent only a small fraction of ancient Jerusalem. Experts believe that a vast quantity of artifacts remains hidden below the ground. Only through the careful work of archaeologists will we become even better informed about the distant past. Even today, hundreds of scholars are engaged in research that will enhance our understanding of the biblical stories and the historical setting in which they were told. Jerusalem, sacred to three religions, is a storehouse of ancient artifacts, but the work of excavation is painstaking and meticulous. In the lifetimes of the students reading this book, many more discoveries will be made, illuminating the stories of the Bible in new ways.

Education

Did the Bible Play a Role in the Development of Public Education?

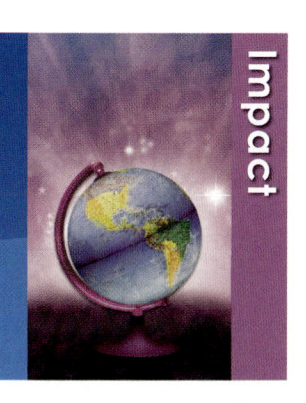

Impact

"Train the young in the way they should go; even when old, they will not swerve from it"

Proverbs 22:6 (NABRE)

Few Readers and Few Books

If you lived anywhere in Europe about 600 years ago, you probably would not have been able to read the words on this page. Literacy (the ability to read and write) was not common. Books had to be copied by hand, which made them extremely expensive. Few families could afford to own them. Even Bibles were few and far between, found only in the wealthiest houses and the largest cathedrals. Ever since the fall of the western Roman Empire, literacy rates in Europe had been very low, with notable exceptions like the Muslim cities of Toledo and Cordoba. They became not only Spanish centers of learning but wielded influence over much of Europe through the ancient texts they preserved. This began to change in the 1450s with the development in Europe of the movable type printing press, a revolutionary innovation in technology that made it faster and cheaper to produce books. As the cost of publishing decreased, the availability of books and other reading material increased, and the ability to read became more important and eventually more common.

There were other factors as well. Early in the 16th century, the Christian church in Europe began a dramatic transformation. Martin Luther (1483–1546) led a popular movement within the church that pressed for numerous reforms. Eventually this caused a rupture between the Roman Catholic Church and emerging "Protestant" groups. Protestants especially believed that people should be able to read the Bible for themselves. Bibles, until that time, were typically available in Latin, the language of the Western church. Luther devoted many years to translating the Bible into German, a project he finally completed in 1534. Even then, very few people could read, but the barriers to reading were beginning to fall.

Vocabulary

> **Protestant Reformation** [noun]
a religious movement in the 16th century that set out to achieve reform in the Roman Catholic Church and led to the establishment of various Protestant denominations

Jewish boys with their teacher in Uzbekistan, by Sergei M. Prokudin-Gorskii, ca. 1910, Library of Congress, Washington, DC.

Talmud Tora, 1937, Russia. Jewish heder, an elementary school where Jewish children are taught to read the Hebrew Bible and other books in Hebrew.

Vocabulary

> **Antiquity** [noun], ancient times, especially the times before the Middle Ages

Ancient Origins of Bible-Based Education

While many people in the West were illiterate and couldn't read the Bible themselves, Jewish rabbis since late antiquity had insisted that families in their communities (including all the various streams of Judaism) should educate their children about what's in the Bible. The importance of this type of instruction is clearly communicated in the Hebrew Bible and the New Testament.

- "Take to heart these words which I command you today. Keep repeating them to your children. Recite them when you are at home and when you are away, when you lie down and when you get up" Deuteronomy 6:6-7 (NABRE).

- "All scripture is inspired by God and is useful for teaching, for refutation, for correction, and for training in righteousness ..." 2 Timothy 3:16 (NABRE).

Some of the sayings and practical advice of the great rabbis who taught between about 200 BC and AD 200, including Simon the Just, Hillel, Gamaliel (mentioned in Acts 5:34-39 and Acts 22:3), and many others, said the same. Shortly before AD 200 these sayings were written down in a famous Jewish book of wisdom called *Pirkei Avot*, translated loosely as *Ethics of the Fathers*. Among many other ethical teachings, *the Pirkei Avot* says that:

- Boys should start learning the Bible when they are five years old (5:22).
- The dignity of your student should be as precious to you as your own (4:12).
- Teachers should not be too strict with their students (2:5).
- Do not look at the vessel, but at what it contains (4:20).

Perhaps it's not surprising that a community so devoted to a written text should place such a strong emphasis on education, scholarship, and the ability to read.

Centers of Education in the Ancient World

The East had centers of learning in ancient times, from imperial academies that trained state officials (such as Taixue in Beijing, China) to centers of religious study (such as Nalanda in India, which may have housed as many as 2,000 teachers and 10,000 students). The Western world also had institutions of higher learning that flourished in the ancient world, in Eastern Christendom after the fall of the Roman Empire, and then again in Western Europe in the High Middle Ages:

The Academy and the Lyceum (Athens, Greece):

The Greek philosopher Plato (ca. 428–348 BC) founded the famous Academy in Athens, which would pass down Platonic teaching for hundreds of years. It was revived in AD 410 to serve another school of thought called Neoplatonism. Also in Athens, the Lyceum was a "gymnasium" (a center for physical exercise, military training, and intellectual development) probably founded in the sixth or fifth century BC. It became most associated with another great philosopher, Aristotle, a tutor of Alexander the Great, when he established a formal school there.

The Musaeum (Alexandria, Egypt):

The Musaeum was founded in the fourth or third century BC, and was dedicated to the Muses. In addition to the famed Library of Alexandria, the Musaeum included a zoo, garden, lecture halls, rooms, and a communal dining hall for scholars. Among the scholars who studied at the Musaeum were Euclid and Archimedes, who are known as the fathers of geometry and engineering, respectively.

Pandidakterion (Constantinople, now Istanbul, Turkey):

Constantinople was the center of the Byzantine Empire and Eastern Christianity. The Pandidakterion, or the "University of Constantinople," was founded in 425 by Byzantine emperor Theodosius II. The government appointed and paid thirty-one teachers. Some taught philosophy and law, but twenty-eight of those professors were appointed to teach Latin and Greek grammar and rhetoric. It was in operation for a few hundred years, even though it was never officially a university.

The Academy of Gondishapur (modern Iran):

The Academy of Gondishapur was established in the fourth century AD, and operated until the ninth century. It became one of the most important centers of medicine in the ancient world, and housed scholars from many regions. A hospital and library were added to the institution, furthering its prestige.

Cathedral Schools and Monastic Schools (Europe):

Prominent cathedrals and monasteries developed schools for training priests and church leaders. They studied theology and philosophy as well as the sciences and ancient languages. As a later chapter will explain, these schools evolved into modern universities in Italy, England, France, Spain, and England in the 11th–13th centuries.

Today, we generally assume that everyone should be able to read. This was not always the case. For children who would operate farms or make shoes or build furniture, it was not clear (especially when books were so rare) that learning to read was a smart use of time. Still, the development of learning and scholarship at centers such as the ones listed above indicate how these societies valued the discovery and preservation of knowledge.

Byzantine society had a type of educational system for children, which helped establish widespread literacy among the population. These educational commitments utilized the same biblical texts studied in this curriculum, and their teaching became part of the culture associated later with Orthodox Christianity. When modern education systems began to develop in the West, they included a biblical emphasis. The study of the Bible was central to cathedral schools, monastic schools, and the original universities. The desire to be able to read the Bible was one significant influence in the spread of education and literacy.

Vocabulary

> **Rhetoric** [noun]
the art of speaking or writing effectively

This monument marks Plymouth Rock in Plymouth, Massachusetts. The spot is not far from where the first Pilgrim scouting party disembarked on December 21, 1620. Pilgrims and Puritans strongly emphasized education, in part because they wanted their children to be able to read and study the Bible.

A rural schoolhouse in Port Sanilac, Michigan. Often eight grades of children would learn together in one room, taught by a single teacher. Into the early 20th century, Bible lessons were included in public education in many regions of America.

Vocabulary

> **Morality** [noun]
conformity to the standards of right conduct

The Bible and Education in Early America

When the Pilgrims landed at Plymouth Rock in 1620, only a small proportion of English children could read. In fact, few attended school at all. Education had been highly prized in England, but mostly reserved for the upper classes. For the Puritans in New England, however, education (at least for white males) was considered so important that it was written into law. They wanted their citizens to be able to read the Bible. In 1647, the Puritans enacted a law in the Massachusetts Bay Colony requiring all children to attend school. The law stated that "that old deluder Satan" wanted to deny people "the knowledge of Scripture." The Puritans believed that establishing education would ensure the community could read the Bible and thus thwart Satan's plans. In any township with at least 50 households, the law required that a person should be appointed to teach the children to read and write. The colony fined any community that failed to provide these educational services. Other colonies enacted similar laws. They were not always enforced, and education was not equal for all. Girls were mostly educated in the home. But a trend had begun: public education would become a central part of American life.

One-room schoolhouses were among the first things settlers constructed in their new towns and villages (along with jails, saloons, and churches) as the nation spread westward. Article 3 of the Northwest Ordinance, an act of the Congress of the Confederation in 1787, asserted: "Religion, morality, and knowledge, being necessary to good government and the happiness of mankind, schools and the means of education shall forever be encouraged." Early state constitutions, such as that of Ohio in 1803, adopted nearly identical language linking learning and literacy to religion and morality. Circumstances were much the same in Canada. By the end of the 18th century, North America had one of the most literate populations in the world.

The New England Primer

The desire to read the Bible inspired many people to want to learn to read and to teach their children to read as well. It also shaped the way in which reading was taught in America. *The New England Primer* is an excellent example.

The earliest English settlers in America used schoolbooks they had brought from England. In the 1680s, however, publishers in Boston began to issue a textbook adapted for the colonies, called *the New England Primer*. Continually reissued in many editions in the 1700s, the primer taught the basics of a classical education as well as Christian character and Bible reading. Various versions of the primer included Bible passages from the King James Version, the "Lord's Prayer" (Matthew 6:9-13), and summaries of basic Christian belief called *catechisms*. Bible stories were rendered in simple rhymes, such as "In Adam's fall, we sinned all." *The New England Primer* gives us a glimpse inside early colonial schoolhouses and shows us how deeply the Bible was embedded in American education. Scholars estimate that 2–3 million copies of the primer were sold over the course of 150 years. Although it was eventually replaced, *The New England Primer* shaped the way many generations of Americans learned to read and think.

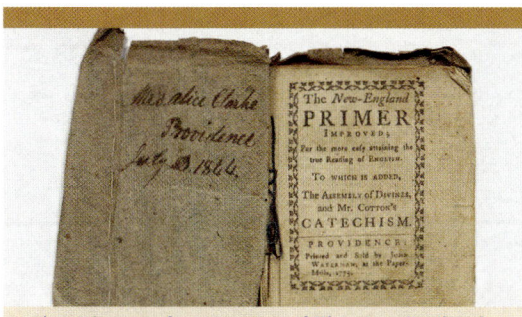

The title page for a version of **The New England Primer**, 1775. Courtesy of the Watkinson Library at Trinity College, Hartford, Connecticut.

Vocabulary

> **Primer** [noun], an elementary book for teaching children to read

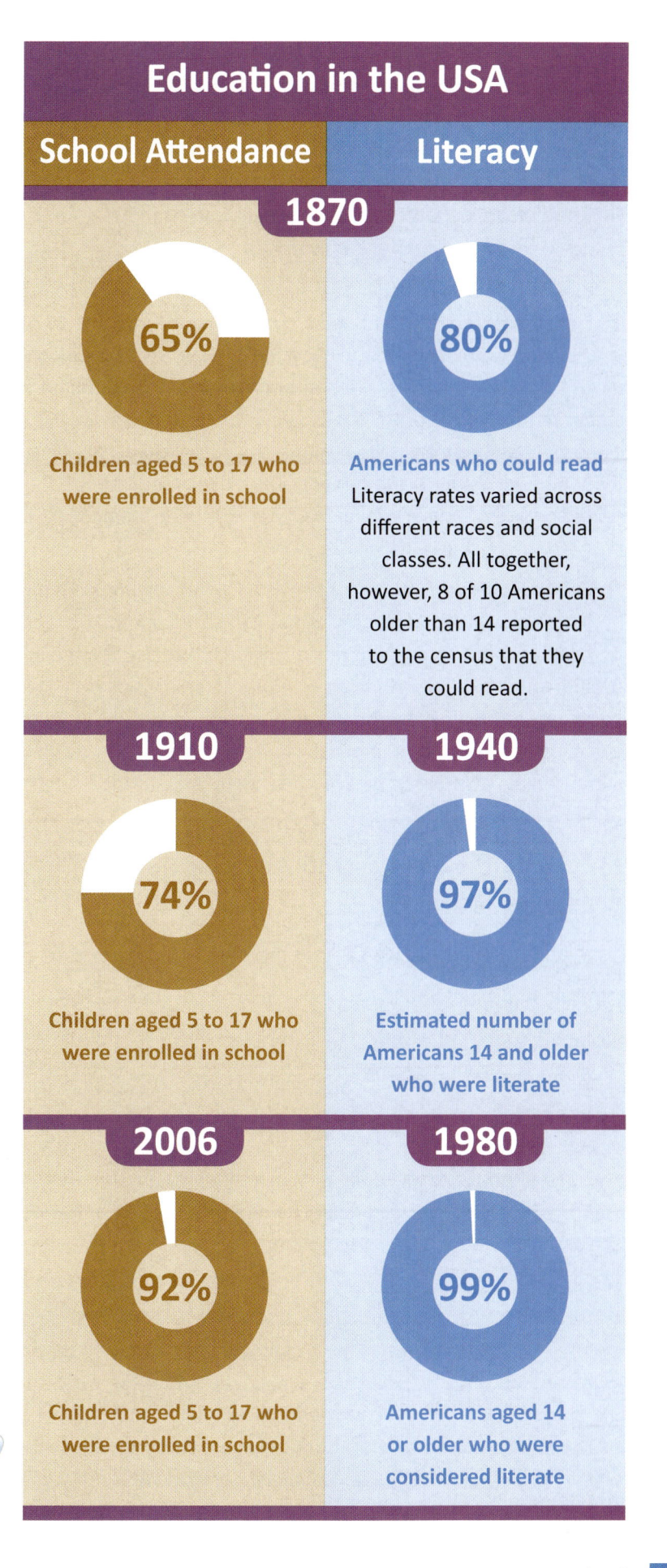

Education in the USA

School Attendance | Literacy

1870

- **65%** — Children aged 5 to 17 who were enrolled in school
- **80%** — Americans who could read. Literacy rates varied across different races and social classes. All together, however, 8 of 10 Americans older than 14 reported to the census that they could read.

1910 | **1940**

- **74%** — Children aged 5 to 17 who were enrolled in school
- **97%** — Estimated number of Americans 14 and older who were literate

2006 | **1980**

- **92%** — Children aged 5 to 17 who were enrolled in school
- **99%** — Americans aged 14 or older who were considered literate

Establishing the Universities

In 1636, the Puritans founded the first formal institution of higher learning in the American colonies. Originally called the New College, it was renamed Harvard College in 1639 and eventually called Harvard University. This launched three centuries of intense competition among other Christian groups and denominations to found their own colleges and universities.

Of the nine "Colonial Colleges"—institutions of higher learning that were chartered and granting college degrees before 1776—each had some degree of Christian affiliation. The College of William and Mary was created in order to prepare Anglican students for ordination in the Church of England. The College of New Jersey (which later became Princeton University) was founded and led by Presbyterians. The Collegiate School (later Yale) originally focused on theology and biblical languages in order to train Congregationalist pastors.

The least sectarian may have been the College of Philadelphia (later the University of Pennsylvania), which Benjamin Franklin founded in order to educate not only clergy but also leaders of business and government. Even here, however, the college grew out of an earlier effort by the famed preacher George Whitefield, and its trustees and first provost (an Anglican priest) disagreed with Franklin and assembled a curriculum that trained young Christian men for ministry.

Early American Colleges With Religious Origins

Institution	Year Founded	Institution	Year Founded
Harvard	1636	Columbia	1754
William and Mary	1693	Brown	1764
Yale	1701	Rutgers	1766
Pennsylvania	1740	Dartmouth	1769
Princeton	1746		

The first Catholic institution of higher learning in the United States, Georgetown University (founded in 1789), followed shortly after the American Revolution.

Many of these schools later cut their denominational ties or relaxed their religious requirements, especially in the 20th century. Still, the desire to train young men in the educated interpretation of the Bible was a major impetus for many of the United States' most renowned educational institutions. The Bible is a part of the story of the founding of these colleges and universities that have gone on to change the world in remarkable ways.

Summary

Cultures shaped by the Bible have shown a marked interest in literacy and education. There are other examples around the world of texts, such as *The Analects of Confucius*, that inspired great concern with education. And there were renowned centers of learning in the classical world. It remains true, however, that the Bible itself, and the desire to read the Bible, has spurred growth in education in many nations and cultures. Especially as books became cheaper and more common, literacy and education rates climbed steeply in nations influenced by the Bible, such as England.

Jewish and Christian communities are examples of how the Bible shaped education over time. So, too, are institutions of higher learning where the Bible was a central part of the course of study. Likewise, are the simple schoolhouses of the American colonies, where public education developed in part to encourage the study of the Bible and where the textbooks drew heavily on Bible stories and teachings.

Later, public schools in the United States would become increasingly neutral on religious matters, accommodating people of all beliefs. Still, the history is important. The Bible and its influence are a part of the story of how education developed in many places around the world, including the United States.

Vocabulary

> **Denomination** [noun]
a particular religious group, especially among Protestants

Early America's Charters and Laws

What Impact Did the Bible Have on the Laws in Colonial America?

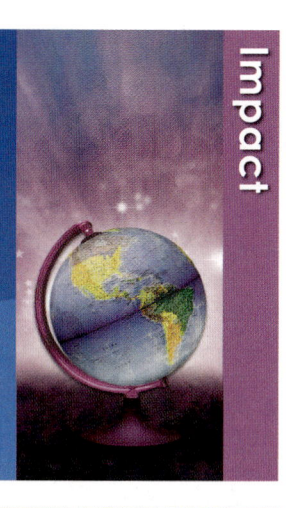

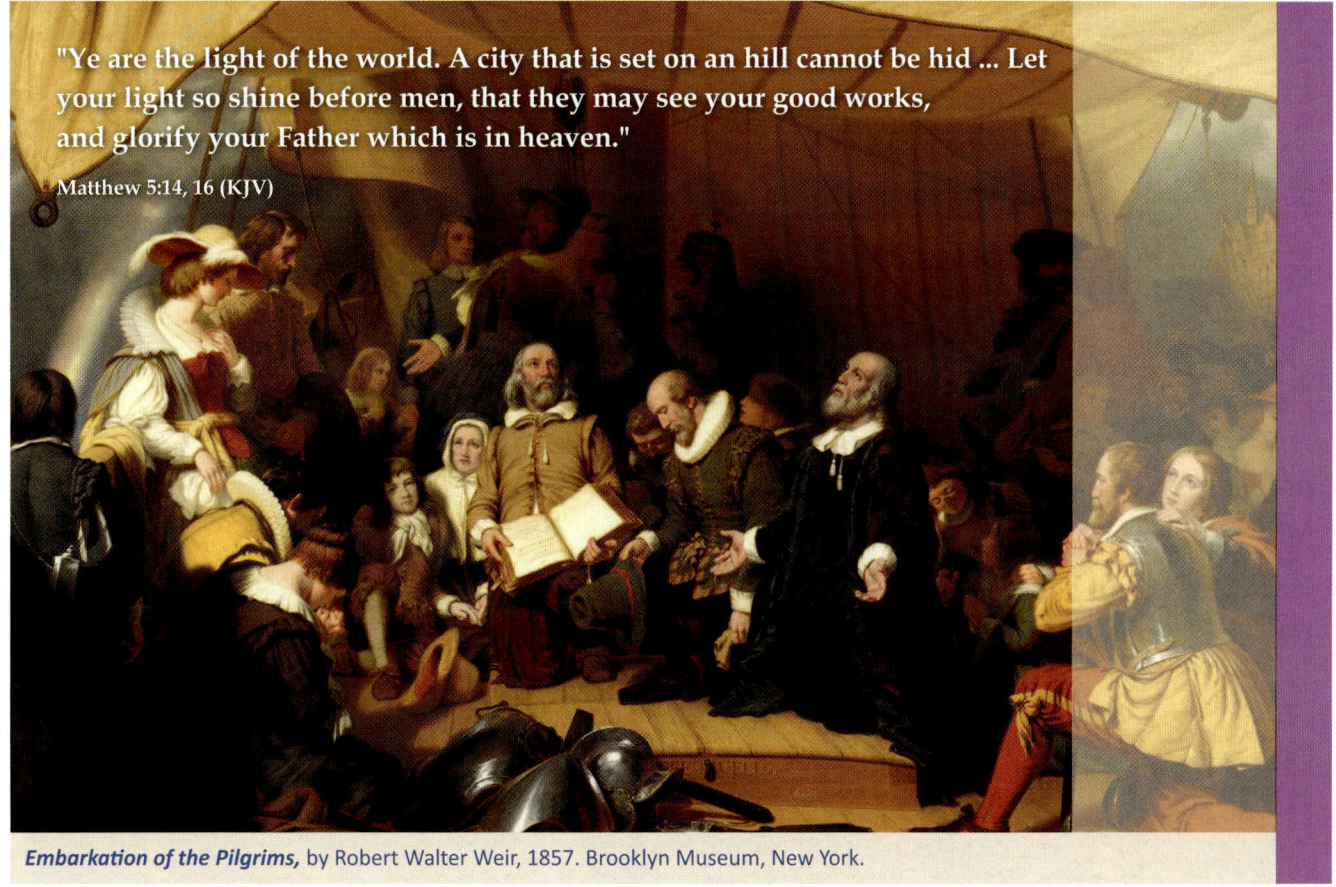

"Ye are the light of the world. A city that is set on an hill cannot be hid ... Let your light so shine before men, that they may see your good works, and glorify your Father which is in heaven."

Matthew 5:14, 16 (KJV)

Embarkation of the Pilgrims, by Robert Walter Weir, 1857. Brooklyn Museum, New York.

The Early Settlers

America received its first large influx of settlers from Europe during the 1600s. Most of these settlers were Protestant Christians for whom the Bible played a significant religious and cultural role. Not surprisingly, as they created the rules and laws that would govern society, the Bible was an important influence.

Many of these settlers came to the New World searching for business opportunities, especially in Virginia and New York. Others sought religious freedom from the official, established churches of Europe, especially the Church of England. Those who came as religious dissidents largely settled in Massachusetts and Connecticut (Pilgrims and Puritans), Maryland (Roman Catholics), and Pennsylvania (Quakers).

Vocabulary

> **Dissident** [noun]
someone in opposition to official policy, especially an authoritarian state or organization

Roger Williams
The Bold Reformer

Roger Williams (ca. 1603–1683) and his wife, Mary, were born in England. Like other Puritans, they had first worked for reform within the Church of England. After experiencing official resistance and persecution, they sailed to Boston, Massachusetts, in 1631 (a year after the city was founded) and joined other Puritans. Interested in languages and culture, Williams studied various Native American dialects and customs. Over the years, he developed close friendships and deep trust among Native Americans, especially the Narragansett tribe.

After a series of conflicts and controversies, Williams was banished from Massachusetts Bay Colony. He and a group of followers purchased land from the native residents and in 1636 established Providence, later part of the colony of Rhode Island. Williams wanted his new settlement to be a safe haven for the "distressed of conscience." He preached that "forced worship stinks in God's nostrils." Quakers and Baptists fled from the Puritan-controlled areas of New England and found religious freedom with Williams and his followers. Although Williams helped found a Baptist church in Providence, which was the first in America, he refused to identify with any one denomination. The first synagogue was also erected in Newport, one of the first cities in America where religious tolerance prevailed. Williams was a strong early proponent of the separation between church and state.

At the left, the Touro Synagogue in Newport, Rhode Island (1763), is the oldest surviving synagogue building in North America. At the right, the First Baptist Church of Providence, Rhode Island. The site of the oldest Baptist congregation in the United States, it was founded by Roger Williams in 1638. The present building was constructed in 1774–1775.

Religious Tolerance Evolves

Full religious liberty, and the dissolution of established churches, didn't come overnight to the American colonies. It was a gradual process that took many years. Nor were the colonies free of religious persecution. Principles we now take for granted as being part of the American system of government—separation of church and state, toleration of religious differences and protection of religious rights, etc.—were being tested in local contexts during the colonial period. Over time, such principles became part of the legal system (with the adoption of the First Amendment, for example); but cycles of trial and error were required before old traditions could be shed and new ones adopted. True religious freedom evolved in some towns and colonies before others.

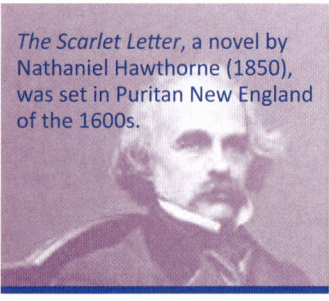

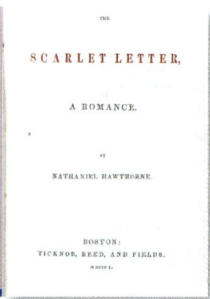

The Scarlet Letter, a novel by Nathaniel Hawthorne (1850), was set in Puritan New England of the 1600s.

Lingering Intolerance

The Puritans were hardly the only group that sought to enforce religious conformity. Almost every colony had dominant groups that did the same. Take, for example, this quote from The Laws of Virginia (1610–1611): "No man shall speak any word or do any act, which may tend to the derision and despite of God's holy word, upon pain of death." Virginians not only assumed the public would respect the Bible, they mandated it—on pain of death! Such laws were common in the colonial era.

Vocabulary

> **Puritan** [noun], a member of a Protestant group in England and New England in the 16th and 17th centuries that opposed and sought to reform aspects of the Church of England

Why the Bible?

The Bible was by far the most widely read book in America during the 1600s. Copies of the Bible were passed down among the most valuable of family heirlooms. Even those who couldn't read the Bible for themselves would hear the Bible read aloud or preached in congregations. For colonists, the Bible was not just a great book; it provided many guiding principles for life. Yale historian Harry Stout has shown that the typical Puritan churchgoer listened to around 7,000 sermons over a lifetime. Given the length of sermons at the time, this came out to some 15,000 hours of listening. The thousands of remaining handwritten copies of these sermons reveal ministers' heavy reliance on the Bible.

Many early Americans believed that any society that openly disobeyed the laws of God (such as the Ten Commandments, listed in Exodus 20) would soon come to ruin, and that it was in everyone's interest to make sure that God and "God's Word" were respected. So, for example, Virginia's early laws did not just prohibit mockery of the Bible. They also banned "taking the name of God in vain." Blasphemers were threatened with having a dagger thrust through their tongues! Virginia's laws also required the colonists to honor Sunday, known as the "Christian Sabbath," and to keep other moral laws and rules. These colonists wanted to make certain that they did not offend God and bring punishment on everyone.

The Bible was at the center of colonial New England communities. Reading and preaching the Bible was a key feature of church services.

Vocabulary

> **Heirloom** [noun], a family possession handed down from generation to generation
> **Blasphemer** [noun], one who speaks or acts disrespectfully toward God

The First Thanksgiving at Plymouth, by Jennie A. Brownscombe, 1914. Pilgrim Hall Museum, Plymouth, Massachusetts.

After a terrible first winter, the Pilgrims who survived—only 50 percent of those who had landed just ten months earlier—gathered in the fall of 1621 for an autumn harvest celebration.

A replica of the *Mayflower*, Plymouth, Massachusetts. During an arduous journey of more than ten weeks, this small ship carried 102 passengers—including 35 Pilgrims—and about 25 crew members, to the New World. After some initial explorations along the coast of New England, they finally landed near present-day Plymouth, Massachusetts, in December 1620. A famous landmark, Plymouth Rock, is thought to be near the spot where the passengers disembarked. They named the place of arrival after the city in southwestern England—Plymouth—from which they had set sail.

The Pilgrims

The Mayflower Compact of 1620, which some regard as America's first written constitution, reflects biblical assumptions about government and morality. Before they made their way to North America, the persecuted Pilgrims had fled England for the relative safety of the Netherlands. Even there the separatists worried about the corrupting effects of Dutch city life, especially on their children. We call them separatists because they physically separated themselves from other members of the Church of England, which in their view retained too many Roman Catholic elements and practices. Some English Protestants were separatists, but many were not. After forming independent Christian churches, they came to the New World in 1620 and quickly wrote the brief Compact to make order and survival more likely, since they were far from England and were not subject to any local laws.

Declaring that they remained loyal to the king of England, the Pilgrims proclaimed that they were founding Plymouth Colony for the "glory of God, and advancement of the Christian faith." Then they agreed to a "covenant" to work together in a "civil body politick, for our better ordering and preservation."

The Puritans Arrive

The Pilgrims who arrived in the New World in 1620 were a small, marginal group of English people. Ten years later, a larger group of Puritans came to North America. Under the leadership of wealthy English lawyer John Winthrop, they traveled in a fleet of 11 ships and totaled about 1,000 people. They first settled in Boston, close to the Pilgrims, and quickly became the dominant group in that part of New England, establishing the Massachusetts Bay Colony.

The Puritans, unlike the separatist Pilgrims, had hoped to purify and complete the reformation of the Church of England. Out of their desire to improve the Church of England rather than separate from it, they remained in the Church of England as long as they were in the Old World. But the church persecuted them. After a while, many decided to leave for New England. (And they kept coming: by 1641, some 21,000 English Puritans had migrated to New England.)

Speaking Biblically from the Beginning

Given the Puritans' expressed motives for establishing Massachusetts, it should be no surprise that this colony's early laws were filled with references to the Bible, biblical concepts, and biblical language. The Laws and Liberties of Massachusetts is one of the most clearly biblical of the early legal codes in America, citing Bible verses throughout. For example, it was stipulated that anyone who worshiped any deity but the God of the Bible should be put to death, consistent with Exodus 22.

Written half a century before the Salem witchcraft trials, the early laws of Massachusetts also threatened those who practiced witchcraft with death, with reference to biblical texts such as Exodus 22:17: "Thou shalt not suffer a witch to live" (NABRE).

The Original City upon a Hill

While en route to the Massachusetts Bay Colony, Puritan leader John Winthrop delivered an address called "A Model of Christian Charity." This outlined his vision for the new colony as one of brotherly generosity and biblical faithfulness (Winthrop served as governor for 12 of the first twenty years of Massachusetts Bay Colony.) His famous metaphor from that address proposed that Massachusetts be a "city upon a hill," echoing Jesus' words from the Sermon on the Mount: "Ye are the light of the world. A city that is set on an hill cannot be hid." Matthew 5:14 (KJV).

John Winthrop (1588–1649) comes ashore in Salem, Massachusetts. Winthrop was one of the major leaders of the newly-formed Massachusetts Bay Colony. Under his direction as a 12-term governor of the colony (each term lasted only one year), Boston was founded and religious and political policies of the early Massachusetts Bay Colony were formulated.

The modern city of Boston, Massachusetts. Founded by Puritan settlers in 1630, Boston is one of the oldest cities in the United States. It was named after the English city of Boston, Lincolnshire, the hometown of several prominent colonists.

Vocabulary

> **Marginal** [adjective], situated on the edge of something
> **Metaphor** [noun], a figure of speech in which a term is applied to one thing in order to suggest a resemblance to something else, such as "A mighty fortress is our God."

Early America's Charters and Laws

Historic home of Judge Corwin, known as Witch House in Salem, Massachusetts. It is the only standing structure in Salem with ties to the witchcraft trials of 1692.

Witch Hill or **The Salem Martyr**, Thomas Satterwhite Nobel, 1869. New York Historical Society, New York City. In this painting, a Salem girl has been found guilty of witchcraft and now walks to the gallows with the hangman and judges.

The Salem Witch Trials

Although the death penalty for blasphemy and other moral offenses was part of the law in most of the American colonies, it was rarely enforced. All over Europe, and especially in Germany and France, state churches executed more than 40,000 people between 1420 and 1750 in widespread witch hunts. In comparison with those numbers, very few were accused of witchcraft or put to death for it in the American colonies. By the 1660s in New England, 15 people had been executed and about 80 accused of practicing witchcraft. The infamous Salem witch trials followed in 1692–1693, in which 19 people were put to death. (A 20th person died during interrogation.)

Most of those who died were upstanding members of the community. Over time, objections were raised to the kinds of evidence used, and the trials were discontinued. Although nothing else like this ever happened again in New England, this tragic event led to a distrust of New England Puritan leadership.

Examination of a Witch by Thompkins H. Matteson, 1853. Peabody Essex Museum, Salem, Massachusetts.
Accused witches (women) and sorcerers (men) were officially checked to see if they had any unusual marks on their bodies. Many of these trials turned into a frenzy of claims and counterclaims.

Early America's Charters and Laws

Maryland and Pennsylvania

Maryland, the only American colony founded as a haven for English Catholics, enjoyed some glimmers of tolerance. Legal codes there did outlaw blasphemy and other crimes, but unlike the Puritan settlements, Maryland allowed the "free exercise" of religion to all Christians in its 1649 Act Concerning Religion. This law guaranteed religious liberty to all its Christian residents, promising that no one would be "compelled to the belief or exercise of any other religion against his or her consent."

Pennsylvania, founded by the much-persecuted Quakers, did offer some small freedom of religious dissent in 1682. All who acknowledged "the one Almighty and eternal God" would suffer no disadvantages because of their faith. Nevertheless, the Pennsylvania Quakers also mandated that a host of offenses against God, such as swearing, cursing, and lying, would be severely punished. Still, this was an improvement over the death penalty!

Simply stated, there was broad agreement in early America that biblical morality was the proper foundation for the law—especially criminal law—and that the Bible itself should be respected. There were, however, disagreements about how government should handle disagreement or "dissent."

Still No Separation of Church and State

Today we think of America as a global pioneer in the defense of religious liberties and in its refusal to establish an official state church. But that development took many years. Long before the American Revolution and long before the Constitution and the Bill of Rights, religious liberties in America were often stifled. Colonial officials regularly threatened to suppress those who did not comply with the doctrines and practices of the established churches.

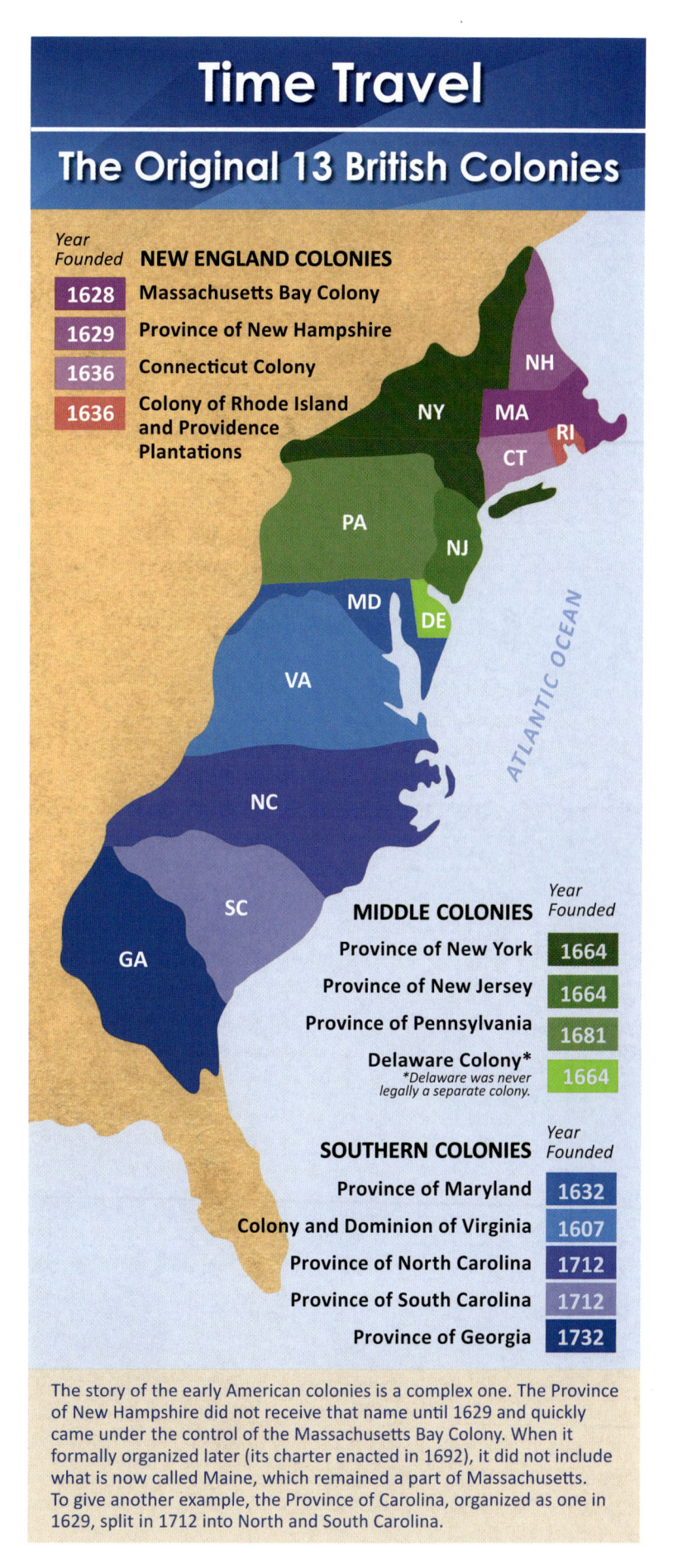

Time Travel

The Original 13 British Colonies

NEW ENGLAND COLONIES — Year Founded
- 1628 Massachusetts Bay Colony
- 1629 Province of New Hampshire
- 1636 Connecticut Colony
- 1636 Colony of Rhode Island and Providence Plantations

MIDDLE COLONIES — Year Founded
- Province of New York — 1664
- Province of New Jersey — 1664
- Province of Pennsylvania — 1681
- Delaware Colony* — 1664
  *Delaware was never legally a separate colony.

SOUTHERN COLONIES — Year Founded
- Province of Maryland — 1632
- Colony and Dominion of Virginia — 1607
- Province of North Carolina — 1712
- Province of South Carolina — 1712
- Province of Georgia — 1732

The story of the early American colonies is a complex one. The Province of New Hampshire did not receive that name until 1629 and quickly came under the control of the Massachusetts Bay Colony. When it formally organized later (its charter enacted in 1692), it did not include what is now called Maine, which remained a part of Massachusetts. To give another example, the Province of Carolina, organized as one in 1629, split in 1712 into North and South Carolina.

Early America's Charters and Laws

Anne Hutchinson

Anne Hutchinson was a devout Puritan and mother of 15 children who lived in the years 1591–1643. Between 1636 and 1638 she was among those who publicly challenged some of the teachings of the Puritans. Her strong religious convictions were at odds with the established Puritan clergy in the Boston area. Her ideas and growing popularity became a threat to them, so the colonial officials of Massachusetts banished her and the Boston Church excommunicated her. Roger Williams was sympathetic to her position and gave her refuge in the Colony of Rhode Island.

Anne Hutchinson on Trial, 1901. Illustration by Edwin Austin Abbey.

John Locke (1632–1704). Engraved by J. Pofselwhite and published in the encyclopedia *The Gallery of Portraits with Memoirs*. United Kingdom, 1836. John Locke, the famous English philosopher, is considered the father of classical liberalism. His work *Letters Concerning Toleration* (1689–1692) outlines his views on religious tolerance. He was influenced by various Baptist theologians and by the Presbyterian poet John Milton.

A Haven of Religious Tolerance

Among the colonies, Massachusetts had some of the most aggressive policies against religious nonconformity. This resulted in protests by dissenters such as Roger Williams and Anne Hutchinson. Eventually both were expelled, and they moved to Rhode Island. Strongly criticizing the Massachusetts government for engaging in "persecution for cause of conscience," Williams believed that government should not punish anyone for what it considered incorrect religious opinions. Williams was the first to argue that the Bible endorses a "hedge or wall of separation between the garden of the church and the wilderness of the world," including the government.

Even before the American revolutionary Thomas Paine or the English philosopher John Locke, Williams was making strong arguments for church-state separation. He believed that religion is too sacred to suffer from government interference. As a result, Rhode Island became unique in the colonies in implementing liberty for all religious groups.

However, even in Rhode Island, the people were only "conditionally free" to exercise and enjoy "their own judgments and consciences in matters of religious concernments." According to the Rhode Island Royal Charter of 1633, the people had freedom of thought regarding religion as long as they behaved "peaceably and quietly" in the community and acted morally and with proper respect toward the religious beliefs of others. No "profaneness" was permitted. While Williams and other dissenters argued that the government should not police religious beliefs, he and virtually everyone else assumed that the government should discourage immoral behavior.

Summary

The Bible was an important influence (along with other sources, including English Common Law) for determining moral behavior in colonial America. All of the early law codes and charters, not only those in Puritan New England, reflected the Bible's influence. Successive waves of European migration brought many settlers to the new colonies. Some (such as Roger Williams and Anne Hutchinson) tested the limits of accepted religious beliefs. Morality and religious conformity were rigorously enforced by the authorities. Biblical laws extended as far as sentencing dissidents and "witches" to exile and death. Religious freedom, as we understand that concept today, was still emerging.

Early State Constitutions

What Shaped the Religious Ideals of the Early Republic?

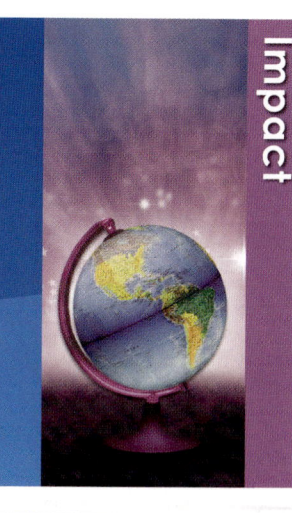

> "And Jesus answering said unto them, Render to Caesar the things that are Caesar's, and to God the things that are God's."
>
> Mark 12:17 (KJV)

Scene at the Signing of the Constitution of the United States, Howard C. Christy, 1940. The Constitutional Convention met in Philadelphia during the summer of 1787, presided over by George Washington. After long debates, the final draft was signed by most of the delegates in September 1787. The painting is now displayed in the House of Representatives wing of the Capitol building in Washington, D.C.

"The Land of the Free and the Home of the Brave"

The promise of religious liberty has made the United States a haven for diverse groups seeking greater freedom. Americans sing about this freedom in their national anthem, declare it on the Statue of Liberty in New York, and have it etched on the Liberty Bell in Philadelphia: "proclaim liberty throughout all the land," a direct quote from the Bible (Leviticus 25:10, KJV). America's guarantee of religious freedom for all is also enshrined in its Constitution.

Yet the right to practice one's religion without fear or hindrance was not easily won. The story of how religious liberty came to be conferred on all American citizens is remarkable. It's a tale of inspiring individuals who were committed to a vision of a new society. They believed it was possible for everyone in the nation to enjoy peace, well-being, and the right to maintain their own faiths and traditions. Here is how it began.

Vocabulary

> **Constitution** [noun], a body of fundamental principles according to which a state or other organization is to be governed

America's First State Constitutions

After the Declaration of Independence in 1776, the colonies had to formulate their own state constitutions. In all 13 colonies, the early American lawmakers faced the same challenge: finding a way to defend religious liberty for all while also acknowledging a common Judeo-Christian heritage among the colonists (where Protestant Christians were in the clear majority).

The history of the United States has been profoundly shaped by tensions between the rights and wishes of the national religious majority (Christians) and the rights and wishes of nonreligious people as well as religious minorities (such as Jews, Buddhists, Muslims, and many others). This tension has also played out between factions within the same faith tradition, such as were created by the stark differences over slavery during the 19th century. At that time preachers joined both sides of the Civil War, sometimes from the same denomination and even the same family.

Religious Freedoms, but Only for the Majority

As we review some of the early state constitutions, it is clear that true religious liberties, as we know them today, usually lost out. At first only one of the 13 states, New York (in 1777), clearly guaranteed religious freedom for minority faiths. This was a major step forward for human rights in New York, which only 70 years earlier had passed some anti-Catholic laws that threatened to imprison any Jesuit priests found in the state!

Taking a Religious Oath

"I believe in one God, the creator and governor of the universe, the rewarder of the good and the punisher of the wicked, and I acknowledge the Scriptures of the Old and New Testament to be given by Divine inspiration."

This oath had to be taken by office holders in Pennsylvania, according to its newly written constitution. Similar oaths were mandatory in most other states. For example, Delaware's 1776 constitution required political leaders to affirm not only the Old and New Testaments, but also to profess their "faith in God the Father, and in Jesus Christ His only Son, and in the Holy Ghost." Such laws meant that only persons who believed in God, as defined by most of Christianity, and in the authority of the complete Bible, could hold office. Such religious oaths discriminated against various sections of the population. The small Jewish community of Philadelphia, for example, protested strongly. Eventually lawmakers amended the oath.

One of the most famous Founders, Benjamin Franklin, chaired Pennsylvania's constitutional convention. Franklin also disagreed with this kind of oath. He contended that a religion could stand on its own if it was good, and did not need special treatment and support from the government.

Writing the Declaration of Independence 1776, Jean Leon Gerome Ferris; Virginia Historical Society. From left to right are three of the main contributors: Benjamin Franklin, John Adams, and Thomas Jefferson.

Benjamin Franklin, David Martin, 1767. White House, Washington, D.C.

Establishing Freedom of Religion in America

Achieving full religious freedom was a long, drawn-out process; it didn't happen overnight. The Virginia colonial legislature had early on passed laws giving Christian doctrine the force of law. For example, a 1705 statute imposed penalties of up to three years in jail without bail for anyone raised as a Christian who "denied the Trinity or the Scriptures to be of divine authority."

In 1776 the Anglican Church was still the official denomination in Virginia. It received tax support for buildings, ministers, and activities related to education and charity work. This preferential treatment made life difficult for Baptists, who at this time were still a minority in America. Their ministers were persecuted, forbidden from preaching, and (as late as 1778) viciously attacked. Progress toward religious freedom came with George Mason's 1776 Virginia Declaration of Rights, when the state affirmed the "free exercise of religion." Yet even this document did not clearly disassociate Virginia from state support for the Church of England.

Patrick Henry, the well-known patriot, introduced a bill in 1784 that would allow Virginia tax funds to be used to support religion. Citizens would be allowed to designate which church would receive their individual tax money. This bill met significant opposition.

In 1786, under James Madison's leadership, the Virginia legislature permanently ended the state's religious establishment by passing a bill for religious freedom. The bill, named the Virginia Statute for Establishing Religious Freedom, was originally written by Thomas Jefferson in 1777. It declared that "no man shall be compelled to frequent or support any religious worship, place, or ministry whatsoever ... or shall otherwise suffer on account of his religious opinions or belief, but that all men shall be free to profess, and by argument to maintain, their opinions in matters of Religion." This ended direct state financial support for any denomination, or the threat of (minor) penalties for religious opinions deemed to be heretical.

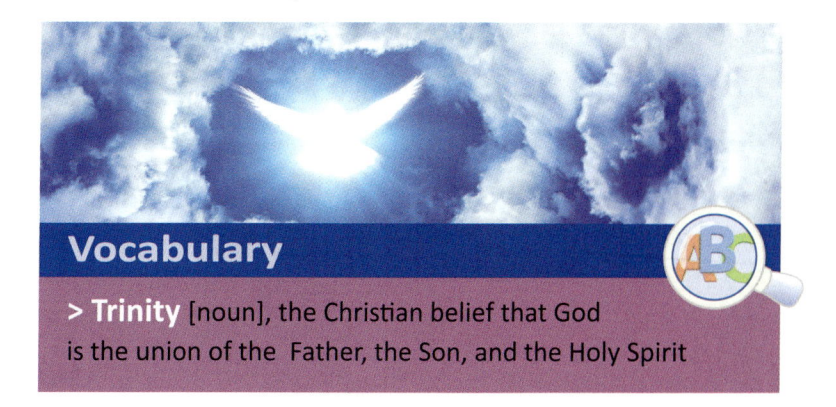

Statue of President Thomas Jefferson at the Jefferson Memorial in Washington, D.C.

Vocabulary

> **Trinity** [noun], the Christian belief that God is the union of the Father, the Son, and the Holy Spirit

Early State Constitutions

Three Key Documents

The three documents shown below each played an important role in securing religious freedom in the early years of the United States: New York's State Constitution (1777); the Virginia Statute for Establishing Religious Freedom (1786); and the Bill of Rights (1791).

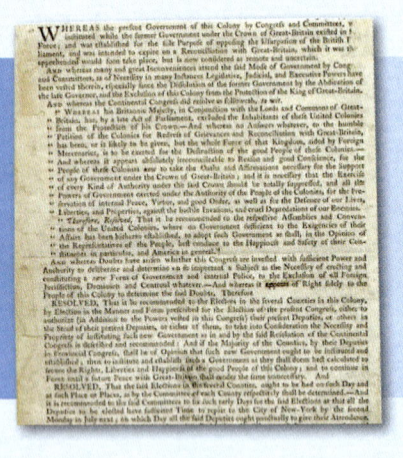

Cover page of the Constitution of the State of New York, 1777.
New York State Archives.

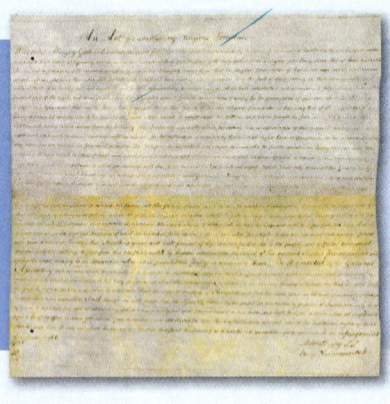

Virginia Statute for Establishing Religious Freedom, 1786.
Library of Virginia.

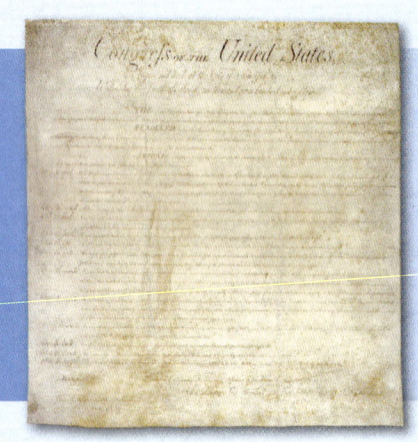

The Bill of Rights, the first ten amendments to the U.S. Constitution, 1791.
U.S. National Archives.

The Great Push for Religious Freedom

The United States Constitution was adopted after the Revolutionary War at the famous Constitutional Convention in Philadelphia in 1787. The Constitution itself said very little about religion; further debate and legislation were required to determine the role that religion would play in the early republic. James Madison was a key figure in this process. In 1789 he took the lead in steering a bill through the First Federal Congress that would explicitly list the rights of American citizens, including rights regarding religion. Two years later, in 1791, ten amendments to the Constitution were ratified; together they form the Bill of Rights. Religion was addressed in the First Amendment: "Congress shall make no law respecting an establishment of religion, or prohibiting the free exercise thereof."

As significant as the First Amendment was, it's important to realize that its protection of religious liberty was really quite limited, since it referred only to Congress; it said nothing about what individual states could or could not do. For that reason, the full implementation of these important new rights throughout the land was a stop-and-go process that took many years to resolve. Connecticut, for example, continued to have a state-endorsed Christian religion until 1818, as did Massachusetts until 1833.

The Fourteenth Amendment, adopted in 1868, prohibited state and local government from depriving citizens of rights of "life, liberty, and property." Because of this amendment, the Supreme Court formally applied the First Amendment protection of the freedom of religion to state governments as well, but not until 1940. Also, immigration and population growth brought more religious diversity to America with a significant increase in the number of Catholics and Jews, other Protestant denominations, as well as people of other faiths.

Vocabulary

> **Illegitimate** [adjective], unlawful; not in line with accepted rules or standards

> **Coercion** [noun], the use of force or threats to get someone to do something

Personal Beliefs of the Founders

The men and women who helped lay the foundations of the new nation held a broad spectrum of views regarding the Bible and how it should be interpreted and applied. The views of many of the best-known Founders lay outside of Christianity's historical norms. This could be rightly said of Thomas Jefferson, who famously produced his own version of the Bible that excluded most miracles and focused on the moral teachings of Jesus. It could also be said of James Madison, Alexander Hamilton, and John Adams, among others. Each of these men was influenced by the ideas of the European Enlightenment, in particular the view known as deism. Deism was a complex strain of thought that emerged in Europe in the 17th and 18th centuries that believed in a Creator God made known in nature and reason. Deism had little impact in early America overall but influenced intellectual elites. Deists tended to reject the notion that God would miraculously intervene in the natural world, but some deists (including some of the Founders) spoke nonetheless about "Providence" and its outworking in human history. Deists often appreciated the Bible, even if they did not consider it revealed by God, and lived fairly traditional religious lives. The Founders generally demonstrated great familiarity with the Bible as well as great respect, even reverence, for its teachings.

Benjamin Franklin was one of only five people to sign both the Declaration of Independence in 1776 and the Constitution in 1787. As a young man, Franklin showed a deep interest in deistic ideas, but he changed course and thereafter kept his religious convictions largely to himself. As is true of many of the Founders, he did not hold a single consistent view throughout his life; nor can we be entirely sure what he believed and practiced. Yet clearly the Bible held an important place for Franklin and his contemporaries. Franklin, for example, proposed (unsuccessfully) that the Great Seal of the United States depict a scene from the Book of Exodus, showing Moses and Pharaoh, with the motto "Rebellion to Tyrants is Obedience to God." (The Great Seal is used to authenticate many official government documents and is seen today on a passport cover or a one-dollar bill.) Perhaps best-known among American writers is Thomas Paine, author of the best-selling pamphlet *Common Sense* (1776). While this work is replete with biblical references and proved formative for America, he later went overseas and wrote rather critical views of biblical teachings. Paine became a controversial figure whose ideas were denounced by many Protestant ministers. Paine sharply criticized what he considered the superstitions of Christianity; only when Christianity was vanquished, he argued, could human happiness and perfectibility be achieved.

The Faith of George Washington

What were George Washington's religious convictions, and how did he regard the Bible? We can't know for certain, but it appears he fit the profile of those known at the time as "liberal" Christians. He attended religious services regularly and was a lay council member in his Episcopal parish, but he rarely took Communion or discussed religion in public. When he did refer to matters of faith, like many of his time, he often spoke of *Providence*, a broad term that encompasses the gifts and guidance of the Creator. Several relatives and acquaintances referred to Washington's personal faith in documents or recorded anecdotes, but it is difficult to know how trustworthy such reports are. Washington insisted, when he was first sworn in as president on April 30, 1789, that he should take his oath of office with his hand upon the Bible. This King James Bible is still owned by Saint John's Freemason Lodge in New York City.

Washington's Inauguration, 1789. Mural by Allyn Cox, 1974, U.S. Capitol. The scene depicts Washington taking the oath of office on the balcony of Federal Hall in New York.

Washington as Statesman at the Constitutional Convention, Junius Brutus Stearns, 1856. Virginia Museum of Fine Arts.

The U.S. Constitution of 1787 has survived, with amendments, for more than 225 years.

The Constitutional Congress of 1787

The 55 delegates to the 1787 Constitutional Convention represented a spectrum of religious beliefs and practices, and a large number of them claimed to hold a high regard for the Bible and its moral guidance. The less famous delegates included Charles Pinckney and John Langdon, who established Bible societies in their home states. Also present was Caleb Strong, one of the founding members of the American Bible Society.

Almost all the delegates were Protestants (mainly Anglicans, Congregationalists, and Presbyterians), and all were white males. Only two Roman Catholics were present; there were no Jews or Native Americans, and no known atheists. There were also no women and no African-Americans. The Constitutional Convention did not have a genuine representative sample of the American population, even though the population at the time was far smaller and more homogeneous.

Despite many challenges, these several dozen delegates were able to craft a written constitution that, along with its later amendments, remains the country's foundational document. The U.S. Constitution of 1787 has survived and withstood more than 225 years of historical development, changing religious demographics, and vigorous debates over the nature of government. Today it is one of the world's oldest written constitutions still in force. The original document comprises one large sheet of paper. Indeed, perhaps its very brevity is partly responsible for its enduring impact.

Two other figures who were influential in the founding period were Elias Boudinot (president of the Continental Congress from 1782 to 1783) and John Jay (the first chief justice of the United States). They became in succession the first two presidents of the American Bible Society, established in 1816.

Vocabulary

> **Homogeneous** [adjective]
of the same kind

Some Facts about the U.S. Population in 1787

While not diverse by today's standards, the delegates who gathered in Philadelphia in 1787 for the Constitutional Convention were considered to be a reasonably representative sample of the voting population of the first 13 states. Consider the following facts:

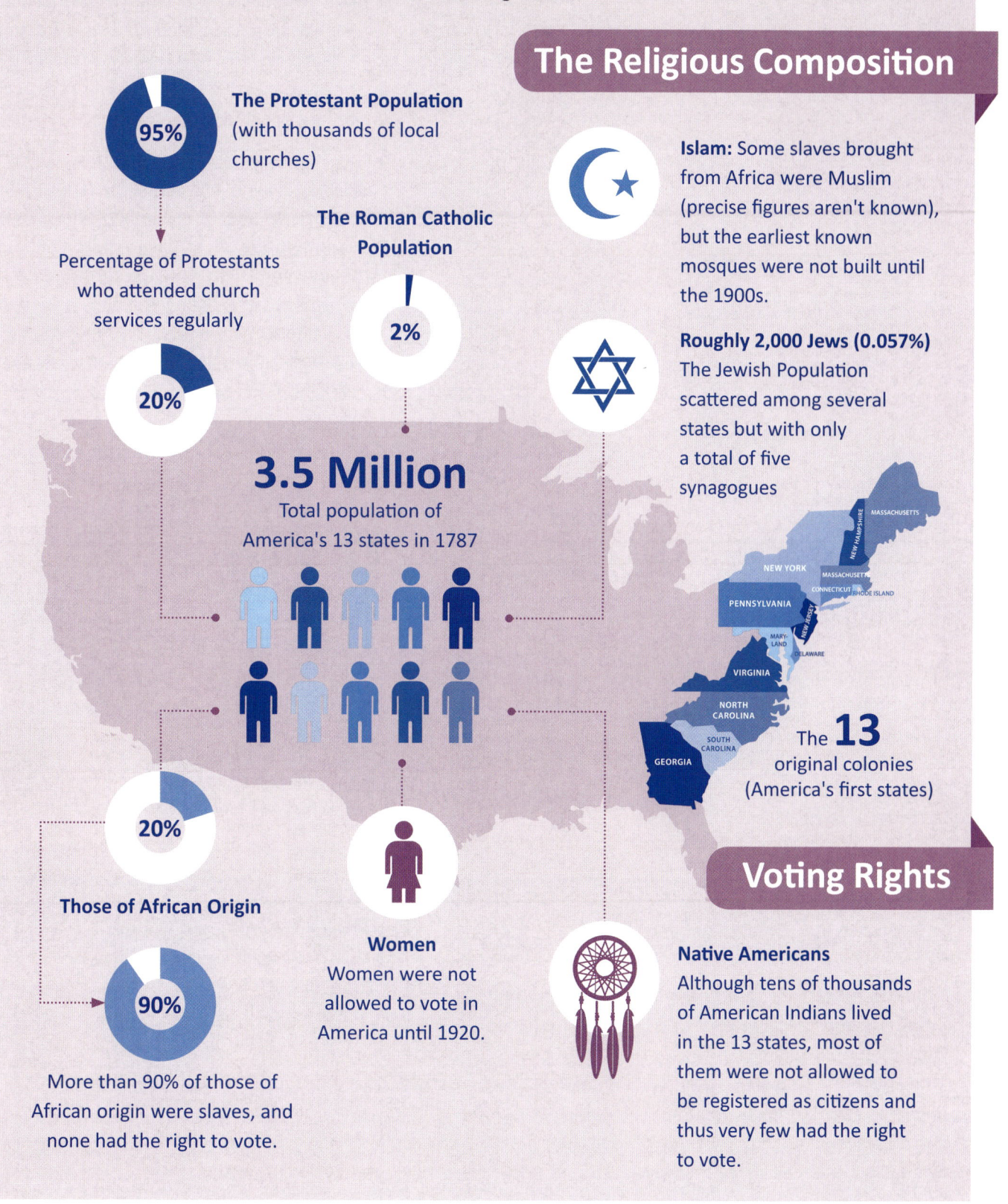

The Religious Composition

The Protestant Population (with thousands of local churches): **95%**

Percentage of Protestants who attended church services regularly: **20%**

The Roman Catholic Population: **2%**

Islam: Some slaves brought from Africa were Muslim (precise figures aren't known), but the earliest known mosques were not built until the 1900s.

Roughly 2,000 Jews (0.057%) The Jewish Population scattered among several states but with only a total of five synagogues

3.5 Million Total population of America's 13 states in 1787

Those of African Origin: 20%

More than **90%** of those of African origin were slaves, and none had the right to vote.

Women Women were not allowed to vote in America until 1920.

The **13** original colonies (America's first states)

States shown: NEW HAMPSHIRE, MASSACHUSETTS, NEW YORK, CONNECTICUT, RHODE ISLAND, PENNSYLVANIA, NEW JERSEY, MARYLAND, DELAWARE, VIRGINIA, NORTH CAROLINA, SOUTH CAROLINA, GEORGIA

Voting Rights

Native Americans Although tens of thousands of American Indians lived in the 13 states, most of them were not allowed to be registered as citizens and thus very few had the right to vote.

Early State Constitutions

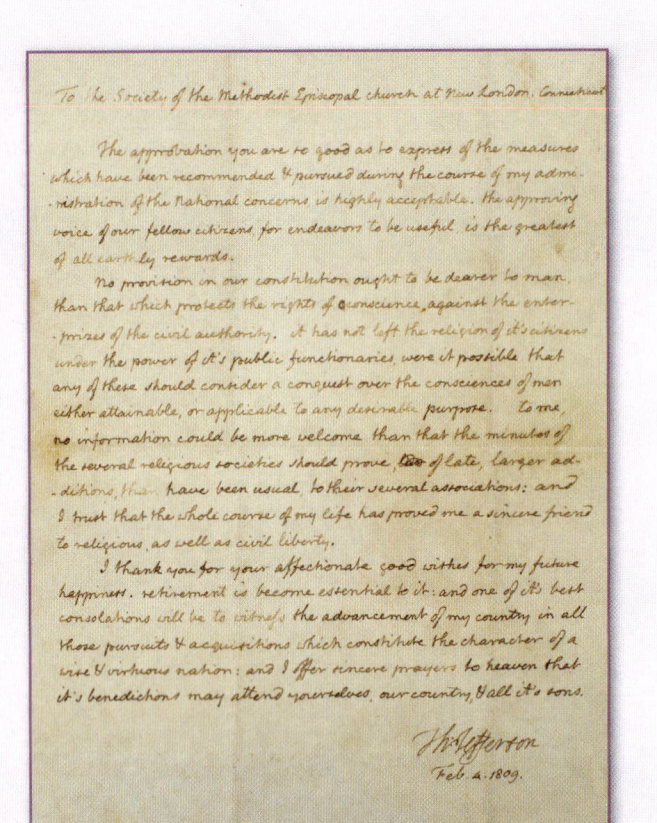

Thomas Jefferson served as the third president of the United States (1801–1809). This is a copy of the letter he wrote on February 4, 1809, to the Society of the Methodist Episcopal Church in New London, Connecticut.
The text contains the following excerpts (spelling modernized):

"No provision in our constitution ought to be dearer to man than that which protects the rights of conscience against the enterprises of the civil authority. It has not left the religion of its citizens under the power of its public functionaries, were it possible that any of these should consider a conquest over the consciences of men either attainable, or applicable to any desirable purpose ... I trust that the whole course of my life has proved me a sincere friend to religious, as well as civil liberty.
"... I offer sincere prayers to heaven that its benedictions may attend yourselves, our country, & all its sons."

The Grand Vision

Following the relative homogeneity of the colonial period, in which Protestant Christianity was the dominant faith of the land, the newly formed United States slowly transitioned into a more religiously diverse society, especially as immigration increased in the 19th and 20th centuries. Not surprisingly, some of the existing laws needed to be revised or replaced in the face of a changing population.

Some states, in their zeal for reform, went so far as to even ban all clergy from public offices for a time in the early 1800s. Even today, the branches of government continue to wrestle with the challenges of living up to the high ideals of religious freedom advocated by the nation's founders. The proper place of the Bible in public life, given its influence in the history of the United States and yet its association with some religious traditions and not others, is very much a matter of ongoing debate.

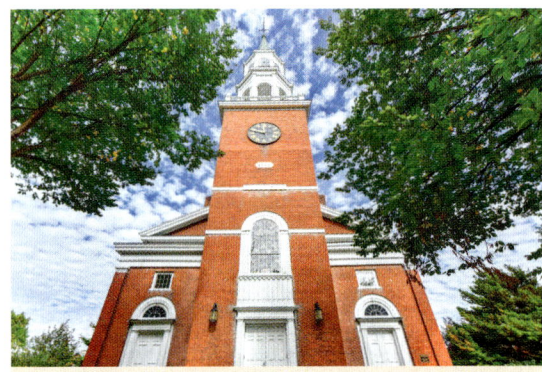

The First Unitarian Church was built in 1816 in Burlington, Vermont.

Summary

The principle of religious freedom was an important matter for the Founders of the United States. James Madison, Thomas Jefferson, and others led efforts to enact laws that would protect religious minorities. Though the Founders shared a common Protestant heritage, and in general they expressed a strong sense of respect for the Bible (especially its moral teachings), most of them also sought to keep a clear distinction between church and state authority. In some states, official church establishment continued until the 1830s. Since then, the ideals of religious freedom have been challenged anew in each generation. Those challenges will continue, especially as the world becomes increasingly diverse and interconnected.

Early American Culture

How Did the Bible Impact Early America?

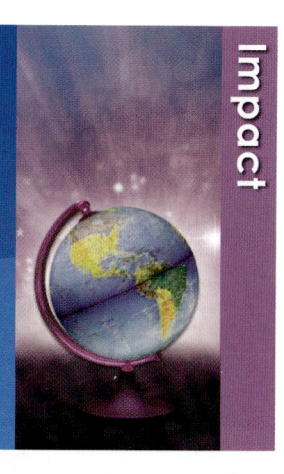

"'Brothers,' he said, 'listen to me.'"
Acts 15:13 (NIV)

Camp-Meeting, Hugh Bridport, ca. 1832, based on an earlier print by Alexander Rider. Division of Home and Community Life, National Museum of American History, Smithsonian Institution. Harry T. Peters, "America on Stone" Lithography Collection.

Introduction

Some of the most penetrating observations of early American culture were made by famous visitors, such as the French writer Alexis de Tocqueville. He toured America extensively in the early 1830s. Although the French government actually sent Tocqueville to study the prison system in the United States, he is best known for his influential book *Democracy in America* (published in two volumes in 1835 and 1840).

In 1833 Tocqueville wrote a lesser-known report, called *On the Penitentiary System of the United States and of Its Application in France*, with Gustave de Beaumont. It describes what they perceived to be the Bible's influence on the American penal system. Tocqueville and Beaumont observed that American prisons were providing inmates with copies of the Bible and that many of them had learned to read as a result. For example, a man of German ancestry arrested for horse stealing was held in a Philadelphia jail. When asked how he passed the time, he answered that there were "but two means—labor, and the Bible." Tocqueville noted that the Bible was the inmate's "greatest consolation." The man exhibited passionate religious convictions and could not "speak long without being agitated, and shedding tears." Tocqueville and Beaumont also noted that the Bible was an important component of American culture.

Why the Bible

Due to the high rate of church affiliation in the early 1800s, great numbers of Americans were at least somewhat familiar with the Bible. If Americans possessed any books in their homes, one was very likely a Bible. Yet some Americans had no church affiliation and some remote areas simply didn't have many pastors. While many Americans might have read the Bible at home, not everyone had access to the robust sermons of the well-known preachers in the cities.

George Whitefield, Joseph Badger, ca. 1750. Harvard University Portrait Collection, Cambridge, Massachusetts.

Vocabulary

> **Robust** [adjective], strong and hardy
> **Great Awakenings** [noun], periods of religious revival where there was a sharp increase of interest in religion

The Great Awakenings

Why were so many Americans affiliated with a church well into the 1800s? Many began attending church during what many historians call the two "Great Awakenings." These spiritual revivals occurred in different parts of America during the 1740s and again in the early 1800s. There was a huge renewal in religious interest at the time. Many people recommitted themselves to the Christian faith, and to Bible reading and study.

The First Great Awakening

The most famous evangelist of the First Great Awakening was an Anglican minister named George Whitefield (pronounced "whitfield"). This English evangelist attracted huge crowds. Many historians say that Whitefield was the best-known person in America prior to the American Revolutionary War. Whitefield, who was already successful in Britain, made an even stronger connection in the colonies. People were eager to hear his preaching, which typically focused on specific passages from the Bible. He was well-known for his extemporaneous and passionate style, speaking in a way that connected with ordinary listeners. One contemporary said that Whitefield could bring a crowd to tears simply by saying "Mesopotamia."

Whitefield crossed the Atlantic 13 times, which is quite remarkable considering how dangerous and expensive these trips were. People in the colonies seemed more comfortable with Whitefield's distinctive outdoor preaching than were his fellow countrymen. Some pastors in America banned him from their churches, but this did not deter Whitefield. He often chose to preach outdoors because America's relatively small churches could not accommodate the crowds of thousands that often gathered to hear him. At one gathering on Boston Common in 1740, for instance, an estimated 20,000 people attended his sermon.

Whitefield resolved early on to make America his "chief scene of action." Although he encouraged the education of slaves, Whitefield was a slaveholder himself and never directly condemned the institution. He died in Massachusetts in 1770, lionized by large numbers of his contemporaries. American Christianity developed a more accessible and democratic character, in part due Whitefield's legacy as a preacher and evangelist.

The Second Great Awakening

The Second Great Awakening was sparked by the Cane Ridge Revival under Barton Stone, a Presbyterian. That revival, in the summer of 1801, drew more than 10,000 people to sparsely populated northeastern Kentucky. Although its influence was mostly in frontier areas, it also spread east under the Presbyterian preacher Charles Finney (1792–1875). The revival continued in waves through the 1830s. Groups such as the American Bible Society (founded in 1816) brought the Bible's influence to ever-larger segments of the American population. Some preachers addressed the injustices of slavery. Finney and others openly encouraged black slaves to seek their freedom. During the 1840s, the widespread revival fervor cooled off and the Second Great Awakening effectively died out. But church affiliation across America remained at high levels for decades.

Barton Stone

Charles G. Finney

Vocabulary

> **Lionize** [verb], to treat somebody as an important person

Cane Ridge Meeting House, Little Rock Road, Paris, Kentucky, Theodore Webb, 1934. Library of Congress, Washington, D.C.

Camp meeting of the Methodists in North America, M. Dubourg, ca. 1819. Library of Congress, Washington, D.C.

A Negro Camp Meeting in the South, 1872, Solomon Eytinge; Schomburg Center for Research in Black Culture, The New York Public Library.

Illustrations from the book *Moody: His Words, Work, and Workers*, 1877.

Birthplace of D.L. Moody; he built the girls school on the adjacent hillside in scenic Northfield, Massachusetts.

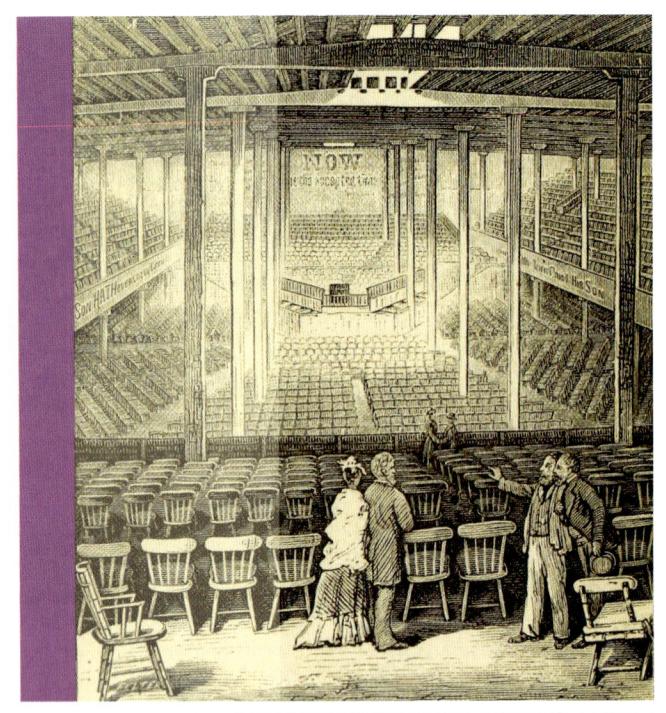

Dwight L. Moody
(1837–1899)

Most historians agree that America's revivalist atmosphere never again reached the heights of the First and Second Great Awakenings. However, other significant (though smaller) waves of religious renewal have rippled throughout American history, even in recent decades. One such wave is associated with the Bible preacher Dwight L. Moody (1837–1899). A shoe salesman and native of Northfield, in the hills of western Massachusetts, Moody moved to Chicago in the late 1850s. In his free time, Moody started a small Bible study class for the city's poor children, many of whom were illiterate and living in slums. Moody's weekly classes soon attracted 1,000 students every Sunday and became the talk of the Midwest. The newly elected president, Abraham Lincoln, visited Moody's Sunday school class in 1860. During that decade, Moody's Bible classes grew into a sizable church, and Moody stopped selling shoes to become a full-time preacher.

After connecting in 1870 with gifted musician and composer, Ira Sankey, Moody's popularity increased all the more. Thousands attended their meetings, and Moody sometimes preached six times a day. Moody and Sankey

Ira Sankey

attracted even larger crowds on one of their first visits to Britain in the early 1870s; more than 15,000 people at a time gathered to hear them. Moody's meetings, with Bible preaching and lively singing, were called evangelistic crusades, and continued to attract large crowds when he returned to Chicago and later traveled around America. Today a Bible school in Chicago named after him has more than 3,000 full-time students. Moody and Sankey helped fund two schools for disadvantaged boys and girls near Northfield. Bible crusades throughout the 20th century by evangelists such as Billy Sunday, Billy Graham, and others have also left an impact on American culture.

Harriet Martineau
(1802–1876)

The Englishwoman Harriet Martineau (1802–1876), who is regarded by some as the world's first female sociologist, published *Society in America* in 1837 following two years of research. She noted Christianity's overwhelming presence in the country. "There are many ways of professing Christianity in the United States," she wrote, "but there are few, very few men, whether speculative or thoughtless, whether studious or ignorant ... who do not carefully profess Christianity, in some form or another." At the time, most Americans of influence at least publicly claimed some affiliation with Christianity. The Jewish population remained very small (only about 10,000).

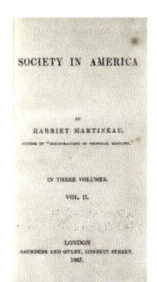

Martineau opposed the idea of official state churches. Like Tocqueville, Martineau credited much of America's religious vitality to the absence of state churches. Rather than the government propping up less popular denominations, Martineau said that in America "every exertion is made to meet the religious wants of the people ... The Mission and Bible Societies exhibit large results. In short, society in the United States offers every conceivable testimony that the religious instincts of the people may be trusted to supply their religious wants."

America's free market of religion has continued today, and the Hartford Institute for Religion Research reported in 2010 that America is home to about 350,000 religious congregations. It is estimated that about 60 million people attend a church or synagogue service in America on most weekends.

Vocabulary

> **Exertion** [noun]
vigorous physical or mental effort

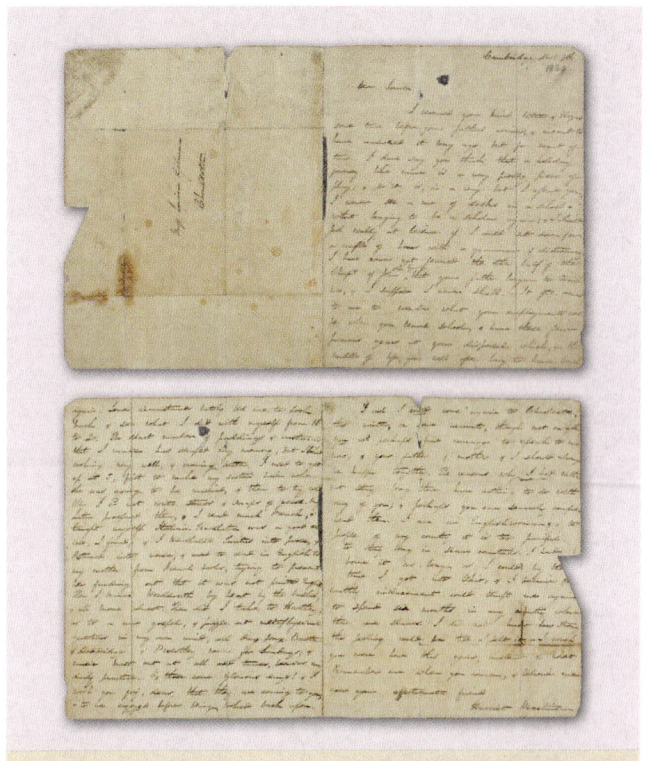

Letter sent in 1834 from Harriet Martineau to Louise Gilman, a schoolgirl. It describes her life and intellectual interests from the age of 16 to 29 and condemns the practice of slavery in the United States.

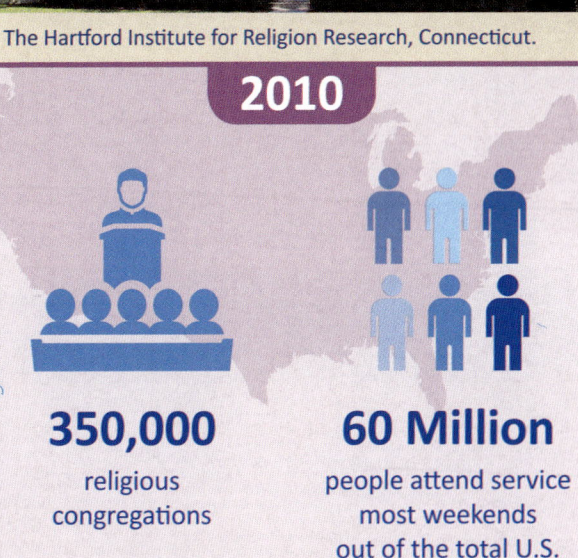

The Hartford Institute for Religion Research, Connecticut.

2010

350,000 religious congregations

60 Million people attend service most weekends out of the total U.S. population of 308 million

Early American Culture

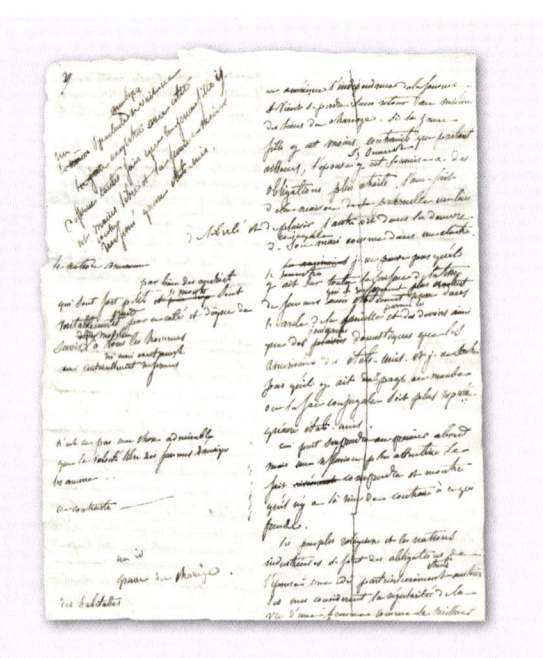

Page from the original working manuscript of *Democracy in America*, Alexis de Tocqueville, ca. 1840. The Beinecke Rare Book and Manuscript Library, Yale University, New Haven, Connecticut.

Pioneer cabin in the backwoods of the American frontier, illustration from Victor Collot's *A Journey in North America*.

Alexis de Tocqueville
(1805–1859)

Writing at the same time as Martineau, Tocqueville too was fascinated by America's vibrant religious life. Tocqueville regarded America in the 1830s as "there is no country in the whole world in which the Christian religion retains a greater influence over the souls of men than in America" (*Democracy in America*). Tocqueville acknowledged that while many Americans might not accept every Christian doctrine, most believed that faith kept the American republic healthy. Tocqueville argued that if the people were to be sovereign in a republic, then they must have a solid ethical grounding, which in America was provided primarily by Christianity and the Bible. He felt that Christianity and liberty were closely intertwined among Americans. Immigrants to the frontier West, especially those who moved from Puritan-influenced New England, brought that connection with them.

Tocqueville was struck by the contrast between the rugged conditions on the American frontier and the literacy of the pioneers. The typical American frontiersman plunged "into the wilds of the New World with the Bible, an axe, and a file of newspapers" in hand. In one instance, Tocqueville visited a family living in a log cabin, who had cleared that spot in the woods themselves. It was "an ark of civilization amidst an ocean of foliage" Tocqueville commented. The books inside their cabin included "a Bible, the six first books of Milton, and two of Shakespeare's plays."

Summary

During the 1830s, two influential foreign visitors studied life in America, Alexis de Tocqueville and Harriet Martineau. They noted the significant influence of the Bible and religion on American culture by observing everything from East Coast prisons to settlements in America's western frontier. Some of this influence can be attributed to what historians now refer to as the First and Second Great Awakenings, associated with a few prominent Bible preachers, such as George Whitefield and Charles Finney.

Acknowledgments

Every effort has been made to secure permissions and provide correct attributions for all images and texts. Most images in the public domain and licensed under Creative Commons licenses were found via the Wikimedia Commons website. Credits listed below relate to the student textbook and the teacher's guide. Omissions brought to our attention will be corrected in subsequent editions.

Chapter 1:
King David
Textbook & Teacher's Guide

David as a Shepherd illustration: © Compedia. **Archaeological Artifact in the Ancient Biblical Sukho,** view to Valley of Elah, Israel: ©Miguel Nicolaevsky/Shutterstock. *David with the Head of Goliath* (oil on wood), 1606–1607, Michelangelo Merisi da Caravaggio; Kunsthistorisches Museum, Vienna, Austria: Public Domain. **Small rocks:** © James Steidl, 123rf.com. **Sheep:** © Attila JANDI/Michal Durinik/Shutterstock. **Detail from a relief on the gate of La Madeleine,** 1837, Baron Henri de Triqueti; Paris, France: © Renata Sedmakova/Shutterstock. **Replica of Michelangelo's famous *David* in front of the Palazzo della Signoria,** Florence, Italy: © ndphoto/Shutterstock. **Artwork from the 16th century on the floor of the Cathedral in Siena, Italy, depicting David's son Absalom hanging by his hair from a tree:** Public Domain. **Ancient Tomb of Absalom** in Jerusalem with two birds on top: © slavapolo/Shutterstock. **King David sculpture:** © mtsyri/Shutterstock. **Silver coin:** © Tal Yanai/Compedia. **Gold coin:** © Tal Yanai/Compedia. **The Rosebery Rolle,** Psalms and Canticles in Latin, ca. 1350–1450; England: Courtesy Museum of the Bible Collection. All rights reserved. © Museum of the Bible, 2016. **Sunshine mountain landscape, Gilboa Mountains, Israel:** © Protasov AN/Shutterstock. **Gold crown isolated on white background:** © Sashkin/Shutterstock. **Ladybugs:** © Tai Chesco/Shutterstock. **Slingshot:** © James Steidl/123rf.com. **Postcard of King David,** 1910-1920: Courtesy of the GFC Trust, from the William Gross Collection.

Joseph and Potiphar's Wife (oil on canvas), 1631, Guido Reni; Collection of the Earl of Leicester, Holkham Hall, Norfolk, England: Public Domain. **Excavations near Temple Mount:** © Giancana/Shutterstock. **Older King David,** an illustration from *The New Testament of our Lord and Savior Jesus Christ...*, 1897: Courtesy Museum of the Bible, Green Collection. All rights reserved. © Museum of the Bible, 2016.

App

Vintage background: © Eky Studio/Shutterstock. **Background tan banner:** © Compedia. *David and Bathsheba* (oil on wood), 1562, Jan Massys; Louvre Museum, Paris, France: Public Domain. **Prophet Nathan and King David** (fresco), ca. 1749-1754, Johann Baptist Zimmermann; Wieskirche, Bavaria, Germany: Public Domain. *The Prophet Nathan Admonishes King David*, ca. 1548-1628, Jacopo Palma il Giovane; Kunsthistorisches Museum, Vienna, Austria: Public Domain. *King David Handing the Letter to Uriah* (oil on panel), 1611, Pieter Lastman; Detroit Institute of Arts, Detroit, Michigan: Public Domain. *King David*: © Zvonimir Atletic/Shutterstock. **3D 360° Model - Tomb Absalom:** ©Compedia. **3D 360° Model - Interactive Harp:** © Compedia. **3D 360° Model - Sling:** © Compedia. **Valley of Elah viewed from the top of Tel Azeka:** Public Domain. *David and Goliath* (watercolor on paper), 1915, Ilya Repin; The Tver Regional Picture Gallery, Russia: Public Domain. ***David Slays Goliath,*** Picture from The Holy Scriptures, Old and New Testaments books collection published in 1885, Stuttgart, Germany. Drawings by Gustave Doré: © Nicku/Shutterstock. **The Biblical City of Suqo in Judea Hills** view to Valley of Elah, the place of David and Goliath Battle: © Miguel Nicolaevsky/Shutterstock.

Chapter 2:
"House of David"
Textbook & Teacher's Guide

David and Goliath illustration: © Compedia. *King David* by Adamo Tadolini on the base of the Colonna dell'Immacolata, Rome, Italy: © Only Fabrizio/Shutterstock. **Portion of the Temple Scroll,** 11Q19, Dead Sea Scrolls, 2nd century BC; The Israel Museum's 'Dead Sea Scrolls Digital Project': Public Domain. **Priestly Blessing fragment,** Image from Tamar Hayardeni, image photoshopped from the Ketef Hinnom Amulet II recto, collage by Aharon Varady, image by Ardon Bar Hama, COJS, and drawing by Gabriel Barkay: Public Domain. **The fragmentary Tel Dan stele;** The Israel Museum, Jerusalem: Image by Oren Rozen, licensed under CC BY-SA 4.0. **Tel Dan Canaanite Gate:** Public Domain. **Holy Grail:** © Magdalena Kucova/Shutterstock. *Jesus and St. John at Last Supper*; St. Michael's Church, Louvain, Belgium: ©Renata Sedmakova/Shutterstock. **Noah's Ark construction:** © photostockam/Shutterstock. **Ten Commandments written on stone tablets in Hebrew:** © James Steidl/Shutterstock. **Ark of the Covenant:** ©James Steidl/Shutterstock. *King David Playing the Harp*, 1622, Gerrit Van Honthorst; Centraal Museum, Utrecht, Netherlands: Public Domain. **The City of David** (from the Model of Jerusalem); Israel Museum, Jerusalem, Israel: Image by Ariely, licensed under CC BY 3.0. **Karnak:** Image by Olaf Tausch, licensed under CC BY 3.0. **The Shishak Inscription** from the Relief of Shoshenq I's campaign list at the southern exterior walls; Temple of Karnak, north of Luxor, Egypt: Image by Olaf Tausch, licensed under CC BY 3.0.

The Mesha Stele, 9th century BC; Louvre Museum, Paris, France: Image by Mbzt 2012, licensed under CC BY 3.0.

App

The Golan Heights in Israel: © Daniel Monterroso/Shutterstock. **Remains of Temple at Tel Dan:** © iStock.com/Joshua Rinehults. **Ancient Israelite Gate in the Biblical City of Dan:** © Miguel Nicolaevsky/Shutterstock. **Front view of the Middle Bronze II mud brick gate at area K in Tel Dan:** Image by Ani Nimi, Public Domain. **3D 360° Model - Tel Dan Inscription:** © Compedia.

Chapter 3:
Psalms

Textbook & Teacher's Guide

Forest creek running through the stones: © Tischenko Irina/Shutterstock. **Donkey:** © poeticpenguin/Shutterstock. **The Rice Psalter in Latin,** 15th century, England: Courtesy Museum of the Bible Collection. All rights reserved. © Museum of the Bible, 2016. **Music notes (2):** © Ramona Kaulitzki/Shutterstock. **King David,** from the Book of Hours (Use of Salisbury), 1512, Simon Vostre; Paris, France: Courtesy Museum of the Bible, National Christian Foundation Collection. All rights reserved. © Museum of the Bible, 2016. **Ethiopian psalter in Ge'ez,** 19th century; Ethiopia: Courtesy Museum of the Bible Collection. All rights reserved. © Museum of the Bible, 2016. **Bible pages:** © Aleksandr Kurganov/Shutterstock. **Miniature psalter,** ca. 1280-1300; Picardy, France: Courtesy Museum of the Bible, Green Collection. All rights reserved. © Museum of the Bible, 2016. *The Musical Instruments,* an illustration from the Macklin Bible, 1800: Courtesy Museum of the Bible, Green Collection. All rights reserved. © Museum of the Bible, 2016. **Sheep (2):** © Khudoliy/Shutterstock. **Light from the clouds:** © JaaoKun/Shutterstock.

App

Text from the Bible: © Leon Rafael/Shutterstock. **King David:** © Zvonimir Atletic/Shutterstock. **Woman's finger presses on old bible book** in a dark room over wooden table and reading a bible: © 4Max/Shutterstock. **Ancient and vintage handwritten Bible pages:** © Maksim Shmeljov/Shutterstock. **Sound bars:** © Compedia. **"House of God, Forever:"** Song courtesy of Jordan Nichole Brown.

Chapter 4:
Music

Textbook & Teacher's Guide

Cello and drums: © sarra22/Shutterstock. **Bono:** Image by Garrettanderson983, licensed under CC BY 3.0. **Bono and The Edge of U2** at Gillette Stadium Foxboro, MA: Image by Garrettanderson983, licensed under CC BY-SA 2.0. **U2 performing in Arlington, Texas:** Image by Jack Newton, licensed under CC BY-SA 2.0. **Psalter in Latin,** ca. 1480-1490, Master of Jacques de Besançon; Paris, France: Courtesy Museum of the Bible, National Christian Foundation Collection. All rights reserved. © Museum of the Bible, 2016. *Miriam* (oil on canvas), 1862, Anselm Feuerbach; Alte Nationalgalerie, Berlin, Germany: Public Domain. **Arch of Titus, Roman Forum:** © Matt Ragen/Shutterstock. **A miniature version of the Temple and Ancient Jerusalem;** The Israel Museum, Jerusalem, Israel: © Flik47/Shutterstock. *Saint John Chrysostom*; Lichfield Cathedral, Staffordshire, England: © A.C. Jones/Shutterstock. *Claudio Monteverdi,* 1597, an anonymous artist; Ashmolean Museum, Oxford, England: Public Domain. **Georg Friedrich Handel** (oil on canvas), ca. 1726-1728, Balthasar Denner; National Portrait Gallery, London, England: Public Domain. **Göttinger Symphonie Orchestera:** Image by Thomas Fries, licensed under CC BY-SA 3.0. **Photoshop of a photo of Lecrae:** Image by Reach Records Management, licensed under CC BY 3.0. **Hand of man reaching towards sky:** © Vladimir Arndt/Shutterstock. **Aretha Franklin performing:** Image by Ryan Arrowsmith, licensed under CC BY 2.5. **Bob Dylan in Barcelona, Spain**: Image by Saibo, licensed under CC BY 2.0. **Leonard Cohen at Edinburgh Castle, Edinburgh, Scotland:** Image by Йо Асакура, licensed under CC BY 2.0. **Headphones on white background:** © Jiri Hera/Shutterstock. **Bono singing during a U2 concert in Portugal:** Flickr, Image by Ângela Antunes, licensed under CC BY 2.0. **Conductor hands:** © Alenavlad/Shutterstock.

App

Music background with piano keys in grunge style. Music concept: © isak55/Shutterstock. **Johann Sebastian Bach,** 1746, Elias Gottlob Haussmann; Bach Archive, Leipzig, Germany: Public Domain. **"Jesu, Joy of Man's Desiring,"** Johann Sebastian Bach; Music by Kevin MacLeod (incompetech.com), licensed under CC BY 3.0. **Georg Friedrich Handel** (oil on canvas), ca. 1726-1728, Balthasar Denner; National Portrait Gallery, London, England: Public Domain. **"Hallelujah Chorus,"** Georg Friedrich Handel, Music by Orchestra Gli Armonici; provided by MUSOPEN, licensed under CC0 1.0, musopen.org. **Joseph Haydn,** 1791, Thomas Hardy; Royal College of Music Museum of Instruments, London, England: Public Domain. *The Creation:* Music by Joseph Haydn, provided by MUSOPEN, licensed under CC0 1.0, musopen.org. **Wolfgang Amadeus Mozart**, 1819, Barbara Krafft: Public Domain. *Mass in C Minor,* Wolfgang Amadeus Mozart; provided by MUSOPEN, licensed under CC0 1.0, musopen.org. **3D Animation - Music in the Temple:** © Compedia.

Chapter 5:
King Solomon

Textbook & Teacher's Guide

Solomon illustration: © Compedia. **Golden nuggets isolated on white:** © Africa Studio/Shutterstock. **The Cathedral of Notre Dame de Paris, France:** © Brian Kinney/Shutterstock. **Exterior of the Hagia Sophia in Sultanahmet, Istanbul**, on a sunny day: © JM Travel Photography/Shutterstock. **Myanmar famous sacred place and tourist attraction landmark - Shwedagon Paya pagoda, Yangon, Myanmar:** © suronin/Shutterstock. **Prambanan temple near Yogyakarta on Java Island, Indonesia:** © Thanwan Singh Pannu/Shutterstock. **The Gates of Paradise, mid-15th century,** Lorenzo Ghiberti; Florence Baptistery, Florence, Italy: © Malgorzata Kistryn/123RF.com. **Jerusalem: Golden Menorah** two meters in height, plated with 43 kg of gold, similar to the one used in Holy Temple: © Rostislav Glinsky/Shutterstock. **Paris: King, Queen of Sheba, King Solomon and St. Peter, details of Notre Dame Cathedral,** Portal of St. Anne: © Zvonimir Atletic/123RF.com. *The Throne of Solomon* (ink on paper print), 1890, Ya'akov Leib Levinsohn; United States: Courtesy of GFC Trust. *Solomon Dedicates the Temple in Jerusalem* (gouache on board), ca. 1896–1902, James Jacques Joseph Tissot; The Jewish Museum, New York City, New York: Public Domain. **Jerusalem: Menorah in front of the Knesset in the Park of Roses:** © Julius fekete/Shutterstock. *Isaac Newton,* engraved by E. Scriven, *The Gallery of Portraits with Memoirs* encyclopedia, United Kingdom, 1837: © Georgios Kollidas/Shutterstock. **Solomon Pillars in Timna National Park in Israel:** © Alexey Stiop/Shutterstock. **Ants:** © schankz/Shutterstock. **Ant rolls heavy stone:** © Andrey Pavlov/Shutterstock. **Solomon's Temple Recreation:** © TurboSquid.com. **The Western Wall in Jerusalem:** © Fat Jackey/Shutterstock. **Unidentified Jewish worshipers pray at the Wailing Wall,** an important Jewish religious site in Jerusalem, Israel: © Flik47/Shutterstock. **Bronze Nugget:** © Andrey Burmakin/Shutterstock.

App

Raster green background with texture of paper: © Chizhovao/Shutterstock. **Vector ancient yellow vertical background with east ornament and texture of paper:** © Chizhovao/Shutterstock. **Nails, hammer and folding ruler:** © STILLFX/Shutterstock. **Heap of new bricks prepared for building:** © sevenke/Shutterstock. **Truck:** © srzaitsev/Shutterstock. **Mason carrying breeze block:** © auremar/Shutterstock. **Builder laying bricks in site:** © hxdbzxy/Shutterstock. **Temple with gold trim:** © Compedia. **Raw logs, ready to be towed and for market floating on Fraser River** surrounds Mitchell Island, British Columbia, Canada: © Trong Nguyen/Shutterstock. *Egyptian Episode of Israel:* **Pyramid Building,** John Clark Ridpath, *Ridpath's Universal History*, Volume 5 (Cincinnati, Ohio: Jones Brothers Publishing Company: 1896): Public Domain. **Crane and building construction:** © SavaSylan/Shutterstock. **Set of under construction icons on a black background.** Vector illustration: © LAUDiseno/Shutterstock. **Notre Dame de Paris Cathedral, Paris, France:** © Brian Kinney/Shutterstock. **Hagia Sophia mosque exterior in Istanbul, Turkey:** © JM Travel Photography/Shutterstock. **Shwedagon Pagoda, Myanmar:** © imgob.net. **Prambanan Temple, Yogyakarta, Indonesia:** © Thanwan Singh Pannu/Shutterstock. **3D 360° Model – The Menorah:** © Compedia. **Winter Fairy Tale:** © Slavoljub Simonovic/

Shutterstock. **Portrait of two lions:** © dejatel/Shutterstock. **Fresh and ripe, green figs on fig leaves:** © acongar/Shutterstock. **3D 360° Model - Jewish Temple:** © Compedia.

Chapter 6:
Hazor, Megiddo, and Gezer
Textbook & Teacher's Guide

Fortifications: © Tal Yanai/Compedia. **Three stones:** © xpixel/Shutterstock. **Hazor** (map insert): Image by האיל הניאוליתי, licensed under CC BY-SA 2.0. **Megiddo** (map insert): © Tal Yanai/Compedia. **Gezer** (map insert): © Tal Yanai/Compedia. **Brick:** © Ivan Nakonechnyy/Shutterstock. **Header background** (stone): © pedrosala/Shutterstock. **Mount Hermon:** © magicinfoto/Shutterstock. **Aerial view of Tel Hazor:** Image by Asaf Z, Public Domain. **Israelite Gate:** © Tal Yanai/Compedia. **Megiddo Altar:** © Tal Yanai/Compedia. **Footer grey stone:** © Tal Yanai/Compedia. **Southern stable at Megiddo:** © Tal Yanai/Compedia. **Gezer Calendar:** Image by oncenawhile, licensed under CC BY-SA 3.0.

App

Blue background: © Compedia. **Projector:** © Compedia. **Casemate wall (double wall with central hollow space between the walls) in the ancient city of Hazor:** Image by Teri C. Peterson. Used with permission. **Israel, Southern Coastal Plain, Solomon's gate at Tel Gezer,** the southern gate of the Israelite city: © Hanan Isachar/Alamy Stock Photo. **Ruins of historic Tel Megiddo, Jizreel Valley, Israel:** © Eunika Sopotnicka/Shutterstock. **Gate of Ashdod:** © Israel Antiquities Authority. **Film reel around photos:** © Compedia. **70-meter-long horizontal tunnel that leads to the spring of water for the inhabitants of Tel-Megiddo:** © Robert Hoetink/Shutterstock. **National park with ancient ruins and history for Israel tourism:** © Pavel Bernshtam/Shutterstock. **Remains and ruins in Tel Megiddo National park in Israel:** © Robert Hoetink/Shutterstock. **The reconstructed southern stables at Tel Megiddo National Park:** © Robert Hoetink/Shutterstock. **Tel Megiddo aerial photo:** Image by אסף.צ, Public Domain.

Chapter 7:
Proverbs
Textbook & Teacher's Guide

Proverbs illustration with ants: © Compedia. **Solomon,** illustration from the Doré Bible, published by Cassell, Petter, and Galpin; London and New York: Public Domain. *The Judgement of Solomon* (or *Jucicio de Salomón*), 1609-1610, Jusepe de Ribera; Borghese Gallery, Rome, Italy: Image by Escarlati, Public Domain. **Head:** © patrice6000/Shutterstock. **Proverbs 4 background:** © FINDEEP/Shutterstock. **Inkwell with quill pen:** © Davydenko Yuliia/Shutterstock. **Black worker ants:** © claffra/Shutterstock. **Some Cape Hyrax basking in the sun,** also known as dassie in Southern Africa: © Nico Traut/Shutterstock. **Locusts:** © Vladimir Wrangel/Shutterstock. **Lizard:** © Pavel L Photo and Video/Shutterstock. **Opening to the Book of Proverbs,** an illustration from the Macklin Bible, 1800: Courtesy Museum of the Bible, Green Collection. All rights reserved. © Museum of the Bible, 2016. **Dandelion abstract background:** © Tiramisu Studio/Shutterstock. **Proverbs 28:6 background:** © Shutterstock. **Hands with seeds background:** © Chepko Danil Vitalevich/Shutterstock.

App

Blue striped background: © Compedia. **Scrolls** (detail from vector illustration): © Macrovector/Shutterstock. **Your choice true or wrong:** © narokzaad/Shutterstock. **White ribbon:** © Compedia. **Tan paper background:** © Compedia. **Pharaoh icon** from Egypt icons and design elements: © Beresnev/Shutterstock. **Set of books in flat design,** vector illustration: © bluelela/Shutterstock.

Chapter 8:
The Song of Songs
Textbook & Teacher's Guide

Song of Songs illustration: © Compedia. **Main waterfalls of En Gedi:** © Tutti Frutti/Shutterstock. **Nubian ibexes:** © Boris Diakovsky/Shutterstock. *The Shulamite Relating the Glories of King Solomon to Her Maidens,* 1894, Albert Joseph Moore; Walker Art Gallery, Liverpool, UK: Public Domain. **Couple walking:** © kak2s/Shutterstock. *A Minstrel Playing Before Solomon,* illumination for the Song of Songs, Rothschild Mahzor, 1492; The Jewish Theological Seminary of America, New York: Public Domain. *Sponsa de Libano,* 1891, Edward Burne-Jones; The

Walter Art Gallery, London, England: Public Domain. **Two rings:** © Gudrun Muenz/Shutterstock. **Two survivors of hurricane Katrina getting married in Houston, Texas:** Image by Ed Edahl/FEMA, Public Domain. **Two white doves:** © df028/Shutterstock. **Heart hands:** © Ditty_about_summer/Shutterstock.

App

Cinnamon sticks and meal close up on wooden table: © Oksana Shufrych/Shutterstock. **Beautiful lilac flowers** isolated on white: © Africa Studio/Shutterstock. **Myrrh as incense** isolated on white background: © unpict/Shutterstock. **Pink rose flower** on white background: © Sutichak/Shutterstock. **Mexican Orange Blossom (Choisya Ternata):** © A & S Aakjaer/Shutterstock. **Henna flowers and seeds** over white background: © Swapan Photography/Shutterstock. **Marigold flower** on a white background: © oksana2010/Shutterstock. **Cherry blossom:** © AVprophoto/Shutterstock. **Sea daffodil on Mediterranean beach:** © Yury Nevalenny/Shutterstock. **Red rose isolated** on white background: © Vitalina Rybakova/Shutterstock. **Branch with spring lilac flowers:** © freya-photographer/Shutterstock. **Viola flower field:** © Smokedsalmon/Shutterstock. **Strelitzia Reginae flower closeup (Bird of Paradise flower), Madeira island:** © symbiot/Shutterstock. **Hedgehog cactus blossoms blooming in the Sonoran Desert:** © Jim Parkin/Shutterstock. **White and yellow narcissus flowers:** © linerpics/Shutterstock. **Yellow dandelion flowers with leaves in green grass, spring photo:** © tinnko/Shutterstock. **Rocky Mountain National Park elk herd:** © Alfie Photography/Shutterstock. **Buffalo grazing on range, Niobrara National Wildlife Refuge, NE:** © Joseph Sohm/Shutterstock. **Male gnu, South Africa:** © Delpixel/Shutterstock. **Thomson's gazelle on savanna in National park. Kenya, Africa:** © Volodymyr Burdiak/Shutterstock. **Magic book:** © LilKar/Shutterstock. **Dove in the air with wings wide open in front of the sun:** © Tischenko Irina/Shutterstock. **Couple in love silhouette:** © Ksenia Bilan/Shutterstock. **Close-up shot of white lilies** isolated on white background: © Vitalina Rybakova/Shutterstock. **Red apples on apple tree branch:** © Alexander Mazurkevich/Shutterstock. **Hand-drawn painted red heart, vector element for your design:** © art_of_sun/Shutterstock. **Colourful Flowerbeds and Winding Grass Pathway in an Attractive English Formal Garden:** © 1000 Words/Shutterstock. **Thomson's gazelle on savanna in national park. Kenya, Africa:** © Volodymyr Burdiak/Shutterstock.

Chapter 9:
Ecclesiastes

Textbook & Teacher's Guide

Hiker in black on the rocky peak: © rdonar/Shutterstock. *Vanitas vanitatum et omnia vanitas (Vanity of Vanities, All is Vanity),* 19th century, Isaak Asknaziy: Public Domain. **Solomon Receiving the Queen of Sheba,** an illustration from the Doré Bible, published by Cassell, Petter, and Galpin; London and New York: © Nicku/Shutterstock. *Marriage Feast of Nastagio degli Onesti* (tempura and oil on panel), ca. 1483, Sandro Botticelli; Private Collection, Florence, Italy: Public Domain. *Jesus Walks in the Portico of Solomon,* ca. 1886-1894, James Jacques Joseph Tissot; Brooklyn Museum, New York City, New York: Public Domain. *The Nature as a Symbol of Vanitas* (oil on canvas), 1665-1679, Abraham Mignon; Hessisches Landesmuseum Darmstadt, Darmstadt, Germany: Public Domain. *Job Confessing His Presumption to God,* ca. 1803-1805, William Blake; Scottish National Gallery, Edinburgh, Scotland: Public Domain. **Skies:** © Triff/Shutterstock. *Shavout* (oil on canvas), 1880, Moritz Daniel Oppenheim; The Jewish Museum, New York City, New York: Public Domain. **An Orthodox Jewish neighborhood in Jerusalem:** Image by kikar hashabat, Public Domain.

App

White banner: © Compedia. **Black avatar profile** on white background: © 10 FACE/Shutterstock. **Official Portrait of President Ronald Reagan:** Public Domain. **Official Portrait of President Gerald Ford:** Public Domain. **Portrait photograph, President John F. Kennedy,** Image by Cecil Stoughton National Archives and Records Administration: Public Domain. **Official Portrait of President George W. Bush,** Image by Eric Draper: Public Domain. **Official Portrait of Senator Barack Obama:** Public Domain. **Official Portrait of President Richard Nixon;** National Archives and Records Administration: Public Domain. **Vice President George H.W. Bush,** ca. 1981-1989, Prints and Photography Division, Library of Congress, Washington, DC, LC-USZC4-1700: Public Domain. **Portrait of President James Earl "Jimmy" Carter;** National Archives and Records Administration: Public Domain. **Portrait of Vice President Dick Cheney:** Public Domain. **Detail of Official portrait of Vice President Joe Biden,** 2013, Image by David Lienemann: Public Domain. **Portrait of Vice President Al Gore:** Public Domain. **Portrait of Vice President J. Danforth Quayle,** 1989: Public Domain. **Israeli Minister of Defense Yitzhak Rabin** arrives in the United States, Andrews Air Force Base, Maryland, 1986, Image by Sgt. Robert G. Clambus: Public Domain. **US President Bill Clinton and Russian President Boris Yeltsin** after a private meeting at the Ciragan Palace in Istanbul, 1999, Image by David Scull: Public Domain. **President Jacques Chirac outside Élysée Palace,** 1999, Image by David Scull: Public Domain. **President Bill Clinton with Nelson Mandela** at the Independence Hall in Philadelphia, PA, 1993, Image by Robert McNeely; National Archives and Records Administration: Public Domain. **Blue background with stripes:** © Compedia. **Quote speech bubble:** © Milan M/Shutterstock. **Scrolls** (detail from vector illustration): © Macrovector/Shutterstock.

Chapter 10:
Elijah

Textbook & Teacher's Guide

Elijah illustration: © Compedia. **Panoramic view of Carmel mountains:** Image by Abreekpano066, with modifications by Oriaaass: Public Domain. **Mount Carmel:** Image by Gidip, licensed CC BY 3.0. *Seal of Jezebel,* 9th Century BC; The Israel Museum, Jerusalem, Israel: Image by RigOLuche, licensed under CC BY-SA 3.0. *Elijah Ascending into Heaven,* an illustration from the Macklin Bible, 1800: Courtesy Museum of the Bible, Green Collection. All rights reserved. © Museum of the Bible, 2016. **Crown:** © RomanenkoAlexey/Shutterstock. *Elijah Resuscitating the Son of the Widow of Sarapeth* (oil on canvas), Louis Hersent; Musee des Beaux-Arts, Angers, France: Public Domain. **Raven:** © Eugene Sergeev/Shutterstock. **Bronze figurine of Baal,** 14th–12th century BC; Louvre Museum, Paris, France: Public Domain. **A statue of Prophet Elijah at the Mukhraka – Israel:** © Asaf Eliason/Shutterstock. *The*

Story of Elijah, an illustration from the German translation of *The Mirror of Human Salvation,* ca. 1450–1460; likely Regensburg, Germany: Courtesy Museum of the Bible, National Christian Foundation Collection. All rights reserved. © Museum of the Bible, 2016. *Elijah Feeding the Ravens,* illustration from The *Bible and Its Story - Volume I,* 1915; Charles Horne and Julius Bewer; Auxiliary Educational League, New York City, New York: Courtesy Museum of the Bible, Green Collection. All rights reserved. © Museum of the Bible, 2016. *Jezebel and Ahab Met by Elijah* (oil on canvas), ca. 1863, Frederic Leighton; Scarborough Art Gallery, Scarborough, North Yorkshire, England. **View of the biblical Mount Tabor and the Arab village:** © irisphoto1/Shutterstock. **A view of snow-covered Mount Hermon, Israel** on a sunny spring day: © Diana Amster/Shutterstock. **Kiddush Cup** (silver), 1890; Germany: Courtesy Museum of the Bible, Green Collection. All rights reserved. © Museum of the Bible, 2016.

App

Elijah and the Widow of Zarephath (oil on panel), Bartholomeus Breenbergh; Private Collection: Public Domain. **Series of adjacent caves in the Mount Carmel region:** Image by Chadner, Public Domain. **Colored postcard of the Jordan River,** ca. 1925: Image by Karimeh Abbud, Public Domain. **Nahal Prat, a nature reserve and park in the Desert of Judea, Israel:** Image by Jewbask, Public Domain. **Egypt, Sinai, Mount Moses. Road on which pilgrims climb the mountain of Moses:** © IGOR ROGOZHNIKOV/Shutterstock. **Pastel map background:** © Compedia. **Vintage background with ripped old paper:** © allegro/Shutterstock. **Cement texture:** © aerogondo2/Shutterstock. **Blue background:** © Compedia. **Projector:** © Compedia. **Film reel border:** © Compedia. *Elijah and the Widow of Zarephath* (oil on canvas), ca. 1640's, Jan Victors; Museum of John Paul II Collection, Warsaw, Poland: Public Domain. *The Prophet Elijah* (oil on canvas), ca. 1550-1560, Daniele da Volterra; Pannocchieschi d'Elci collection: Image by The Yorck Project, Public Domain. *Elisha Raises the Shunammite's Son* (oil on canvas)**,** 1766, Benjamin West; Speed Art Museum, Louisville, Kentucky: Public Domain. *Elijah Revives the Son of the Widow of Zarephath,* 1842, Julius Schnorr von Carolsfeld; Getty Center, Los Angeles, CA: Public Domain. *Elijah Resuscitating the Son of the Widow of Sarepta* (oil on canvas), Louis Hersent; Musée des Beaux-Arts, Angers, France: Public Domain. **3D 360° Model - Baal:** © Compedia. **Empty white wall with 5 spot lights and wooden floor:** © Santiago Cornejo/Shutterstock. *An Angel Awakens the Prophet Elijah* (oil on canvas), 1667, Juan Antonio Frias y Escalante; Gemäldegalerie, Berlin, Germany: Public Domain. *The Running of Elijah*, W. Montague Carey, The Bible and Its Story, Volume 5, edited by Charles F. Horne (1909); © 2016 Christian Image Source *The Prophets of Baal Are Slaughtered*, 1866, Gustave Doré, Illustration from *The Holy Scriptures, Old and New Testaments*, 1866: Public Domain.

Chapter 11:
Sennacherib's Assault

Textbook & Teacher's Guide

Ancient Assyrian clay relief depicting a row of warriors with weapons and text written in cuneiform writing: © kamira/Shutterstock. **Assyria - Siege of Lachisch**: The assault on Lachish. Assyrian, about 700-692 BC. From Nineveh, South-West Palace, Room XXXVI, panel 7: British Museum, London, England: Photograph by Mike Peel (www.mikepeel.net), licensed under CC-BY-SA 4.0. **Sennacherib Stele (Taylor Prism),** 686 BC; British Museum, London, England: Image by David Castor, Public Domain. **Lachish relief,** 700-681 BC; Israel Museum, Jerusalem: © Lev Tsimbler/Alamy Stock Photo. **Tel Lachish Gate:** Image by Hanay, licensed under CC BY 2.5. *King Hezekiah Displays His Treasure,* 1789, Vicente López y Portaña; Museo de Bellas Artes, Valencia, Spain: Public Domain. **Replica of the Shiloah (Siloam) inscription:** Image by Wikikati, Public Domain. **Hezekiah tunnel:** Image by Tamar Hayardeni, licensed under CC BY 3.0. **Da Vinci Code cover:** © Penguin Random House LLC, used with permission. **The knights' temple church as made famous by Dan Brown's novel *Da Vinci Code*:** © Chris Harvey/Shutterstock. **Combination puzzle box or Cryptex w/a secret message inside:** ©Amy Walters/Shutterstock.

App

Aerial photo of Tel Megiddo: Image by אס.פץ, Public Domain. **Sebastia ancient Israel excavation on Palestinian territory:** © Pavel Bernshtam/Shutterstock. **Green background, crown emblem:** © Compedia. **Golden crown, vector**: © mona redshinestudio/Shutterstock. **Worshipers pray at the western wall.** © Sean Pavone/Shutterstock. **The Iron Age city gate of Lachish:** Image by Juha Pakkala, Public Domain. **Purple background, crown emblem:** © Compedia. **3D 360° Model - Lachish Relief:** © Compedia.

Chapter 12:
King Josiah's Reform

Textbook & Teacher's Guide

Josiah illustration: © Compedia. **Tel Dan altar:** Image by תמר מרום- Pikiwiki Israel, licensed under CC BY 2.5. **Statuette of *King Necho*** (bronze), ca. 610-595 BCE, 5½ x 2¼ x 2¾ in. (14 x 5.7 x 7 cm); Edwin Wilbour Fund, (Photo: 71.11_threequarter_PS1.jpg): Image by Brooklyn Museum, licensed under CC BY 3.0. *Moses with His Rod and Brazen Serpent* (engraving), 1793, John Hall after Benjamin West; Wellcome Library, London, England: Image by Wellcome Images, licensed under CC BY-SA 4.0. **Basalt stela of Nabonidus**; British Museum, London, England: Public Domain. **Cylinder of Nabondius,** Image by John Lendering, Public Domain. *Akenhaten and Nefertiti and Their Children* (limestone bust), ca. 1340 BC, Amarna; Neues Museum, Berlin, Germany: © tkachuk/Shutterstock. **Alter to the god Aten, Tel el-Amarna:** Image by Olaf Tausch, licensed under CC BY-SA 3.0. *Miniature in two registers: Moses receiving the tablets of law; Moses addressing Aaron and the Israelites (Exodus):* Moutier-Grandval Bible, ca. 834-843; Tours [St. Martin]; British Library, London (file: add_ms_10546_f025v; source; Add. 10546; creator: Anon): © The British Library Board 08/31/2016. **Tel Arad altar:** Image by Lior Golgher, licensed under CC BY-SA 3.0. **Tel Beersheba:** Image by gugganij, licensed under CC BY-SA 3.0. **Restored altar of Tel Beersheba:** Image by Dr. Avishai Teicher, Pikiwiki Israel, licensed under CC BY 2.5. **The colorful souk in the old city of Jerusalem Israel:** © Ana del Castillo/Shutterstock.

App

Holy City, Middle East Town, Jerusalem, Vector illustration: © vividvic/Shutterstock. **Scrolls** (detail from vector illustration): © Macrovector/Shutterstock. **Skyline of the Old City at the Western Wall and Temple Mount in Jerusalem, Israel:** © Sean Pavone/Shutterstock. *The Judgment of Solomon* (paint on ceramic), 18th century; Lille Museum of Fine Arts, Castile, Italy: Image by Vassil, Public Domain. *Asa Destroys the Idols and Forbids Worship in Local Shrines,* from Petrus Comestro's *Bible Historiale*, 1372; France: Public Domain. **King Jehoshaphat,** 17th century, unknown artist; Choir of Sankta Maria kyrka in Åhus, Sweden: Image by David Castor, Public Domain. **King Hezekiah,** 17th century, unknown artist; Choir of Sankta Maria kyrka in Åhus, Sweden: Image by David Castor, Public Domain. **King Josiah,** 17th century, unknown artist; Choir of Sankta Maria kyrka in Åhus, Sweden: Image by David Castor, Public Domain. **King Solomon,** ca. 1866, from Doré's illustrations for the Book of Proverbs: Public Domain. **White ribbon:** © Compedia. **Pictograph of justice scales:** © iDesign/Shutterstock. **Monochrome vintage antique crowns - icons and silhouettes:** © Ezepov Dmitry/Shutterstock. **Icons collection for World Religions** on white background: © Strejman/Shutterstock.

Chapter 13:
Prophets of a Future Hope

Textbook & Teacher's Guide

Prophets of a Future Hope illustration: ©Compedia. **Opening to the Book of Isaiah,** an illustration from the Macklin Bible, 1800: Courtesy Museum of the Bible, Green Collection. All rights reserved. © Museum of the Bible, 2016. **Tower of David in the old city of Jerusalem, Israel:** © Pete Spiro/Shutterstock. *Ezekiel* by Carlo Chelli on the base of the Colonna dell'Immacolata, Rome, Italy: © Only Fabrizio/Shutterstock & © Pavel Bernshtam/Shutterstock. **Jaffa gate in Jerusalem old city:** © Pavel Bernshtam/Shutterstock. **Jerusalem March on Oct 02, 2007:** © ChameleonsEye/Shutterstock. *Isaiah* by Salvatore Revelli on the base of the Colonna dell'Immacolata, Rome, Italy: © Only Fabrizio/Shutterstock. **Jerusalem, Israel, the remains of ancient Roman pillars located in Jewish Quarter:** © Phish Photography/Shutterstock. **The front façade of the United States Supreme Court in Washington, DC** © Joe Ravi/Shutterstock. **U.S. Capitol building in Washington, DC:** © Ferhat/Shutterstock. **A reconstruction of the Ishtar Gate of ancient Babylon;** Pergamon Museum, Berlin, Germany: Image by Radomir Vrbobsky, licensed under CC BY-SA 4.0. **Assyrian palace relief,** Nimrud NW Palace B-18; British Museum, London, London, England: Image by Capillon, Public Domain. *Jonah and the Whale* (oil on oak), 1621, Pieter Lastman; Museum Kunstpalast, Düsseldorf, Germany: Public Domain. *Let Us Beat Our Swords into Plowshares* (bronze), 1959, Yevgeny Vuchetich; North Garden of the United Nations Headquarters, New York City, New York: Public Domain.

App

Congratulation gold vector retro background with red heart: © Alkestida/Shutterstock. **Pink banner:** © Compedia. *Bar Kochba* (watercolor and gouache on paper), 1927, Arthur Szyk: Image by The Arthur Szyk Society, Burlingame, CA (www.szyk.org), licensed under CC BY-SA 4.0. *Shabtai Zvi,* an illustration from *Jewish Encyclopedia* (Brockhaus and Efron, 1906-1913): Public Domain. *Jacob Frank*, 1895, an illustration from Alexander Kraushar, *Frank i frankiści polscy 1726-1816. Monografia historyczna* (Kraków: Skl. gł. u G. Gebethnera i spółki, 1895): Public Domain. **Moses Maimonides** (portrait), 1744, Blaisio Ugolino; Rambam Institute, Safed, Israel: Public Domain. **Banner** (detail from vintage background vector file): © limbi007/Shutterstock. **Three abstract vintage old paper banners** (detail from vector illustration): © foxie/Shutterstock. **White border:** © Compedia. **Opening to The Book of the Prophet Isaiah,** an illustration from the Macklin Bible, 1800: Courtesy Museum of the Bible, Green Collection. All rights reserved. © Museum of the Bible, 2016. **Dirty male feet on dried earth:** © Denis and Yulia Pogostins/Shutterstock. **Wooden yoke in a vintage flea market:** © FPWing/Shutterstock. **Fabric of linen:** © AmyLv/Shutterstock. **Fragments of broken floor tiles:** © Chaikom/Shutterstock. **Beggar on the ground with straw bales:** © lafoto/Shutterstock. **Empty white wall with 5 spot lights and wooden floor:** © Santiago Cornejo/Shutterstock. **Law scales on table. Symbol of justice:** © BrAt82/Shutterstock. **Tan background:** © Compedia. **Green background:** © Compedia. **Tan border:** © Compedia. **Scales** (detail from vector illustration): © Macrovector/Shutterstock. **Old brass weight scale near books and feather on dark background:** © cosma/Shutterstock. *Elijah, The Great Prophet to King Ahab,* an illustration from *Bible Primer* (Rock Island, IL: The Augustana Synod: 1919): Public Domain. **United States Constitution with flag in background:** © Kasia/Shutterstock. *Nathan Advises King David,* 1672, Matthias Scheits: Public Domain. **United States Capitol, Washington, D.C.:** © holbox/Shutterstock. **3D Animation – Ishtar Gate-Babylon:** © Compedia. **Background music," Accralate:"** Music by Kevin MacLeod, Incompetech, licensed under CC BY-SA 3.0, https://incompetech.com/.

Chapter 14:
Job

Textbook & Teacher's Guide

Job and His Friends illustration: © Compedia. *Job Rebuked by His Friends* (pen and black ink, gray wash, and watercolor, over traces of graphite), 1805, William Blake; Morgan Library and Museum, New York City, New York: Public Domain. **Opening to the Book of Job,** an illustration from the Macklin Bible, 1800: Courtesy Museum of the Bible, Green Collection. All rights reserved. © Museum of the Bible, 2016. **Bible open to Job:** © Joe Fallico/Shutterstock. **Fountain of Job in the Hinnom Valley,** 1841, image by David Roberts (artist) and Louis Haghe (lithographer); Prints and Photographs Division, Library of Congress, Washington, DC, LC-USZC4-3442: Public Domain. *Ludlul bēl nēmeqi (Praise the Lord of Wisdom),* 930 BC; Library of Ashurbanipal, Neo-Assyrian, Kouyunji British Museum, London, England: © The Trustees of the British Museum. All rights reserved. **Young girl in sorrow with a friend consoling her:** © Anchiy/Shutterstock. *Job* (statue), 1968, Nathan Rapoport; Yad Vashem, Jerusalem, Israel: Image by Dr. Avishai Teicher, pikiwiki.org.il, licensed under CC BY 2.5. **Job,** 1880, Leon Bonnat; Musee Bonnat-Helleu, Bayonne, France: Public Domain. *Job and His Friends* (oil on canvas), 1869, Ilya Repin; the State Russian Museum, St. Petersburg, Russia: Public Domain. Statue of *Job*, 1983, Dallas Anderson; Christ Cathedral, Garden Grove, California: Used with permission from Lynn L. Kauer. **Fiddler on the Roof:** © Eugene Ivanov/Shutterstock.

App

Seamless background with cuneiform: © Sidhe/Shutterstock. **Vector icon book:** © Nadin3d/Shutterstock. **Quiz icons.** Human brain think. Checklist with check mark symbol. Survey poll or questionnaire feedback form sign. Circle concept web buttons. Vector: © Blan-k/Shutterstock. **Lock vector icon:** © Vector.design/Shutterstock. **Blue box:** © Compedia. **Purple box:** © Compedia. **Dark purple around padlock symbol:** © Compedia. **Ludlul bēl nēmeqi (Praise the Lord of Wisdom),** 930 BC; Library of Ashurbanipal, Neo-Assyrian, Kouyunji; British Museum, London, England: © The Trustees of the British Museum. All rights reserved. **Detail of Anzu-bird and Ninurta from Bas-Reliefs at an Entrance to a Small Temple** (plate 19/83) from Austen Henry Layard, *Second Series of the Monuments of Nineveh; Including Bas-reliefs from the Palace of Sennacherib and Bronzes from the Ruins of Nimroud.* (London: J. Murray, 1853): Public Domain. **Ancient Assyrian winged god carved in stone:** © Kamira/Shutterstock. **King Esarhaddon of Assyria and his mother Naqi'a-Zakutu in the temple of Marduk.** Relief commemorating the restoration of Babylon by Esarhaddon (bronze, originally gold-plated), ca. 681-669 BC; Louvre Museum, Paris, France: Photo by Jastrow, Public Domain. **Job,** 1880, Leon Bonnat; Musee Bonnat-Helleu, Bayonne, France: Public Domain. **Vintage background with old books:** © Vadim Georgiev/Shutterstock. **Flat Design Call-To-Action Buttons:** © Tracie Andrews/Shutterstock. **Digital scrapbooking kit:** old paper - different aged paper: © AKaiser/Shutterstock. **Aristotle statue located at Stageira of Greece:** © Panos Karas/Shutterstock. **Friedrich Nietzsche,** Professor of Classical Philology at the University of Basel in Switzerland, Basel Hartmann, 1872: Public Domain. **52-year-old Bertrand Russell in America,** 1924: Public Domain. **Unidentified child in the front of the Nelson Mandela mural in Williamsburg section in Brooklyn:** C Leonard Zhukovsky/Shutterstock. **Tan background:** © Compedia.

Text

Safire, William. *The First Dissident: The Book of Job in Today's Politics.* New York: Random House, 1992. Used by permission.

Chapter 15:
Esther

Textbook & Teacher's Guide

Esther illustration: © Compedia. ***Queen Vashti*** (oil on linen), 2012: © Ann Manry Kenyon: Used with permission. **Ruins of ancient Achaemenid palace in Sush (Susa), Iran:** © Matyas Rehak/Shutterstock. **Hamedan, Iran: An Iranian Jewish woman prays at the tomb of the heroine of the biblical Book of Esther:** © Damon Lynch/Shutterstock. **Jerusalem: Ethiopian Jewish woman prays, facing the old city:** © RnDmS/Shutterstock. **Hamantashen:** © Maglara/Shutterstock. ***Illustrated Scroll of Esther*** Handwritten in Hebrew (ink and pigment on parchment), 1615, Ferrara, Italy. Courtesy of the Gross Family Collection, Tel Aviv, Israel. Photograph by Ardon Bar-Hama. Depiction of ***Bigthan and Teresh*** from the Book of Esther, 1590, Antoine Caron; Munich Culture Institute, Munich, Germany: Public Domain. **Illustrated Scroll of Esther** in an ornamental case: Courtesy Museum of the Bible Collection. All rights reserved. © Museum of the Bible, 2016. **Purim carnival in Jerusalem:** © Ekaterina Lin/Shutterstock. **Purim gragger (noise maker)** - A toy for Purim: © Mordechai Meiri/Shutterstock. **Two old bronze Kiddush wine cups isolated:** © Borya Galperin/Shutterstock. **Albert Einstein,** 1947, image by Oren Jack Turner; Prints and Photographs Division, Library of Congress, Washington, DC, LC-USZ62-60242: Public Domain. Photo of **Dr. Jonas Salk:** Image by SAS Scandinavian Airlines, Public Domain.

App

Stone bas-relief in ancient city Persepolis, Iran: © MielnickiStudio/Shutterstock. **Ancient city of Meybod in Iran:** © Anton Ivanov/Shutterstock. **King's private apartments, central part of the palace.** Susa, Iran: Image by Pentocelo, Public Domain. **Abstract black background:** © kak2s/Shutterstock. **The Torah in a synagogue:** © Oleg Ivanov IL/Shutterstock. **Fast of Esther:** © Compedia. **Haman ears cookies for Jewish festival of Purim:** © Maglara/Shutterstock. **Hamantaschen cookies or hamans ears Purim celebration:** © tomertu/Shutterstock. **Hamantaschen cookies in bucket with grogger noise maker and carnival mask:** © Maglara/Shutterstock.

Chapter 16:
Daniel

Textbook & Teacher's Guide

Daniel in the Lions' Den (oil on canvas), 1615, Peter Paul Rubens; Alisa Mellon Bruce Fund, National Gallery of Art, Washington, DC: Public Domain. ***Daniel Interprets the Dream of King Nebuchadnezzar and Wins His Favor*** by Grant Romney Clawson: © By Intellectual Reserve, Inc. **Kosher Grill serves kosher food** at 2013 US Open: © lev radin/Shutterstock. ***Belshazzar's Feast*** (oil on canvas), 1636, Rembrandt Harmenszoon van Rijn; The National Gallery, London, England: Public Domain. ***Daniel's Answer to the King*** (color mezzotint), 1890, Briton Rivière; Manchester Art Gallery, Manchester, England: Public Domain. **Daniel in the lions' den** (architectural detail); facade of the church of St. Trophime, Arles, Provence, France: © Elena Dijour/Shutterstock. **Lion:** © Stepan Kapl/Shutterstock. **Daniel Bomberg Bible,** 1527; Venice, Italy: Courtesy Museum of the Bible, Green Collection. All rights reserved. © Museum of the Bible, 2016. **City graphic:** © Giancana/Shutterstock. **Lion statues:** © kulikovv/Shutterstock.

App

3D 360° Model - Belshazzar's Feast (*Belshazzar's Feast* (oil on canvas), 1636, Rembrandt Harmenszoon van Rijn; The National Gallery, London, UK): © Compedia. ***Daniel's Answer to the King*** (color mezzotint), 1890, Briton Rivière; Manchester Art Gallery, Manchester, England: Public Domain. **Timeline arrow:** © Compedia. **Answer block outlines:** © Compedia. **Number markers:** © Compedia.

Chapter 17:
Coming Home from Babylon

Textbook & Teacher's Guide

Temple building illustration: © Compedia. **Jerusalem Old City Wall:** © Pete Spiro/Shutterstock. **Wall relief on the Arch of Titus** reveals Roman soldiers after the destruction of the Temple of Jerusalem in 70 A.D. including the Temple Menorah, the Table of the Shewbread and silver trumpets: © Matt Ragen/Shutterstock. **Ark of the Covenant:** © James Steidl/Shutterstock. **Ruins of ancient synagogue in Baram, Israel:** © -V-/Shutterstock.

Jerusalem; **Israeli Jewish students learn Torah:** © ChameleonsEye/Shutterstock. **Red wine in glass** isolated on white background: © Chursina Viktoriia/Shutterstock. **Tomb of Cyrus the Great,** the burial place of Cyrus the Great of Persia; Pasargadae, UNESCO World Heritage Site: © Aleksandar Todorovic/Shutterstock. **Olympic Park – Cyrus (Cyrus II of Persia);** Sydney Olympic Park, Sydney, Australia: Original image by Siamax, licensed under CC BY-SA 3.0, cropped by TRAJAN 117. **Opening of the Book of Nehemiah,** from the Macklin Bible, 1800: Courtesy Museum of the Bible, Green Collection. All rights reserved. © Museum of the Bible, 2016. *Israel in Egypt* (oil on canvas), 1867, Edward Poynter; Guildhall Art Gallery, London, England: Public Domain. *The Flight of the Prisoners* (gouache on board), 1902, James Jacques Joseph Tissot; Jewish Museum, New York City, New York: Public Domain. *The Destruction of the Temple of Jerusalem* (oil on canvas), 1867, Francesco Hayez; Gallerie dell'Accademia, Venice, Italy: Public Domain. **Beautiful landscape of the mountains of Galilee and Golan Heights via Jordan River:** © Guy Zidel/Shutterstock. **A lovely sunny day in Jerusalem, walls and towers against the sky and clouds:** © kavram/Shutterstock. **The Palmach, Immigration to Israel, 1947:** Image from the Palmach Photo Gallery via WikiPiki, Public Domain. **Model of the Second Ancient Jerusalem Temple:** © Flik47/Shutterstock.

App

3D 360° Model - Arch of Titus: © Compedia. **Vintage background with ripped old paper.** Vector illustration: © allegro/Shutterstock. **Tower of Babel as religion concept:** © Elena Schweitzer/Shutterstock. *The Tower of Babel* (oil on panel), ca. 1563-1565, Pieter Bruegel the Elder; Museum Boijmans Van Beuningen, Rotterdam, Netherlands: Public Domain. **Timeline Infographic** with diagrams and text in retro style: © MSSA/Shutterstock. **Cement texture:** © aerogondo2/Shutterstock. **Digital scrapbooking kit:** old paper - different aged paper objects for your layouts: © AKaiser/Shutterstock. **Scrolls** (detail from vector illustration): © Macrovector/Shutterstock. **Ruins of an Ancient Synagogue at Kafr Bir'im:** Public Domain. **The ruins of the ancient synagogue in Israel:** © Oleg Lopatkin/Shutterstock. **Ancient Baram synagogue in Israel:** © Ariy/Shutterstock. **Prayers at the newly renovated "Hurva" synagogue at the Old City of Jerusalem** © Asaf Eliason/Shutterstock. **Puzzle piece:** © Compedia. **White banner:** © Compedia. **Your choice true or wrong:** © narokzaad/Shutterstock. *Cyrus and Astyages* (oil on canvas), ca. second half of 18th century, Jean-Charles Nicaise Perrin; Private Collection: Public Domain. Web Gallery of Art. *Daniel and Cyrus Before the Idol Bel* (oil on panel), 1633, from Rembrandt and his Collections of Art in America, The J. Paul Getty Trust; Los Angeles, California: Public Domain. *Zerubbabel Displays a Plan of Jerusalem to Cyrus the Great* (oil on canvas), ca. 1640-1670, Jacob van Loo; Musee des Beaux-Arts, Orleans, France: Public Domain. *La clémence de Cyrus II le Grand envers les Hébreux* (illumination on parchment), ca. 1470-1475, Jean Fouquet; Bibliothèque nationale de France, Paris, France: Public Domain. *Childhood of King Cyrus* (oil on canvas), ca. second half of 17th century, Antonio Maria Vassallo; Hermitage Museum, St. Petersburg, Russia, Web Gallery of Art: Public Domain. **Blue background** (detail from vector illustration): © Macrovector/Shutterstock. **Green background:** © Compedia. **Unknown avatar:** © Compedia.

Chapter 18:
Rediscovered People

Textbook & Teacher's Guide

Archaeological dig site: © Pepe Ramirez/Shutterstock. **Archaeology: a thin layer stripping, one of the stages of excavation:** © krugloff/Shutterstock. **Ancient jug with coins:** © Sergey Kamshylin/Shutterstock. **Middle East under magnifier:** © Popartic/Shutterstock. **Archeological dig at the caves of Qumran site:** © ChameleonsEye/Shutterstock. **An archeologist examining some ancient crocks on a desk:** © Dario Lo Presti/Shutterstock. **Archeologists at work in ancient Caesarea, Israel:** © Aleksandar Todorovic/Shutterstock. **Ancient Citadel in Kirkuk, Iraq**: Image by Chad.r.hill, Public Domain. **Clay tablet and envelope** (A11878), discovered in Nuzi, Iraq, late 1400s BC: Courtesy of the Oriental Institute Museum at the University of Chicago, Chicago, Illinois. **Ruins of ancient city Hattusha, Turkey,** UNESCO: © Libor Píška/Shutterstock. **Ruins of ancient city Hattusha,** the Hittite Capital, Lion's Gate, Turkey, UNESCO: © Pecold/Shutterstock. **Hittite Storm God at Karatepe:** © bumihills/Shutterstock. *Paul-Émile Botta, Orientalist* (oil on canvas), 1840, Charles-Émile-Callande de Champmartin; Louvre Museum, Paris, France: Public Domain. *Palace of Khorsabad,* sketch by Sellier and Meunier: © Morphart Creation/Shutterstock. **Near Eastern Antiquities** - Louvre Museum, Paris, France: © bond girl/Shutterstock. **The Cyrus Cylinder,** 539–530 BC; British Museum, London, England: Image by Mike Peel, changes by مانفی, licensed under CC BY-SA 4.0. **The Nabonidus Chronicle,** 556-539 BC; British Museum, London, England: Image by ChrisO, licensed under CC BY-SA 3.0. **Lion hunt,** from an ancient Assyrian relief, 645-635 BC; British Museum, London, England: © Krikkiat/Shutterstock. A terracotta statue of the prophet **Balaam,** 1575–1578, Tommaso Porlezza della Porta; Rijksmuseum, Amsterdam, Holland. Purchased with the support of the BankGiro Loterij, a private collector, and the Migelien Gerritzen Fonds/Rijksmuseum Fonds/ Rijksmuseum, Amsterdam: Public Domain. **Jehoiachin Ration Cuneiform tablet,** 595–570 BC; Pergamon Museum, Berlin, Germany: © Livius.org. Used with permission. **Elephantine Island, Aswan, Egypt:** © Elzbieta Sekowska/Shutterstock. **A letter written on papyrus from the Jewish community in Elephantine in Egypt,** 407 BC; Egyptian Museum, Berlin, Germany: Letter by Yedoniah, photographer unknown, Public Domain. **Jericho:** © WDG Photo/Shutterstock.

App

Mesha Stele (Moabite Stone) (plaster replica of basalt original), ca. 830 BC, Louvre, Dhiban, Jordan; Oriental Institute Museum, University of Chicago, Chicago, Illinois: Image by Daderot, Public Domain. **Rubber stamp collection:** © Simo988/Shutterstock. **Temple of Hercules in antique citadel in Amman, Jordan:** © vvoe/Shutterstock. **Clay tablet - one of the Armana Letters from Aziru of Amurru to the Pharaoh found at the site of Akhetaten,** the new capital city built by the Pharaoh Akhenaten as his capital and center of worship of the monotheistic god Aten: Public Domain. **Background blue abstract website pattern – Vector:** © HorenkO/Shutterstock (photoshopped). **Old open book with magic light on a dark abstract background:** © Robert_s/Shutterstock (photoshopped). **Hebrew**

Bible Text: © Scott Rothstein/Shutterstock. **Nuzi map:** © Compedia. **Clay tablet and envelope (A11878), discovered in Nuzi, Iraq,** late 1400s BC: Courtesy of the Oriental Institute of the University of Chicago, Chicago, Illinois. **Cuneiform writing of the ancient Sumerian or Assyrian civilization in Iraq:** © Fedor Selivanov/Shutterstock. **The Great temple, Hattusas archeological site, Turkey:** © vlas2000/Shutterstock. **Ruins of old Hittite capital Hattusa, Turkey:** © Alexander A.Trofimov/Shutterstock. **Reconstruction of Hittite Fortress:** © Oez/Shutterstock. **The tablet containing the Qadesh treaty between the Hittites and the Egyptians,** 1269 BC; Istanbul Archaeological Museum, Istanbul, Turkey: Photo by Giovanni Dall'Orto, Public Domain. **Ruins of old Hittite capital Hattusa, Turkey:** © Matyas Rehak/Shutterstock. **Ruins of ancient city Hattusha, the Hittite Capital, Lion's Gate, Turkey, UNESCO:** © Pecold/Shutterstock. **3D 360° Model - The Cyrus Cylinder:** © Compedia. **Abstract texture:** © rinitka/Shutterstock. **Archaeological research in ancient Roman city:** © Moni84/Shutterstock. *Balaam and the Angel* (oil on canvas), 1836, Gustav Jaeger: Public Domain. **Cleaning of a thin layer from an old neolithic ceramic vessel:** © Moni84/Shutterstock. **Black student hat isolated on white background:** © Serafima82/Shutterstock. **True grunge seal:** © Artist_G/Shutterstock. **False rubber seal:** © Artist_G/Shutterstock.

Chapter 19:
The Septuagint

Textbook & Teacher's Guide

Scribe illustration: © Compedia. **Hands on typewriter background:** © MJgraphics/Shutterstock. **Shelf of Bibles** in different versions and languages: © Kenneth Sponsler/Shutterstock. **Torah Scroll:** © Stavchansky Yakov/Shutterstock. **Praying Jew with Torah scroll at Passover:** © Boris Diakovsky/Shutterstock. **New library building on sunny day in Alexandria, Egypt:** © Baloncici/Shutterstock. **Interior of Egyptian Library in Alexandria, Egypt:** © RiumaLab/Shutterstock. **Hebrew characters:** © Yuriy Chertok/Shutterstock. **TANAKH:** © Lindsay Basson/Shutterstock. **Marble Statue of Greek King Ptolemy II Philadelphus** at Alexandria, Egypt: © MidoSemsem/Shutterstock. **Leaf from P. Bodmer XXIV** (manuscript on papyrus), Psalm 108:16 - 109:4 in Greek, 3rd-4th century AD; Pabau, Egypt: Courtesy Museum of the Bible Collection. All rights reserved. © Museum of the Bible, 2016. **Greek Orthodox Church in Santorini, Greece:** © stocker1970/Shutterstock. **Alexander the Great:** © Aleksandar Kamasi/Shutterstock.

App

Sogut on the Brozburun Peninsula in Turkey: © Gordon Bell/Shutterstock. **Famous ancient Egypt Cheops pyramid and sphinx in Giza Cairo:** © Kokhanchikov/Shutterstock. **Model of the Second Ancient Jerusalem Temple:** © Boris Diakovsky/Shutterstock. **Persepolis, The magnificent ruin of Persian, Achaemenid Empire, Iran:** © Kochatornranapat/Shutterstock. **Panorama of green Indus valley from ascend to Kardung La pass;** Ladakh, India: © f9photos/Shutterstock. **Open old book, close-up, on top:** © RrraumShutterstock. **Egypt's Alexandria Library:** © ylq/Shutterstock. **Close up of old books with weathered leather backs:** © IsakBA/Shutterstock. ***Ptolemy with the Sages,*** 1672, Jean Baptiste de Champaigne; Palace of Versailles, Versailles, France: Public Domain. ***The Burning of the Library at Alexandria in 391 AD*** (illustration), 1910, Ambrose Dudely, from *Hutchinsons History of the Nations* (London: Hutchinson & Co., Ltd.): Public Domain. **A panoramic view of Bibliotheca Alexandrina** showing the library in front of the Mediterranean Sea: Image by Bebo106, Public Domain.

Chapter 20:
The Hebrew Bible

Textbook & Teacher's Guide

Jewish Holy Scriptures: © Leon Forado/Shutterstock. **Torah Scroll** (ink on gevil), 17th century, North Africa: Courtesy Museum of the Bible Collection. All rights reserved. © Museum of the Bible, 2016. **Kippah and Torah:** © Anneka/Shutterstock. **Photo of two women:** © Compedia. **Torah Scroll** (ink on gevil), 15th century; Spain: Courtesy Museum of the Bible, Green Collection. All rights reserved. © Museum of the Bible, 2016. *The Torah Scribe* (oil on cardboard), 1876, Maurycy Gottlieb; National Museum, Wrocław, Poland: Public Domain. **Dead Sea Scrolls; Shrine of the Book, Jerusalem, Israel:** © ChameleonsEye/Shutterstock. **Dead Sea Scroll fragment** (circle): © ChameleonsEye/Shutterstock. **The desert cliffs near the Dead Sea:** © Tal Yanai/Compedia. **Feather:** © Roman Malyshev/Shutterstock.

App

3D 360° Model - Torah Scroll: © Compedia. **Old paper textures - background with space for text:** pashabo/Shutterstock. **Old manuscript scroll with ink and writing feather. High quality vector illustration:** © sinvuka/Shutterstock. **Pink buttons** (Multicolored Scroll Banner Ribbons Vector Collection): © A.Lachney/Shutterstock. **Hanging scroll:** © KID_A/Shutterstock.

Chapter 21:
The "Obscure" Books of the Bible

Textbook & Teacher's Guide

Maccabees illustration: © Compedia. **King James Bible,** The Great "She" Bible, 1611: Courtesy Museum of the Bible, Green Collection. All rights reserved. © Museum of the Bible, 2016. *Angel of Maccabees*, 1866, illustration from the Doré Bible, published by Cassell, Petter, and Galpin; London and New York: Public Domain. *Sirach,* illustration from the Doré Bible, published by Cassell, Petter, and Galpin; London and New York: Public Domain. *Solomon,* illustration from the Doré Bible, published by Cassell, Petter, and Galpin; London and New York: Public Domain. *The Angel Raphael and the Family of Tobit*, illustration from the Picture from The Holy Scriptures, Old and New Testaments books collection, 1885, Stuttgart, Germany; drawings by Gustave Dore: © Nicku/Shutterstock. *Judith Shows the Head of Holofernes*, illustration from The Holy Scriptures, Old and New Testaments books collection, 1885, Stuttgart, Germany; drawings by Gustave Dore: © Nicku/Shutterstock. **Old vintage scroll** isolated on white background: © Vadim Sadovski/Shutterstock. **Hourglass** (from "Spending money or out of money concept" vendor illustration): © koya979/Shutterstock. **Vector illustration of cross section of the trunk:** © Nicola M/Shutterstock. **Antique books isolated:** © MIGUEL GARCIA SAAVEDRA/Shutterstock. **Jackfruit leaves on white background:** © Noppharat46/Shutterstock. **Golden nuggets** isolated on white: © Africa Studio/Shutterstock.

App

Birthday design over blue background, vector illustration: © grmark/Shutterstock. **White banner and Pink ribbon** (Vintage background with emblem, foliage, ribbon and text Happy Thanksgiving): © style-photography/Shutterstock. **Stack of books symbol:** © Shutterstock. **3D 360° Model - The Maccabees:** © Compedia.

Chapter 22:
Daily Life in Bible Times
Textbook & Teacher's Guide

Daily Life illustration: © Compedia. **Caravan of camels:** © Zazaa Mongolia/Shutterstock. **Car with luggage:** © Africa Studio/Shutterstock. **Rock carvings:** © Wollertz/Shutterstock. **Laptop:** © Alex Brylov/Shutterstock. *Jacob Urging Leah and Rachel to Flee from Laban*, 1638, Pieter Symonsz Potter; Saint Catherine's Convent Museum, Utrecht, Netherlands: Public Domain. **Shepherd illustration:** © Canicula/Shutterstock. *Abraham's Servant Meets Rebecca,* 1902, James Jacques Joseph Tissot; The Jewish Museum, New York City, New York: Public Domain. **Bedouin Camps:** © Eliane Haykal/Shutterstock. *Bedouin Wedding Series, Bedouin Tent*, ca. 1900-1920, image by American Colony (Jerusalem) Photo Department; G. Eric and Edith Matson Photograph Collection, Prints and Photography Division, Library of Congress, Washington, DC, LC-DIG-matpc-15116: Public Domain. *Bedouin Girls*, ca. 1898-1946; G. Eric and Edith Matson Photograph Collection, Prints and Photography division, Library of Congress, Washington, DC, LC-DIG-matpc-04635: Public Domain. *Pedagogue and Boy* (terracotta statue), third - second century BC (Hellenistic Period), Greece; The Walters Art Gallery, Baltimore, Maryland: Public Domain. *Bedouin Girl Weaving*, ca. 1898-1946, image by American Colony (Jerusalem) Photo Department or Matson Photo Service; G. Eric and Edith Matson Photograph Collection, Prints and Photography Division, Library of Congress, Washington, DC, LC-DIG-matpc-05414: Public Domain. **Family Meal at Nazareth Village:** Image by מוחמד מוסא שהואן, licensed under CC BY 2.5. **Dish of Salt from Masada:** Image by Clara Amit, courtesy of Israel Antiquities Authority. **Olive seeds from Masada:** Image by Clara Amit, courtesy of Israel Antiquities Authority. **Carpenter at Nazareth Village:** Image by מוחמד מוסא שהואן, licensed under CC BY 2.5. **Olive oil illustration:** © Canicula/Shutterstock.

App

Old paper textures – background with space for text: © pashabo/Shutterstock. **Skyline graphic and Jet Plane** (Big collection of banners in flat style vector design): © sir.Enity/Shutterstock. **Ribbons:** © Compedia. **Man on donkey** (Vector Illustration. Branding Identity Corporate logo design template Isolated on a white background): © Steinar/Shutterstock. **The man holding the smartphone** (Internet communication. Vector illustration style flat design): © Kochkanyan Juliya/Shutterstock. **An illustration of an Arabic man leading a camel through a desert**: © pandora64/Shutterstock. **Instructor** (Business college education icons vector): © VoodooDot/Shutterstock. **Teacher icons** (School college university education flat 3d web isometric infographic concept vector): © Sentavio/Shutterstock. **3D 360° Model of Painting:** *Jacob Urging Leah and Rachel to Flee from Laban*, 1638, Pieter Symonsz Potter; Saint Catherine's Convent Museum, Utrecht, Netherlands: © Compedia. **Blue background:** (Supreme court judge and blindfolded justice with sword and scales people law flat horizontal banners vector illustration): © Macrovector/Shutterstock. **Family flat icons set** with married couples parents and children isolated vector illustration: © Macrovector/Shutterstock. **Wedding rings and wedding bouquet** of red roses on wooden table: © Rustle/Shutterstock. **Ketubbah (marriage contract)** dated 6 June 1838: Image courtesy of the Asian Collection, Wellcome Images, licensed under CC BY 4.0. **Silk curtain on the window:** © antoni halim/Shutterstock. **Hindu Indian wedding ceremony** in a temple: © Nadina/Shutterstock. **Four-room house;** used with permission from Prof. A. Ben-Tor, Institute of Archaeology, The Hebrew University of Jerusalem. **Four-room Israelite House;** used with permission from Prof. A. Ben-Tor, Institute of Archaeology, The Hebrew University of Jerusalem. **A reconstructed Israelite house,** 10th-7th century BCE; Eretz Israel Museum, Tel Aviv, Israel: Image by Yair Talmor, Public Domain. **A reconstructed Israelite house,** 10th-7th century BCE; Eretz Israel Museum, Tel Aviv, Israel: Image by Yair Talmor, Public Domain. **Livestock room – stalls, hay:** used with permission from Prof. A. Ben-Tor, Institute of Archaeology, The Hebrew University of Jerusalem. **Bedroom;** used with permission from Prof. A. Ben-Tor, Institute of Archaeology, The Hebrew University of Jerusalem. **Tan background:** © Compedia. *Moses with the Tablets of the Law* (oil on canvas), Rembrandt; Gemäldegalerie, Berlin, Germany: Image by the The Yorck Project, Public Domain. *Moses Striking the Rock* (oil on canvas), ca. 1630, Pieter de Grebber; Musée des Beaux-Arts, Tourcoing, France: Public Domain. **Vector illustration of Moses standing for Passover:** © Liron Peer/Shutterstock. **Crowd, chariots, towers:** © Compedia. *King Solomon*, from Doré's illustrations for the Book of Proverbs, 1866, Gustave Doré: Public Domain. *The Idolatry of King Solomon* (oil on panel), ca. 1630-1648, Willem de Poorter; Rijksmuseum, Amsterdam, Netherlands: Public Domain. **Icon of** *Christ Pantocrator* 1384, Metropolitan Jovan Zograf; Church of the Monastery of the Holy Transfiguration, Zrze- Prilep: Image courtesy of orthodoxphotos.com, Public Domain. *Jesus Walks in the Portico of Solomon* (opaque watercolor over graphite on gray wove paper), ca. 1886-1894, James Jacques Joseph Tissot; Brooklyn Museum, Brooklyn, New York: Public Domain. *Saint Paul*, 1482, Bartolomeo Montagna; Museo Poldi Pezzoli, Milan, Italy: Public Domain. *Saint Paul Preaching in Athens*, 1515-1516, Raphael; Royal Collection of the United Kingdom, Victoria & Albert Museum, London, England: Public Domain.

Chapter 23:
The Dead Sea Scrolls
Textbook & Teacher's Guide

Dead Sea Scroll illustration: © Compedia. **Dubai desert camel safari landscape:** © Banana Republic images/Shutterstock. **The Leningrad Codex,** 1008; National Library of Russia, St. Petersburg, Russia: Image by Shmuel ben Ya'akov: Public Domain. **Deuteronomy 32:50-33:29, Aleppo Codex,** 10th century CE; Ben-Zvi Institute and the Hebrew University, Jerusalem, Israel: Image by David Ezra, Public Domain. **Qumran caves in Qumran National Park, Israel:** © Ella Hanochi/Shutterstock. **One of the caves in which the Dead Sea scrolls were found at the ruins of Qumran** in the desert of Israel (circle): © Aprilphoto/

Shutterstock. **View of the archaeological site at Qumran,** looking from the west: © Tal Yanai/Compedia. **Shrine of the Book, Museum of Israel, Jerusalem:** © Borya Galperin/Shutterstock. **Roland de Vaux,** director of the French Biblical and Archaeological School, and co-director of excavations at Qumran in the 1940s and 1950s: Image courtesy of École biblique et archéologique française de Jérusalem. **Roland De Vaux, handling small finds from the field:** Image courtesy of École biblique et archéologique française de Jérusalem. **Excavation worker holding a large storage jar with Hebrew inscription:** Image courtesy of École biblique et archéologique française de Jérusalem. **Roland De Vaux and his excavation team** in discussion with local Bedouin men: Image courtesy of École biblique et archéologique française de Jérusalem. **Dead Sea Scroll Fragment, Genesis 32,** ca. AD 50, Qumran: Courtesy Museum of the Bible Collection. All rights reserved. © Museum of the Bible, 2016. **Large storage jar exposed in its original setting at Khirbet Qumran:** Image courtesy of École biblique et archéologique française de Jérusalem. **Scroll jar with small ceramic lamp and other pottery,** following reconstruction: Image courtesy of École biblique et archéologique française de Jérusalem. **Scene of Khirbet Qumran being excavated,** looking east toward the Dead Sea: Image courtesy of École biblique et archéologique française de Jérusalem. **Storage Jar:** © flik47/123RF.com.

App

3D Map – Dead Sea Area: © Compedia. **3D 360° Model - Isaiah Scroll:** © Compedia.

Chapter 24:
Digging Up Jerusalem

Textbook & Teacher's Guide

Jerusalem: © photo.ua/Shutterstock. **Panoramic of Jerusalem:** © Evgeniy Ayupov/Shutterstock. **Hills of Jerusalem:** © S1001/Shutterstock. **Herod's Gate:** Image by Herwig Reidlinger, licensed under CC BY-SA 3.0. **Golden Gate:** Image by Mark A. Wilson, Public Domain. **Southern Walls:** Image by Oren Rozen, licensed under CC BY 3.0. **Zion's Gate:** Image by Berthold Werner, licensed under CC BY-SA 3.0. **Outside Western Wall:** © Boris Stroujko/Shutterstock. **Part of the Jaffa gate at the old city of Jerusalem:** Image by Miriam Sommer, licensed under CC BY-SA 3.0 DE. **Northern Wall:** Image by Deror Avi, licensed under CC BY-SA 3.0. **Ivory Pomegranate:** Image by Wikkikati, Public Domain. **Archaeological Site at the Givati Parking Lot Dig,** Image by תמר הירדני, Public Domain. **Bulla bearing the Hebrew inscription 'belonging to Gemaryahu ben Shaphan',** Iron Age II, City of David ('House of the Bullae'): Courtesy of Israel Antiquities Authority. **Stone wall:** © Fat Jackey/Shutterstock. **The Jerusalem Archeological Park:** Image by Tamar Hayardeni, Public Domain. **Cobbled street on Jerusalem Pilgrim Road:** Image by Tamar Jordan, Public Domain. **Flavius Josephus** (woodcut engraving) from William Whiston, *The Genuine Works of Flavius Josephus,* Volume 1 (Boston: S. Walker, 1849): Public Domain. **Robinson Arch:** Image by eman, Public Domain. **Reconstruction Model of Robinson's Arch:** Image by Водник, licensed under CC BY-SA 2.5. **Second Temple diagram:** © Compedia. **Hebrew inscription: "For the place of trumpeting...":** Image by יעל ', licensed under CC BY-SA 3.0. **Ancient Jerusalem: a remnant of the Temple Walls, with Hebrew inscription: "For the place of trumpeting...":** Image by Ekeidar, licensed under CC BY-SA 3.0. **Temple Mount"...son of the High Priest.":** Image by Archaeological Staff Officer - Civil Administration in Judea and Samaria. **Model of Second Temple,** Dig: Benjamin Har-Even and Naftali Isaac: © Joseph Calev/Shutterstock. **An inscription bearing the name of Pontius Pilate**, Procurator of Judea, in the time of Yeshua of Nazareth; Israel Museum, Jerusalem, Israel: Image by BR Burton, Public Domain. **Bulla with partial paleo- Hebrew text: "(Belonging) to Gaalyahu son of Imer:"** Courtesy of the Temple Mount Sifting Project, Jerusalem, Israel. **The Ossuary of Kayafa:** Image by BR Burton, Public Domain. **2,700-year-old personal seal:** Image by Clara Amit, courtesy of Israel Antiquities Authority. **Walls:** © Joseph Calev/Shutterstock.

App

Jerusalem at night: © Alexey Stiop/Shutterstock. **Vintage background with ripped old paper.** Vector illustration: © allegro/Shutterstock. **Timeline Infographic with diagrams and text in retro style:** © MSA/Shutterstock. **Cement texture:** © aerogondo2/Shutterstock. **View on main entrance in at the Church of the Holy Sepulchre in Old City of Jerusalem:** © Nickolay Vinokurov/Shutterstock. **Via Dolorosa, Jerusalem, Israel:** © Anton_Ivanov/Shutterstock. **The Western Wall in Jerusalem:** © Asaf Eliason/Shutterstock. **Dome of the Rock and Dome of the Chain on the Temple Mount in Jerusalem, Israel:** © Mikhail Markovskiy/Shutterstock. **Dormition Abbey at Mount Zion. Jerusalem. Israel:** © Protasov AN/Shutterstock. **3D Map – The Evolution of Jerusalem's Borders:** © Compedia. **Ruins of the ancient city in the desert:** © Oleksandr Lysenko/Shutterstock. **Beautiful scenic view of massive wall in ancient crusader fortress** - The Al Karak (UNESCO World Heritage Site) in Jordan, Middle East: © Natalia Davidovich/Shutterstock. **Wall of the old city of Jerusalem:** © S1001/Shutterstock. **Background aerial of city:** Image by קנוי מעיר דוד. **The City of David aerial:** Image by קנוי מעיר דוד. **Excavation in City of David Givaty parking lot Jerusalem:** Image by אני, Public Domain. **The pool of Siloam at the end of Hezekiah's tunnel** is a rock-cut pool on the southern slope of 'the City David' in Jerusalem: © Robert Hoetink/Shutterstock. **Excavations on Ophel. Wall of the Jebusites,** ca. 1900-1920, image by American Colony (Jerusalem) Photo Department; G. Eric and Edith Matson Photograph collection, Prints and Photographs Division, Library of Congress, Washington, DC, LC-DIG-matpc-05478: Public Domain. **Village de Siloam, Jerusalem,** 1856, Aguste Salzmann; Dorot Jewish Division, The New York Public Library, The New York Public Library Digital Collections: Public Domain. **Temple Mount: Royal Stoa:** © Compedia. **Market and stores:** © Compedia. **Court of the Gentiles:** © Compedia. **General:** © Compedia. **Hall of Hewn Stones:** © Compedia. **Antonia Fortress:** © Compedia.

Chapter 25:
Education

Textbook & Teacher's Guide

Open book with glowing letters on concrete background and image: © Syda Productions/Shutterstock. **Group of Jewish Children with a Teacher in** Samarkand (digital color rendering), 1910, image by Sergei Mikhailovich Prokudin-Gorskii; Prokudin-Gorskii Collection, Print and Photographs Division, Library of Congress, Washington, DC, LC-DIG-ppmsc-04442. **Talmud Torah School,** 1937, Bendery,

Modlova (modern Tighina, Moldova): Public Domain. **The Plymouth Rock:** © Marcio Jose Bastos Silva/Shutterstock. **One room rural schoolhouse bathed in sunlight,** Pt. Sanilac Historical Village, Pt. Sanilac, Michigan: © ehrlif/Shutterstock. **Inside the Port Sanilac schoolhouse:** © Lowe Llaguno/Shutterstock. *The New England Primer* (title page), 1775; Courtesy of the Watkinson Library at Trinity College, Hartford, Connecticut.

App

3D Book - Luther's Bible: © Compedia. **World Map:** © ekler/Shutterstock. **Positive cute kid in the school, writing on table, red apple in front of him:** © ZouZou/Shutterstock. **Kids sitting on the street of Kathmandu Nepal:** © nevenm/Shutterstock. **Very Cute African School Girl Toothy Smile in Bamako, Mali:** © Riccardo Mayer/Shutterstock. **Group of Muslim Kids:** © Distinctive Images/Shutterstock. **Group of teen boys looking at the camera:** © v.s.anandhakrishna/Shutterstock.

Chapter 26:
Early America's Charters and Laws

Textbook & Teacher's Guide

Embarkation of the Pilgrims (oil on canvas), 1857; Brooklyn Museum, A. Augustus Healy Fund and Healy Purchase Fund B, 75.188: Public Domain. *Roger Williams Statue;* Promenade de la Treille, Geneva, Switzerland: Image by Traumrune, licenced under CC BY 3.0. **Touro Synagogue:** © Daniel M. Silva/Shutterstock. **View of the First Baptist Church in America** and partial skyline of Providence, Rhode Island, from College Hill against a bright blue sky: © Stephen B. Goodwin/Shutterstock. **Hawthorne portrait:** © Everett Historical/Shutterstock. **Title page of Nathaniel Hawthorne,** *The Scarlet Letter*, First Edition (Boston: Ticknor, Reed & Fields:1850): Public Domain. *Roger Williams in a New England Church*, Arthur C. Perry American History (New York, NY: American Book Company, 1913): Courtesy of the Congregational Library & Archives, Boston, Massachusetts, Public Domain. *The First Thanksgiving at Plymouth*, 1914, Jennie Augusta Brownscombe; Pilgrim Hall Museum, Plymouth, Massachusetts: Public Domain. **Replica of the** *Mayflower:* © Joseph Sohm/Shutterstock. **Landing of Governor** *Winthrop at Salem* (wood engraving), 1630, from *A Treasury of Knowledge and Cyclopedia of History, Science and Art* (Robert Sears, 1850; Art and Picture Collection, The New York Public Library Digital Collections: Public Domain. **Boston:** © Sean Pavone/Shutterstock. **Salem, MA - July 25: Historic home of Judge Corwin,** known as Witch House in Salem, MA, as seen on July 25, 2011. Witch House is the only standing structure with ties to the Witchcraft Trials of 1692: © littleny/Shutterstock. *Witch Hill* or *The Salem Martyr*, 1869, Thomas Satterthwite Nobel; Collection of the New York Historical Society, New York City, New York: Public Domain. *Examination of a Witch*, 1853, Tompkins Harrison Matteson; Peabody Essex Museum, Salem, Massachusetts: Public Domain. *Anne Hutchinson on Trial*, 1901, Edwin Austin Abbey: Public Domain. **John Locke,** engraved by J. Pofselwhite and published in *The Gallery of Portraits with Memoirs* encyclopedia, United Kingdom, 1836: © Georgios Kollidas/Shutterstock.

App

Vector illustration of a High Detail USA Map: © nale/Shutterstock. **San Miguel Church; Santa Fe, New Mexico:** © pmphoto/Shutterstock. **Looking west across Broadway at St Paul's Chapel on a sunny midday:** Image by Jim Henderson: Public Domain. **Photographic view of the northeast rear elevation of Old Ship Church, Hingham, Massachusetts,** Image by Frank O. Branzetti, Historic American Buildings Survey; Prints and Photographs Division, Library of Congress, Washington, DC, HABS MASS,12-HING,5--20: Public Domain. **St. Luke's Church near Smithfield, VA, built ca. 1632:** Image by Greg Vassilakos, Public Domain. **Abstract black background:** © kaks2/Shutterstock. **Country church in New England:** © Leena Robinson/Shutterstock. **Law code, gavel and books:** © FikMik/Shutterstock. **Line art drawing of a Ducking Stool:** Image by the Archives of Pearson Scott Foresman, Public Domain. **A boy trapped in a medieval torture device:** © Aigars Reinholds/Shutterstock. **Young pigs on the farm:** © Igor Stramyk/Shutterstock. **3D 360° Model** - *The First Thanksgiving at Plymouth,* 1914, Jennie Augusta Brownscombe; Pilgrim Hall Museum, Plymouth, Massachusetts: © Compedia. **Salem Witch Trials.** A woman protests as one of her accusers, a young girl, appears to have convulsions.: © Everett Historical/Shutterstock. **Martha Corey,** illustration by John W. Ehninger, "Giles Corey of the Salem Farms", 1868, *The Complete Poetical Works of Henry Wadsworth Longfellow* (Boston, MA: Houghton, 1902): Public Domain. **Two alleged witches being tried in Salem, Massachusetts as part of the infamous witch hunts,** 17th century, artist unknown: Private collection, Public Domain. **Bacon's Rebellion, Virginia 1677.** Wife of Edmund Cheeseman faints as Governor Berkeley rejects her plea to spare her husband's life. © Everett Historical/Shutterstock. **"The Sheriff brought the witch up the broad aisle, her chains clanking as she stepped."** From John R. Musick, *The Witch of Salem*, or *Credulity Run Mad* (New York: Funk & Wagnalls Company, 1893): Public Domain. **Flag of the Commonwealth of Virginia:** © Xrmap, Public Domain. **Flag of Maryland;** from the Open Clip Art Library: Image by Michael Wheeler, Public Domain. **Flag of Rhode Island and Providence Plantations**: Image by Xrmap, Public Domain. **Flag of Massachusetts:** Public Domain. **Flag of South Carolina,** from the Open Clip Art Library: Public Domain. **Flag of North Carolina**: Public Domain. **Flag of Delaware:** Image by Xrmap, Public Domain. **Flag of New Jersey:** Image by Xrmap, Public Domain. **Georgia state flag,** isolated on white background: © Atlaspix/Shutterstock. **Flag of the state of New York:** Image by Xrmap, Public Domain.

Chapter 27:
Early State Constitutions

Textbook & Teacher's Guide

The Signing of the Constitution of the United States (oil on canvas), 1940, Howard Chandler Christy; United States House of Representatives, Washington, DC: Public Domain. *Writing the Declaration of Independence, 1776*: Benjamin Franklin, John Adams and Thomas Jefferson review a draft of the Declaration of Independence, by J.L.G. Ferris. From a 1909 lithograph by Wolf & Co.: © Victorian Traditions/Shutterstock. Ferris *Benjamin Franklin* (oil on canvas), 1767, David Martin; White House, Washington, DC: Public Domain. **Statue of President Thomas Jefferson** (bronze), 1949, Rudulph Evans; Jefferson Memorial, Washington, DC: © Vacclav/Shutterstock. **Dove in clouds:** © isak55/Shutterstock. **Cover page of the Constitution of the State of New York,**

1777, New York State Secretary of State, Record Series A1802, First Constitution of the State of New York, 1777; New York State Archives, Albany, New York: Public Domain. **Virginia Statute for Establishing Religious Freedom**, 1786; Library of Virginia, Richmond, Virginia: Used with permission from the Library of Virginia. **The Bill of Rights**, the first ten amendments to the US Constitution, 1791; U.S. National Archives, Washington, DC: Public Domain. *George Washington* (oil on canvas), 1797, Gilbert Stuart; Clark Art Institute, Williamstown, Massachusetts: Public Domain. *Washington's Inauguration*, 1789 (oil on canvas), 1974, Allyn Cox; U.S. Capitol Building, Washington, DC: Public Domain. *Washington as Statesman at Constitutional Convention* (oil on canvas), 1856, Junius Brutus Stearns; Virginia Museum of Fine Arts, Richmond, Virginia: Public Domain. **Constitution: Focus on We the People Wording in Document:** © Sean Locke Photography/Shutterstock. **Thomas Jefferson,** Letter to the Society of the Methodist Episcopal Church in New London, Connecticut, (February 4, 1809): Courtesy Museum of the Bible, National Christian Foundation Collection. All rights reserved. © Museum of the Bible, 2016. **The First Unitarian Church**: © Felix Lipov/Shutterstock.

App

3D 360° Model - The Bill of Rights: © Compedia. **Constitution: USA Constitution Document with American Flag Behind:** © Sean Locke Photography/Shutterstock. *William Floyd*, ca. 1793, Ralph Earl; Independence National Historical Park; Philadelphia, Pennsylvania: Public Domain. *Francis Hopkinson,* illustration from Ellis Paxson Oberholtzer, *The Literary History of Philadelphia* (Philadelphia: George W. Jacobs & Co., 1906): Public Domain. *Joseph Galloway, member of the Congress of 1774* (etching), 1885, Max Rosenthal; The Miriam and Ira D. Wallach Division of Art, Prints and Photographs: Print Collection, The New York Public Library, They New York Public Library Digital Collections: Public Domain. **Portrait of *Benjamin Franklin*** (oil on canvas), 1778, Joseph Duplessis; Metropolitan Museum of Art, New York City, New York: Public Domain. **Vertical striped background:** © Compedia. **Blue ribbon:** © Compedia. *Daniel Carroll* (oil), ca. 1758, John Wollaston; Maryland Historical Society, Baltimore, Maryland: Public Domain. *Samuel Adams* (oil on canvas), ca. 1772, John Singleton Copley; Museum of Fine Arts, Boston, MA: Public Domain. *John Rutledge*, artist unknown: Public Domain. *George Mason* (oil), 1750, John Hesselius: Public Domain. *James Madison,* 1816, John Vanderlyn; White House Historical Collection, Washington, DC: Public Domain. *Patrick Henry* (oil on canvas), 1891, George Bagby Matthews after Thomas Sully; United States Senate, Washington, DC: Public Domain. *Richard Dobbs Spaight, Jr.,* ca. prior to 1850; North Carolina Office of Archives and History, Raleigh, North Carolina: Public Domain. *Carter Braxton* (oil), 1901, by Albert Rosenthal; Independence National Historical Park, Philadelphia, Pennsylvania: Public Domain. *Eliphalet Dyer,* member of the Continental Congress (etching), 1886, Albert Rosenthal; The Miriam and Ira D. Wallach Division of Art, Prints and Photographs: Print Collection, The New York Public Library, The New York Public Library Digital Collections: Public Domain. *George Washington* (oil on canvas), 1797, Gilbert Stuart; Clark Art Institute, Williamstown, Massachusetts: Public Domain. *John Knox Witherspoon* (oil on canvas), 1783-1784, Charles Willson Peale, after Charles Willson Peale; Independence National Historical Park, Philadelphia, Pennsylvania: Public Domain. *Lyman Hall* (detail from the lithograph "Portraits & autographs of the signers of the Declaration of Independence"), 1876, Ole Erekson; Prints and Photographs Division, Library of Congress, Washington, DC, LC-DIG-ppmsca-07837: Public Domain. *Elbridge Gerry,* 1861, James Bogle after John Vanderlyn; Independence National Historical Park, Philadelphia, Pennsylvania: Public Domain. *Nicholas Van Dyke* (oil on canvas), Jefferson David Chalfant; United States Senate, Washington, DC: Public Domain. *Thomas Jefferson,* 1800, Rembrandt Peale, White House Collection/White House Historical Association, Washington, DC: Public Domain. *Samuel Huntington* (oil on canvas) 1783, Charles Willson Peale; Independence National Historical Park, Philadelphia, Pennsylvania: Public Domain.

Chapter 28:
Early American Culture

Textbook & Teacher's Guide

Camp-Meeting, ca. 1832, Kennedy & Lucas, Alexander Rider, and Hugh Bridport; Philadelphia, Pennsylvania: The Harry T. Peters Collection, National Museum of American History, Smithsonian Institution. Used with permission. *George Whitefield*, ca. 1750, attributed to Joseph Badger; Harvard University Portrait Collection, Cambridge, Massachusetts: Public Domain. **Cane Ridge Meeting House,** Little Rock Road, Bourbon County, Kentucky, image by Thomas Webb; Prints and Photographs Division, Library of Congress, Washington, DC, HABS KY, 9-CANRI: Public Domain. **Barton Stone**; pioneers in the great religious reformation of the nineteenth century; Prints and Photographs Division, Library of Congress, Washington, DC, LC-DIG-pga-03590: Public Domain. **Charles G. Finney:** The Miriam and Ira D. Wallach Division of Art, Prints and Photographs: Photography Collection, The New York Public Library, The New York Public Library Digital Collections: Public Domain. *Camp Meeting of the Methodists in North America,* ca. 1817, image by M. Dubourg; Prints and Photographs Division, Library of Congress, Washington, DC, LC-USZC4-772: Public Domain. **A Negro Camp Meeting in the South,** 1872, Solomon Eytinge; Schomburg Center for Research in Black Culture, Photographs and Prints Division, The New York Public Library Digital Collections: Public Domain. **Dwight L. Moody,** 1900, image by Barron Fredericks; Prints and Photographs Division, Library of Congress, Washington, DC, LC-USZ62-122752: Public Domain. **"Interior of Chicago Tabernacle" and "Mr. Moody Preaching in the Opera House Haymarket,"** Illustrations from *Moody: His Words, Work, and Workers* (New York: Nelson & Phillips, 1877): Images from Internet Archive Book Images, Flickr Commons, Public Domain. **Ira Sankey,** 1895, image by Davis Garber; Prints and Photographs Division, Library of Congress, Washington, DC, LC-USZ61-265: Public Domain. **Birthplace of D.L. Moody:** Courtesy of Jerry Pattengale, PhD. **Harriet Martineau** (engraving), 1837, unknown artist: Public Domain. **Letter from Harriet Martineau to Louise Gilman:** Image courtesy of Norfolk Record Office, NRO, 267/2 684X6. *Society in America,* by

Harriet Martineau (New York: Saunders and Otley: 1837): Public Domain. **The Hartford Institute for Religion Research, Connecticut:** Image by Sage Ross, licensed under CC BY-SA 3.0. *Alexis de Tocqueville* (oil), 1850, Théodore Chassériau: Public Domain. **Page from the original working manuscript of *De La Democratie en Amerique*,** ca. 1840, Alexis de Tocqueville; GEN MSS 82, Beinecke Rare Book and Manuscript Library, Yale University: Public Domain. **Pioneer homestead** in the backwoods of the American frontier; illustration from *A Journey in North America*, 1796, Victor Collot: © Everett Historical/Shutterstock. **Stack of cut logs fire wood from Common Alder tree** (Alnus glutinosa): © Kletr/Shutterstock.

App

3D 360° Model – Painting: *Camp-Meeting,* ca. 1832, Kennedy & Lucas, Alexander Rider, and Hugh Bridport; Philadelphia, Pennsylvania; The Harry T. Peters Collection, National Museum of American History, Smithsonian Institution, used with permission: © Compedia. **Vintage background,** (ornamental pattern template for design): © Megin/Shutterstock. **Old Bible and illuminated cross:** © Triff/Shutterstock. **"Barton Stone"** from "Pioneers in the Great Religious Reformation of the Nineteenth Century," ca. 1885, engraved by J.C. Buttre, designed by J.D.C. McFarland, engraved by John Chester; Prints and Photographs Division, Library of Congress, Washington, DC, LC-DIG-pga-03590: Public Domain. **Dwight L. Moody,** 1900, image by Barron Fredericks; Prints and Photographs Division, Library of Congress, Washington, DC, LC-USZ62-122752. **Ira Sankey,** 1895, Davis Garber; Prints and Photographs division, Library of Congress, Washington, DC, LC-USZ61-265: Public Domain. ***Charles Grandison Finney***, unknown artist, from *The Spirit of Reform*, Joshua Wakefield: Public Domain. **George Whitefield:** © Everett Historical/Shutterstock.

Chapter Summary Quizzes – Bible Champ Host

Happy successful young man in glasses standing: © Sergey Furtaev/Shutterstock. **Mr. Really Happy Guy:** © Sergey Furtaev/Shutterstock. **Smiling Latin student with black glasses showing forefinger on something:** © Sergey Furtaev/Shutterstock. **Smiling Latin college student with tablet PC showing forefinger:** © Sergey Furtaev/Shutterstock. **Cheerful Latin young man showing ok sign:** © Sergey Furtaev/Shutterstock. **Portrait of tired college student in checkered shirt and black glasses:** © Sergey Furtaev/Shutterstock.

Maps

Maps by Eli Itzak, Ph.D., Bar Ilan University. Sources: Esri Arcgi Online based on information provided by a third party; Aharoni, Yohanan, ed. *Carta Atlas of the History of the land Israel - Part A: the Biblical Period*. Jerusalem, Israel: Carta, 1964, 1974; Ziv, Michael, ed. *Atlas of the History of the Nations and Israel*. 3rd edition. Israel: Stematsky, 1986.